Praise for
Church on Sunday, Work on Monday

"This is a very important discussion on the relation between business and religion in contemporary America. It should be required reading, especially for businesspeople worried about the Church and church people worried about business."

—Peter L. Berger, director, ISEC

"Nash and McLennan unlock the door between Christian beliefs and the day-to-day realities of the business world. This book is must reading for Christians working in the private sector and the clergy struggling to effectively minister to them."

—Samuel L. Hayes III, Jacob H. Schiff Professor of Investment Banking–Emeritus, Harvard University

"Extremely useful in breaking down the walls between business and religion, and will be equally valuable to religious and business leaders alike."

—Bowen H. "Buzz" McCoy, author of the award-winning Harvard Business Review article *The Parable of the Sadhu*

"Laura Nash shares her unparalleled depth of insight about why the Christian faith is failing to engage the core activities of the business enterprise. No one can make any real progress until they come to grips with the realities she and Scotty McLennan so fluently explore. Read it—whatever your perspective about faith and business."

—William Messenger, director, Mockler Center for Faith and Ethics in the Workplace and Gordon-Conwell Theological Seminary

"Manna from heaven! Nash and McLennan couple empirical evidence with personal anecdotes to articulate and analyze the nature of the divide that many people of faith find between their Sunday worship and their Monday work. This is a must-read for clergy who take their congregation's work seriously, and for laypeople who take their worship seriously."

—David W. Miller, president, The Avodah Insitute

"This is a much-needed and important book. In an area that has been shockingly devoid of empirical research, Nash and McLennan add to our knowledge of one of the most important aspects of life. They are to be strongly applauded."

—Ian Mitroff, coauthor, A Spiritual Audit of Corporate America

"The line between the sacred and the secular often separates the thinking and understanding among Christian leaders and leaders in business who are also Christian. The essence of the faith requires integration in all areas of life, so why isn't there more common ground? This book represents a careful study and review of this question. It is a must-read for those who are serious about teaching and living their faith."

—C. William Pollard, chairman, The ServiceMaster Company and author of Soul of the Firm

"A bold book with a clear wake-up call to businesspeople and churchgoers to cease seeing one another as incompatible adversaries and begin to recognize that, as a source of strength and perspective, religion offers businesspeople a foundation on which to take risks and do good work. And business offers people of faith an opportunity to let their beliefs drive their behavior and accountability in the workplace. Laura Nash and Scotty McLennan use stories of real people to ground their book. The result is a heartening, indispensable guide for anyone making critical decisions in business today."

—Jeffrey Seglin, author, The Good, The Bad, and Your Business: Choosing Right When Ethical Dilemmas Pull You Apart

"With incisive intelligence, Laura Nash and Scotty McLennan lift the curtain on the mistrust, hostility even, between the church and business. A groundbreaking book."

—A.J. Vogl, editor, Across the Board magazine

"This book's particularly thoughtful analysis comes at a crucial time(when more businesspeople are seeking deeper spiritual understandings and commitments and also when churches are seeking to engage the challenging problems of our communities that businesspeople are well equipped to help resolve."

—J. McDonald Williams, chairman, Trammell Crow Company

Other Books by Laura Nash

Good Intentions Aside: A Manager's Guide to Resolving Ethical Problems

Believers in Business

Policies and Persons: A Casebook in Business Ethics
with Kenneth E. Goodpaster

Other Books by Scotty McLennan

Finding Your Religion: When the Faith You Grew up with Has Lost Its Meaning

Church on Sunday, Work on Monday

The Challenge of Fusing Christian Values with Business Life

Laura Nash and Scotty McLennan

JOSSEY-BASS
A Wiley Company
San Francisco

Published by

JOSSEY-BASS
A Wiley Company
989 Market Street
San Francisco, CA 94103-1741

www.josseybass.com

Jossey-Bass books and products are available through most bookstores. To contact Jossey-Bass directly, call (888) 378-2537, fax to (800) 605-2665, or visit our website at www.josseybass.com.

Substantial discounts on bulk quantities of Jossey-Bass books are available to corporations, professional associations, and other organizations. For details and discount information, contact the special sales department at Jossey-Bass.

We at Jossey-Bass strive to use the most environmentally sensitive paper stocks available to us. Our publications are printed on acid-free recycled stock whenever possible, and our paper always meets or exceeds minimum GPO and EPA requirements.

Library of Congress Cataloging-in-Publication Data

Nash, Laura L.
Church on Sunday, work on Monday: the challenge of fusing
   Christian values with business life / Laura Nash and Scotty
   McLennan; foreword by Ken Blanchard.—1st ed.
      p. cm.
   Includes bibliographical references and index.
   ISBN 0-7879-5698-8 (alk. paper)
   1. Businesspeople—Religious life.   2. Business—Religious
aspects—Christianity.   I. McLennan, Scotty.   II. Title.

BV4596.B8 N37 2001
248.8'8—dc21   2001003014

FIRST EDITION
HB Printing   10 9 8 7 6 5 4 3 2 1

Contents

Foreword

When Laura Nash and Scotty McLennan asked me to write a fore-word to their book *Church on Sunday, Work on Monday: The Challenge of Fusing Christian Values with Business Life*, I was thrilled. Why? Because today more than ever before people are living in constant white water. Nowadays changes are occurring rapid fire—one on top of another. There's no rest and there's no getting ready. In the heat of this chaos, it's hard for people to maintain perspective, particularly when they tend to get stuck in the thinking that got them to where they are today even though that thinking can't be used to get them to where they need to be tomorrow. Enter this wonderful book.

Business leaders need help and they need the kind of help that they can get from the leadership message of Jesus. Although the meaning of Jesus' life goes beyond the ways in which people earn a living, it shouldn't be forgotten that he was the greatest leader of all time. He took on twelve inexperienced people and developed them to the point that they were able to carry on without him and build a

God-centered spiritual movement that has flourished over centuries and provided a moral compass for billions of people.

Churches need help to meet the challenges of change and the fierce competition in their domain. Business leaders know things that can help church leaders. They know about marketing, they know about finance, they know all kinds of things that are necessary to effectively manage a business—and a church is a faith-based business.

If business leaders need help from church leaders and church leaders need help from business leaders, why aren't they getting together? That's what Laura Nash and Scotty McLennan are asking. And rather than pointing fingers to find fault, they are saying "Let's come together." "Let's work together." "Let's make each other more effective in doing our work in the world."

Why is a business writer and an entrepreneur like me interested in this subject? First of all I am a follower of Jesus. I was named after a Presbyterian minister. As a kid, I did the Sunday School bit but never really understood the power of the church because the impression I got was that Christianity was "something to know" and "something to do." As a result, as a young man I turned my back on the church as irrelevant because it didn't seem to give me any guidance for life. In most churches I attended they mentioned Jesus once in a while but never highlighted him as a model for all our behavior.

I finally got the potential of the church in my forties. When *The One Minute Manager* came out it was so successful I was either going to get a big head or wonder what was going on. I chose wonderment. I began to look again at my original Christian roots. With that, all kinds of believers started to enter my life and began to teach me that true Christianity was "someone to know" and "someone to follow." Putting Jesus front and center in my faith makes sense to me and motivates me to learn about his teachings.

As I began to read the Bible, I realized that much of what I had taught was consistent with the values that Jesus taught by example, even though his life extended far beyond business or management. As examples, his actions reflected many of the guidelines suggested in *The One Minute Manager,* and he embodied all the thinking around Situational Leadership. Name anything that promotes effective leadership and Jesus did it, including encouraging his followers to think beyond their own personal needs and goals: to feed the hungry, shelter the homeless, and visit the sick and imprisoned.

Concurrent with my realization that Jesus was a leadership model for all leaders, Phil Hodges and I founded the Center for FaithWalk Leadership, a nonprofit enterprise committed to helping leaders of faith walk their faith in the marketplace. In many ways we are doing the church's work, but in the process we are encouraging clergy throughout the country to take Jesus out of wraps and get his inspirational and effective leadership approach into the business world. Our motivation is not to soften leaders but to enable them in a caring way to live out Christian values *and* success in the marketplace. At the same time, others like Bob Buford are exposing clergy to wonderful market leaders that are helping them create growing and successful churches.

As a result of my experiences with FaithWalk Leadership, I think Nash and McLennan are on the right track. Read this book! They are Christians, and they are part of the world of business and the academy that cannot be easily classified in all the usual ways. Their faith and their experiences make their message important to people of all kinds of faith—in both the pulpit and the pew.

Christian values and business life are synergistic. One plus one is greater than two. Both sides of this equation have to remember that "none of us is as smart as all of us." Thanks, Laura and Scotty.

Ken Blanchard
Coauthor of *The One Minute Manager*

Acknowledgments

The seeds of this book were planted during the research stage of *Believers in Business*, Laura Nash's previous book on evangelical CEOs in business, published in 1994. At that time, Scotty McLennan was teaching a popular elective course on spirituality at Harvard Business School, and Laura was becoming aware that interest in spirituality and business was on the increase. Both of us were seeing evidence of serious challenges to examining faith and work, but there was little indication of new academic research or even interest in the question. Support for this book came at a critical time. It allowed us to follow the spirituality and business movement as it exploded in the latter part of the 1990s, and to keep a Christian focus despite cultural pressure to secularize the business ethics questions.

We are especially grateful to Peter L. Berger, director of Boston University's Institute for the Study of Economic Culture; and to Craig Dykstra, Chris Coble, and the Lilly Endowment for their early and substantive support of this project. Another private foundation, which wishes to remain anonymous, also provided funds in the start-up stage. Harvard University's Graduate School of Business Administration made additional research assistance available for the completion of this book. Harvard Divinity School's Center for the Study of Values in Public Life released some of Laura's time for the same purpose.

A great number of people contributed to the discussion and findings presented here, many of whom will remain anonymous. Among them, we are particularly indebted to the congregants and pastors who made themselves available for reflection on faith and business, and to the seminaries that participated in our survey. Although some were willing to be identified, we have disguised all such participants to ensure confidentiality. A great debt is also owed to the interviewees at our case sites, who again are not always named. Others who can be named, and to whom we are indebted for their assistance in presenting or evaluating our findings, are Nancy Ammerman, Robert Anderson, Joseph Badaracco, Robert Banks, John Beckett, David Berndt, Kenneth Blanchard, Matthew Budman, Robert Buford, Frederic Burnham, Stephen Caldwell, Allen Callahan, Tom Chappell, Brent Coffin, James Connor, Harvey Cox, William Crozier, Diana Dale, Melissa Daniels, Max De Pree, Donna Dial, Amy Dominik, Thomas Dunfee, Craig Dykstra, William H. Farley, Howard Good, Rick Goosen, Os Guinness, John Hamill, Pete Hammond, J. Bryan Hehir, Phil Hodges, Elmer Johnson, Linda Karpowich, Martin Marty, Bowen McCoy, Al McDonald, William Messenger, David Miller, Richard Mouw, James L. Nolan, Lynn Paine, Thomas Phillips, Thomas Piper, C. William Pollard, David Purdy, Peter Quek, Michael Rion, Peter S. Robinson, Gail Ross, Diana Rowen, Jeffrey Seglin, Donald Shriver, Timothy Smith, David Specht, Ben Sprunger, Max L. Stackhouse, Michael Stebbins, Paul Stevens, Al Vogl, Jim Wallis, George Weigel, Oliver Williams, Preston Williams, Richard Wood, and Mike Yoshino.

Research and administrative help was given by Annabel Beerel, John Berthrong, Virginia Cervantes, Bernice Ledbetter, Dolores Markey, Ann McLenahan, Sarah Orwig, Michal Sobieszcyk, Andrea Truax, Donna Verscheuren, and Laurel Whelan.

We also want to thank the people at Jossey-Bass for their strong and sympathetic editorial assistance: Sheryl Fullerton, Andrea Flint, and Naomi Lucks for heroic editing; Sarah Polster for her initial interest; and Mark Kerr and Jessica Egbert for encouragement and support in reaching you, our reader.

Finally, we thank all the students, faculty, and friends who patiently acted as a thoughtful sounding board for the several stages of this book. Their interest and encouragement made the task especially meaningful. Our spouses and children have offered patience and love that can never be fully acknowledged but is most important of all.

Preface

In 1636, a Boston merchant named Robert Keayne was brought up before the General Court of what was then known as the Bible Commonwealth on charges of usury. His story is one of the earliest recorded skirmishes between church officials and businesspeople in the American colonies over proper execution of religious duty in the marketplace.

Keayne was charged in court for allegedly making excessive gains in the matter of horse bridles, gold buttons, and nails, and of falsifying his books. Despite his vigorous protestation, Keayne was found guilty and the Commonwealth levied a stiff fine. The church voted to censure Keayne and demanded he make a public "penitential acknowledgment" of his sin.

Keayne, however, felt that the elders had misunderstood both his motives and the actual facts of the case. In a final and wickedly ingenious move to set the record straight, Keayne wrote a fifty-thousand-word document detailing every transaction during his career. He filed this account in probate as part of his last will and testament, thereby ensuring its irrevocable publication.[1]

In this document, commonly referred to as *The Apologia of Robert Keayne*, the merchant offered a meticulous accounting of the transactions that had brought on his censure. He argued that his profits were not excessive, that others had charged even more for goods of lesser quality. He stressed his lifelong diligence, avoidance of leisure, and numerous acts of public good and charity—all of which he claimed to have done out of his private sense of Christian duty and pious gratitude for the bounties he had received in New England.

He did not stop with a demonstration of his own piety and diligence. He responded to his accusers in kind, claiming their motives were entirely inconsistent with the religious principles they purported to represent. He charged representatives of his church with meanness of spirit and denounced their zeal as being out of all proportion, "as if they had had some of the greatest sins in the world to censure." Through it all, however, Robert Keayne remained a strong member of that church and a minor civic leader of the Bible Commonwealth.

Thus was laid down—more than 350 years ago—a pattern of alienation and détente between the devout American businessperson and the Church that is still in a state of constant renegotiation. Hoping for the possibility of consistency between their Christianity and their careers, many businesspeople find themselves instead locked in surprising conflict with their own church's attitudes toward business, or locked out of the church's approval of their role as business leader.

A church that baptizes (and later marries) your children, helps you worship God weekly, and buries your friends and family members at the end of their lives can also be a church that leaves you unsupported when it comes to who you are as a businessperson. If you yourself have felt that the church is not of substantive help in navigating faith and work, you are not alone. As we found in our research, most businesspeople report less-than-satisfactory connections between religion and business in their lives. Their spiritual selves are not fulfilled at work; they want more. They want to realize their spiritual potential or discover a sense of meaning in business activities that give them no sense of spiritual possibility whatsoever. Yet they are not at all certain that they want to go *to* the church for an answer.

The Church could be one of the strongest resources we have for leading a balanced and effective business life. In most cases, it is not. It could provide spiritual and ethical insight about work that would revolutionize business life. In most cases, it does not. At the heart of these problems are fundamental tensions between Christian ideals and the realities of business life that have created a significant gap between our life at church and our life at work.

Exploring why this gap exists, and what the Christian Church and businesspeople can do to bridge that gap, is the subject of this book. Our goal is not to convince the church that it should be the handmaiden of business—in fact, we argue for less, rather than more, engagement of the institutional church in economics. But we do argue that the church should help businesspeople develop a *process* for personally engaging their faith in the management arena.

Along the way, we look at how Americans think about religion in the workplace, how they might make their faith a part of their whole life—especially their work life—and not just something that pertains when they're in church. Most of all, we want to locate the connection between institutional Christianity and the workplace: How can we bring together these opposite and distant worlds?

We do not attempt to dictate a blueprint for how to make this integration occur. Rather, we propose a framework for thinking and talking about the issues, a critical first step toward connection. We hope that our findings help you recommit to the vitality of the Church, and that clergy and congregations begin to work together to develop sophisticated spiritual fulfillment in the professional lives of businesspeople.

Cambridge, Massachusetts   *Laura Nash*
Palo Alto, California   *Scotty McLennan*
July 2001

Introduction

In the past decade, American business has experienced revolutionary changes in how it defines markets, composes institutions, communicates between people, and adapts to changing expectations in society. Not surprisingly, these change have occasioned an intense quest for new forms of guidance to help businesspeople deal with the marketplace and its impact on people's lives inside and outside the corporation.

Perhaps more surprisingly, the quest has led many people to a new interest in spirituality. People of all faiths (and of no faith) consult with spirituality gurus on managing for the twenty-first century. They gather in discussion groups to explore the spiritual aspects of successful leadership and a successful life. At a conservative estimate, corporations and individuals are investing hundreds of millions of dollars in management advice with some spiritual content. New seminars and workshops for executives on values and leadership are springing up weekly. Major news media, from the *Wall Street Journal* to *Business Week*, have followed the trend with increasing frequency and a continuing air of amazement. Religion, it seems, is news—and startling news in the context of business.

The diversity and popularity of spirituality and religion as they relate to work issues have been remarkable. What first seemed like a marginal faction of New Age crystal gazers and holistic health nuts quickly burgeoned into a mainstream trend that included some of the best business gurus in the United States. In a parallel but less broadly sponsored development, there has been a sudden resurgence of motivational programs from the conservative Christian evangelical movement, offering an updated revival of previous movements connecting business and faith, such as Norman Vincent Peale's power of positive thinking and Robert Greenleaf's servant leadership.

Capitalizing on both trends, publishers with large business customer bases dramatically increased the number of religious titles they were carrying—even as they destroyed all previous notions of what a "religion" book would be about. Barnes and Noble reported a 35 percent increase in the bookseller's religious titles between 1993 and 1995. By the end of 1999, Amazon.com was carrying more than nine thousand titles under the subject heading of spirituality and religion. Many of these were how-to books attempting to popularize spiritual concepts or give daily guidance.

Though they differ dramatically in style and religious content, both the secularized and overtly Christian strands of this trend have many similarities to the business religious climate in the late 1800s. Then, as now, radical technological change, explosive innovation, and new concentrations of extreme wealth characterized the market. Then, as now, people were both eager to participate in the economic boom and morally disturbed by its excesses. They turned to religion in their quest for higher meaning and personal effectiveness. Religion was adapted to these new longings. Building on the intense emotionalism and social activism of the Second Great Awakening at the start of the nineteenth century, the so-called Third Great Awakening (approximately 1890 to 1920) heralded a notably personalized and pragmatic religious interest. Old-money social-gospel advocates and new-climber positive thinkers joined in diversifying the religious scene, while crossing swords over the traumas and opportunities of the new industrial age. Newer forms of spirituality and commonsense morality flourished, from the popular Horatio Alger novels to the optimistic mind-cure and positive-thinker movements.

As today, many of the popular religious programs offered a convergence of sources: mainstream Protestantism was mixed with Emersonian transcendentalism, Berkeleyan idealism—and even Hinduism—to create an exotic resource for Americans seeking business and spiritual success.[1] These programs suggested an intimate connection between mind and body and the ability to cope with the new economic and social problems of the time.

Despite extraordinary similarities with the religious and economic landscape at the turn of the nineteenth century, there has been a radical change in the *sources* from which American businesspeople are now developing their religious understanding, particularly in terms of its relation to their working lives. A Fourth Awakening of sorts has occurred, marked by dramatic economic and social change and intense interest in personalized, experiential religious awareness. The dimensions of this awakening are debated. Nobel prize winner Robert Fogel has suggested that its chief proponents are the "enthusiastic" Christian faiths, from the Pentecostals to the evangelical groups in mainstream denominations.[2] He notes that beyond the cacophony of political exploiters, there is a great commonality in the search for religious rootedness or what futurist Faith Popcorn calls "anchoring."

We suggest that this spiritual awakening is even more widespread and diverse than is normally thought, especially among businesspeople. The great divide between conservative religious faith and the new spirituality is regularly being crossed. Despite sometimes radical differences in their political or religious leanings, conservative Christian groups share many commonalities with the so-called secular spirituality adherents, and also with people who have an increasing interest in religious heritage but not institutional religious membership. Jews and interested non-Jews read Torah together at lunchtime; Christians and unaffiliated "questers"[3] participate in online Benedictine services at sunrise; people of many faiths are reciting Buddhist chants before a heavy workday. Spirituality is the first common denominator; not surprisingly, interest in business effectiveness is the second.

The variety of this movement confuses development of a common understanding of *religion* and its role in life more than ever before—especially for questers with some Christian belief. Not only are more believers "unchurched" and eclectic in their religious views,[4] but they also have available a variety of competing institutions to facilitate their social and spiritual interests, especially when placed in a business context. Fueled by extensive business media coverage of the new sciences, ethics, and health, business culture is now inundated with activities that are not labeled as religion but are hardly distinguishable from the traditional concerns of religious institutions. Businesspeople need look no further than their own corporations for advice and tangible help on parenting practices, ethical behavior, elderly care, health and wellness, psychology, wholeness, intellectual development, community service, and even cosmological guidance concerning the nature of life and intelligence in the face of new scientific models.

No better indication of the new conflation between business and spirituality can be found than the list of resource gurus who were scheduled to lead *Fortune* magazine's 1999 Leadership Seminars. Of the five speakers set to talk on leadership, at least three run extensive training programs that include spirituality as a key component (Ken Blanchard, Stephen Covey, and Margaret Wheatley), and the other two (Tom Peters and Robert Cooper) have participated in many "inspirational" programs that feature the positive themes of this movement. Spirituality, it seems, is the new resource for business creativity, personal leadership, and social harmony. It is regularly enlisted to empower the manager to be a better person, create a better business, and contribute to a better society.

Most of the management spirituality programs are "secularized," reflecting American attitudes toward religion in the public arena. Universalizing many aspects of Eastern religion, humanistic ethics, and psychology, they focus on the self-expressive and the pragmatic. They explicate ultimate concerns in a curious combination of the scientific and evocative—a language that is part science fiction and part clothing advertisement. Many offer psychological solace and metaphysical meaning. They stress self-empowerment and universal respect. Contrary to general reports, most do not advocate greed and selfishness. Rather, they encourage business success while reinforcing the importance of social conscience and ethical standards. They do not, however, tell people which specific religion to believe in. In fact, many suggest that their programs are highly compatible with all religions, as well as secular viewpoints.

Curiously, mainstream Christianity (until recently the religion of choice for the majority of Americans) is notably absent on the new road to Canterbury. Some evangelical groups have eagerly sought to be part of the current spiritual pilgrimage of businesspeople, but it is fair to say that undisguised emphasis on Jesus has *not* achieved a significant connection with the management culture of mainstream corporate America. As a result, the spirituality-in-business movement is changing not only the face of American business but the face of American religion as well. The absence of supportive church engagement in today's spiritual quest and the presence of many alternative spiritual expressions have posed deep problems for both the businessperson and the Christian church. Already favoring syncretistic approaches to faith, the baby boomers who cannot find any meaningful message on economic life in the church of their childhood look elsewhere to feed their spiritual hunger. Even businesspeople of deep Christian faith find it difficult to understand what Christianity has to say to their professional concerns.

As one business executive with strong affection for his child-hood religion commented: "I love the Church, but sometimes I look at what we do in the company, the nonprofits we work with, the family policies, and I believe in many cases we [business] have found a more effective vehicle for these concerns *outside* the church. I begin to wonder, you know, What *is* the 'religion' part of social action or business ethics, when so much of what we do resembles what the church does but without the involvement of any formal religion?"

Such confusion is not unusual. Absent any significant ecclesias-tical engagement in the businessperson's concerns, businesspeople become frustrated by the current chaos of institutionalized forms of conscience and meaning in modern society. They wonder what it *means* to be a Christian and a businessperson. The way they think about this, however, is all too likely to reduce religion to narrow coping strategies to stay in business and still feel good. Unfortu-nately, the church's response, if any, is often a turn-off: too abstract, too uninformed, or too antagonistic to be practical. In a language long on polemics and short on conflict resolution, the church fails to enhance the business community's ability to *engage* with the sacred as it conducts its daily work.

Coming off the mountain of their own spiritual search, busi-nesspeople find themselves left to go it alone in the workplace. Their support of the church is undermined, as Robert Wuthnow has so amply demonstrated, and a great potential for real change in the workplace is lost.

The urgency of this situation, reinforced by a thirty-year decline in mainstream church membership[5] and continuing cynicism about business ethics, has caused us to take the unorthodox route of try-ing to speak to two audiences—businesspeople of faith as well as church professionals—to advance our understanding of Christian-ity's potential message for business as quickly as possible in both realms. Thus we take up two closely related topics: the nature of today's spiritual quest among businesspeople, and the forces preventing a productive inclusion of religion—particularly the churches—in this quest.

We seek to sound a wake-up call to the churches and to businesspeople to take the relation of spirituality, faith, and business more seriously. The new spirituality has many indications of religious spillover, which seems inevitable but is also likely to trickle away, lost in confused and contradictory attitudes toward business and formal religion in America. The new collision of spiritual and business attention is exciting and widespread, yet the churches have been slow to respond. Meanwhile, recurring assumptions about the outdated nature of religion and Christian views in economic life encourage the already strong tendency among businesspeople to go it alone in the spiritual quest.

If church professionals fail to detect and address deeply ingrained assumptions that are hostile to business or hopelessly devoid of practical implementation, they will engage in one of the largest acts of self-marginalization since their support of national prohibition. It is urgent that the new spiritual interest be understood both for its spiritual *potential* as well as its limits.

Based on extensive interviews of clergy and businesspeople,[6] as well as a thorough review of the new spirituality literature and executive programming, this book attempts to shed a helpful light on the mental frameworks that seem to abort serious consideration and application of faith in the workplace today. We explore where and why so many people's faith suffers a bifurcation when set in a business context. We also pay attention to the coping strategies that businesspeople and the church develop to withstand the pressures of bifurcation by putting religion in a private box, never to be taken out in the corporation. Most important, we profile the key trigger points that have caused businesspeople and clergy to turn off to each other's message. Knowing this terrain is essential if spirituality is to develop into an actively engaged faith.

This book is intended to be of use to a broad group of Christian businesspeople, clergy, and religious educators of all denominations, whether or not their experience precisely coincides with that of the people profiled here. Our frameworks are generalized to transcend the denominations, just as many Americans are themselves constructing a belief system that draws on multiple sources.

Among the key questions we ask are these:

- What is today's spiritual interest about in relation to business?

- What is being claimed?

- Why does it strike such a chord?

- Are there commonalities among the many sources of wisdom being represented?

- What is the church's potential role in this movement?

- How does the church cope with its own limitation of influence over the economic choices of a religiously diverse public?

- How have certain classic attitudes about Christianity caused believers to enter a blind alley in their quest to be good Christians and good businesspeople?

Some businesspeople will want to use this book as a private resource for exploring their own assumptions about integrating faith and work. Clergy who have separated their own management role from a true sense of calling may also find the frameworks helpful in administrative roles. Ultimately, however, our goal is to provide substantive help to the church at large—ecclesiastics and congregants—to effect *mutual engagement* in the questions of faith and work. To this purpose, we have created a detailed study guide for congregations and seminar groups. It offers practical advice for creating the right conditions for any type of clergy-congregant discussion and a twelve-part program for discussing and acting on the ideas in this book. In following the suggested program, congregations and seminaries may be able to address uncomfortable aspects of the distanced relationship in concert. In so doing, they will fashion a new voice for the religious dimensions of life.

Brief Overview of the Book

The terrain we cover is notably short of common definitions. Spiritual quests seem to be everywhere, but no two people have the same definition of spirituality. So, too, the meaning of being religious has always varied in America, especially in terms of practical action and state of consciousness during business hours. We need to clarify our own terms.

After reviewing the many understandings of spirituality in use today—including the eleven definitions recently reported by Gallup in *The Next American Spirituality*[7]—we define *spirituality* as access to the sacred force that impels life. Much of the new spirituality movement is about this accessing process, which (as many have noted) leans toward a personalized, experiential form of religious engagement. Stressing discovery of the inner, sacred self and self-discovery of the connection between the sacred force impelling life and one's own life, spirituality is not the same as organized religion. Indeed, many people are clear about seeing a great difference between the two.[8]

The parameters of religion, in our opinion, include spirituality, but they also go beyond the personal and experienced forms of the transcendent. By *religious understanding*, we mean three basic concerns:

1. The *source narratives* by which people explain their ultimate concerns and cosmological questions

2. The *source disciplines, rituals, and communities* through which they personally discover and stay in touch with these truths and apply them to daily life

3. The *ethical rules and practices* that they believe are demanded by these understandings

Some questers are most comfortable with a strategy of partial engagement. They cherry pick the methods and content of religion that are described here while proclaiming a profound difference between who they are as spiritual people in the real world and what specific religions claim. In our opinion, spirituality cannot help but spill over into religion at some point, despite the resistance of the business community. We already see a religiously spiritual market in the making as people seek out earlier forms of Christian practices and beliefs and a new formation of religious community via Web sites, adult bible classes, and new collections of literature. At the same time, the churches are in great danger of missing the boat. One of the most disturbing findings in our interviews was the pervasive lack of awareness or interest among ecclesiastics in how deeply anticapitalist the message continues to be among many liberal and conservative clergy, however much they cultivate a warm relationship with members of their congregation. Under such conditions, the seminaries are not innovating new courses, nor is the ministry attracting people who offer a voice and meaningful religious dimension to business issues that their own communities face.

Thus a self-destructive pattern emerges: the businesspeople turned off by "clueless" economic statements have no confidence in investing in any divinity school program that aims at economics for ecclesiastics or laity. This simply reinforces the isolation of the professional religious community and its tendency to look only to other academics and clergy for signs of success. On the conservative right, businesspeople support new lay efforts but carry such an espoused agenda that their good discoveries of catalytic Christianity are destined to be severely limited in terms of carryover to the whole corporation.

In *God and Mammon in America*, Robert Wuthnow discussed the many ways in which changing economics are shaping American religion. Based on surveys conducted in 1992, his book largely pre-dated the full-blown business and spirituality movement, whose explosion in the 1990s only confirmed Wuthnow's understanding that there is an important relationship between economic life and the functions of the church. In *Church on Sunday, Work on Monday*, we have turned to the topic again, not only to reinforce the need for rethinking how churches are approaching business but also to understand where they are most needed and might best fit with the keen spiritual interest exhibited by businesspeople today.

Understanding the nature of the new spiritual interest, and the dynamics of traditional churches in respect to business issues, is crit-ical to the church's reentry into the arena of the marketplace. Our conclusion is that few divinity schools or congregations have taken serious note of the many factors addressed here, and that they must do so if the type of full integration of the religious dimension that we suggest as a New Way is to occur. The current lack of commu-nication is real, alarming, and unacceptable.

Equally distressing is the degree to which church leaders have allowed an antibusiness attitude to influence their own negativity toward the responsibility to manage the church itself. Faith-based nonprofits suffer a similar fate. There are many good efforts today to improve the management of churches, but without serious explo-ration of underlying assumptions about the relationship of faith and management these programs are sadly inadequate to their goals.

Business is a central concern of America, but it is often forgot-ten that Calvin Coolidge included an addendum to his famous assertion: "The business of America is business, *but we also want much more.*" As the new spirituality shows, that "much more" has all the optimism, self-reliance, and desire to be good of an earlier time. These good intentions need sustenance and hard scrutiny. This book challenges the churches to do more in providing both.

Church on Sunday, Work on Monday

PART I

In Separate Worlds

Exploring the Gap Between Church and Business

1

Spirituality Goes
to Work, the Church
Stays Away

Religious Disconnects
in American Business Lives

*I see many tensions between my Christian beliefs and
what I do at work, and I feel deeply responsible to be
a "good Christian" in my daily life. But my pastor is
the last person I'd discuss this with.*

—Protestant businessperson

"We are not human beings having a spiritual experience, but
spiritual beings having a human experience." So the Covey
Leadership Center facilitator advised the twenty-two businesspeople and professionals sitting before him in the spring of 1997, quoting the late Jesuit priest Pierre Teilhard de Chardin.

We were in the first few minutes of a three-day "principle-
centered leadership" workshop dedicated to improving managerial

---

All opening epigraphs are taken from interviews we conducted with business executives and church professionals on the topic of religion, business, and the role of
the church. For more information on our research, see "A Note on Methodology"
at the back of the book.

and organizational effectiveness. During our time together, the facilitator would recite the Prayer of St. Francis of Assisi in its entirety, refer more than once to his experiences as a Presbyterian youth minister, explain how to bring love into the workplace, examine the role of personal conscience, and describe in some depth the spiritual dimension of life in relation to the physical, emotional, and intellectual. However, this management seminar—and all of the Covey Leadership Center's work—is explicitly secular, not religious. The public relations manager at Covey's headquarters in Provo, Utah, told us: "We are not a religious organization. The principles we teach are universal and can be found in virtually all traditions, secular and religious."

No doubt about it: there has been a sea change in the way businesspeople are approaching the problems of business and work. Spirituality—however defined—is now a popular resource for business needs, whether for sparking creativity or for being a better person on the job. Tap a search engine for business and spirituality, and fifteen hundred Web sites are likely to pop up.

The dry, hyperrational paradigms that long held sway over financial decision making have failed to inspire or even adequately source nonrational intelligence, or satisfy the universal need for personal meaning—dynamics that were patently beneath the surface of seemingly impersonal market forces. New spirituality programs and their gurus—such as Covey, Deepak Chopra, Robert Greenleaf, and others—are engaged in a strong partnership with the business community, as evidenced by the popularity of corporate seminars and the abundance of bestsellers aimed at transforming the lives of businesspeople. Some form of spiritual practice can be found in most business settings today: people meditating at their desks, calling on faith to help them stay the course during hard times, silently calling on angels, acting out of faith-based compassion, or simply striving for a Buddha-like mindfulness. At more than one company, meetings begin with the lighting of a candle to "focus" the group mentally and emotionally. Office rooms are reserved for meditation and quiet time. Companies sponsor dramatic retreats for executives and distribute commonsense guidelines for holistic living.

Despite all this spiritual interest, mainstream Christianity has not been a notable force in the businessperson's pilgrimage. Traditional mainstream religion, it seems, has failed to deliver on the desire for experiential, personalized ways of knowing God in one's work.

This is not to say that businesspeople do not consider themselves Christians. Ironically, the majority of church members in mainstream Protestant congregations are middle-class people who spend most of their waking hours at a business or are married to people in business. They are looking for ways to live their Christian beliefs and values at work, as they do at home and at church. Yet when they look to the church for guidance, they find one of two responses: clergy who are indifferent to the idea or who are wildly interested but stumped as to how to begin. As we discovered in our interviews, even deeply faithful Christians in business tend to feel a strong disconnect between their experience of the church or private faith, and the spirit-challenging conditions of the workplace:

- A prominent business leader in his sixties, very active in Catholic charity work, asks, "Can't the church offer just a little more help to those of us who want to be good Catholics at work?"
- A liberal Protestant manager in her forties stops at an Episcopal monastery to pray several times a week. She reports that this practice gives her "spiritual focus." She is convinced that it helps her at work, but she cannot be more specific.
- A Christian-Buddhist computer engineer is unaffiliated with any formal church but attends several services and meditation sessions around the city. He takes his spirituality very seriously but does not want to entrust its guidance to any clerical authority: "They mean well, but they don't understand the world I live in. I don't get much from church."
- The owner of a medium-sized insurance agency organizes a monthly prayer-and-discussion session at lunchtime for a group of

businesspeople from a variety of Christian denominations. He feels the sessions are a personal ministry to "people in pain, people who want to do the right thing but who feel abandoned and lost in their workplace." His pastor is enthusiastic about this effort but has never attended a session.

- An accountant in his mid-forties suddenly decides to take time off to attend divinity school. Though he has never been asked to cheat or lie at work, his company cultivates a doggedly dehumanized culture. He has no desire to be a preacher but wants to enrich his understanding of religion and theology. He would like to devote himself to some other kind of business with a different balance of values, and he hopes that divinity school will reawaken his spiritual life and help prepare him for the task of applying his Christian faith more actively to his business work. So far, he hasn't seen the connection.

Plainly, businesspeople of faith are seeking a deeper spiritual life and a greater degree of integration of faith and work. Some are in deep despair, stressed by financial and family issues. Unable to access the inner peace they believe is possible, they strive to recover their souls. Others have experienced financial success but are dissatisfied by the wealth. They want something more out of life than a paycheck—both for themselves and for those less fortunate who seem abandoned or even abused by the economic system. Some are outraged by unethical business practices, or by the morality of their leaders; they want to follow a higher standard of conduct, one presumably closer to a religious ethic. Others seek community, or increased effectiveness in their lives, or help in creating a leadership vision from that uplifting connection to the divine we call inspiration.

For regular churchgoers and unchurched nonpracticing believers alike, career maturity has not necessarily brought equivalent spiritual maturity. They express feelings of radical disconnection between Sunday services and Monday morning activities, describing a sense of living in two worlds that never touch each other. When they are deeply involved in business affairs, they long for the settings that have in the past occasioned deep spiritual faith and certainty about what is right from a religious standpoint. But when they retire to an overtly sacred state of mind, they are unable to see a way to carry out the real-world goals they feel are important. The changing world of business poses problems their religious upbringing never touched on.

This split poses significant psychological and moral uncertainty. The spiritual questers politely dismiss the church from intruding on their lives and entertain reservations about its ability to offer practical advice. They struggle with how they can act on, articulate, and symbolize Christian spirituality within a secular social context. To disguise faith seems inauthentic, but taking it out of the closet may provoke conflict or accusations of being inappropriate. As businesspeople struggle with these problems, they rarely look to the church for help. As we heard in the epigraph that opens this chapter, the words of one executive are echoed by many others: "I see many tensions between my Christian beliefs and what I do at work, and I feel deeply responsible to be a 'good Christian' in my daily life. But my pastor is the last person I'd discuss this with."

Despite his affection for many aspects of his church, this man has taken his spiritual development into his own hands.[1] He feels that to do otherwise invites a conflict with his pastor that would be extremely painful to them both. In making this choice, he cuts himself off from the possibility of fully supporting the church and being supported by it. How much easier it is to patch in secular spirituality, with its empowering claims of being able to evoke many of the states of consciousness associated with religion: peak experience, "flow," a transformational frame of consciousness, emotional and physical wellness, and new cognitive skills.

For many reasons (which we explore in later chapters), the ecclesiastics have in large part found it difficult to adopt such a supportive relationship to business-centered activity. Their reluctance, however justified in their own theological terms, may miss the main import of the business and spirituality movement: it is not the ruthless ethic of excessive greed that is the church's chief competitor in the struggle for people's souls; it is the new spirituality-in-business movement that has taken hold with such vigor.

Making It Up as We Go Along

The surprising force with which the concept of spirituality struck a chord among businesspeople in the 1990s has caused many Americans to revise their understanding of work, performance, and the good life. Starved for meaning and eager for new sources of power in their working lives, they are not willing to remain hungry. Today, whether basking in sudden wealth or hurting from new competition, businesspeople actively seek new clues and mental paradigms to solve the frightening quandaries and meaning of the global, cybernetic economy. In the midst of this search, they are particularly drawn to spirituality in its many forms, hoping for self-awareness, meaning, moral goodness, and effectiveness in their vocational activities.

With remarkable determination, businesspeople are making it up as they go along, relying on authorities outside their religious tradition, and hoping for a cognitive leap of faith between these frameworks and their religious belief. They use code words to cope with the distance: calling themselves spiritual but not religious, or citing their denominational affiliation but saying it should be separated from their work life. Underlying this phenomenon is the new blending of domestic and working life that forms the reality of most American workers today. The social cosmologies that marked the early church have collapsed in terms of gender, race, and vocational hierarchies. Americans now entertain the possibility of holistic, personalized religious experience in all walks of life. To many, this is not a lesser religious goal; it *is* religion—and in a form that has meaning in daily affairs.

Where's the Clergy?

Even when clergy, congregants, and the general business population hold the same concerns about the challenges of economic life, they cannot share these concerns with each other. Instead, they maintain a polite but distanced relationship. Congregants in business who said they felt very close to their pastors on issues of family, personal well-being, or community outreach told us a different story when it came to their role as businesspeople. Here they often felt ignored, disdained, or simply beyond the comprehension and experience of most clergy.

One man's comment is quite representative: "You have to expect the clergy to haul you over the coals a little. Otherwise, why would you go to church? To be told you're doing everything right? But when you hear this stuff, it's just so off base. They don't understand what business does. It's such a turn off!"

Such sentiments are a tragic glimpse into the extreme sense of separation that many businesspeople feel concerning the moral authority and personal sustenance of the church. The church's skepticism over the more commercialized or cooptive forms of spiritual guidance can be well justified; but its often-dismissive response to the layperson's optimistic desire to integrate faith and career is not. In fact, this attitude may be the largest act of self-marginalization mainstream churches have ever engaged in.[2]

Why has the church failed to develop an engaging response to the interest in spirituality that businesspeople are exhibiting? What is preventing active integration of Christian principles and religious consciousness in businesspeople's lives, in the workplace as well as in the home and community?

Many of the ecclesiastics whom we interviewed did not realize how deeply they were distanced from practical economic dilemmas, or why the Church was not a more significant influence on the business culture. Strong in their own distaste for the false god of the marketplace, they failed to see their own participation in cutting the church off from significant parts of the lay Christian community.

Indeed, many clergy reported that they felt ignored or simply powerless to have a significant impact on businesspeople, but they did not know why. They would assume, for example, that business-people were simply too greedy or indifferent to care about real spiritual issues, and that the predominance of a market mentality in society was simply overwhelming their flock.

Gone are the days of the medieval town or the Bible Common-wealth of early Massachusetts, when churches were intimately involved in regulating state and economy. Today's Americans are more independent of their churches, and churches are more independent of the mainstream economy. What remains is spiritual hunger and the search for rootedness, meaning, a sense of balance, and perspective. Whether this search takes the form of cashing out to lead a simpler life, or engaging in exciting new transformations of the business basics, the church has the opportunity to shape the quest.

It is clear that we desperately need new strategies and paradigms for thinking about Christianity at work. Our goal in this book is to try to understand the fundamental areas in which the church is failing to engage. First, however, we need to look at the context for these problems: the social and economic factors that underlie the current obsession with workplace spirituality, the felt needs of Christians in business today, and how the new spirituality answers these needs in a way that mainstream Christianity currently does not.

The Social-Economic Foundations of the New Spirituality

American business has always tended to structure its religious views around its economic concerns. The business community has seized on the new spirituality out of an essentially pragmatic idealism in the face of new social and economic trends. We believe six major realities have particularly influenced the shape of new spirituality programs and the terms on which they have based their broad, popular appeal: (1) the baby boomers, (2) the global economy, (3) increasing work-related stress, (4) new scientific concepts, (5) postmodern paradigms, and (6) the rise of the business guru.

The Baby Boomers Have Come of Age

That enormously influential generation, the baby boomers—born between 1946 and 1964—are now occupying leadership roles in corporations and dominate the business population. They have reached a stage of life where the feeling that work should be about something more than a paycheck is becoming urgent. As they have done all their lives, they are having a major cultural impact.

This generation highly values individualism, egalitarianism, self-expression, personal fulfillment, antiauthoritarianism, diversity, tolerance, and holistic thinking. The new programs frame spiritual concerns not only to emphasize all these values but also to suggest ways of using them to overthrow outdated techniques for business success and exclusionary, nonexperiential formats for religious interest. As best-selling futurist Kevin Kelly asserts, we must anticipate an economy where all the normal rules will be turned upside down.[3]

The Rise of the Global Economy

The new global economic environment has created the perfect platform for affirming that boomer values are not just compatible with economic success; they are *essential*. Globalism demands tolerance, openness to novelty, and intuitive ability to adapt quickly to unforeseen administrative problems—a call for a whole new mind-set in the marketplace. Cookie-cutter solutions from an Anglo-Western tradition simply won't do. This attitude has extended to dismissing authoritarian forms of Christianity as delivered by traditional churches.

From an economic and technological standpoint, increasing global connectivity is essential for business success, and globalism offers an exciting new scale of connection opportunities. Necessary cognitive connections between mind, spirit, and body—including psychological well-being—are enhanced by the ability to draw on multiple ways of knowing, multiple religious traditions, and multiple cultural connections. Globalism also plays into the need for stronger community and ethics in business, and it offers a new model for social connectedness that does not rely on the already mistrusted large institution.

Increasing Sense of Psychological Stress at Work

The pace of business grows ever faster, more capricious, and multidirectional. New technologies and new sources of production from overseas constantly threaten existing products and markets; unstable new financial markets, constant mergers, hubristically high benchmarks for compensation, two-career families, and changing social values add to the uncertainty about personal worth. Spirituality offers new hope of accessing alternative solutions to problems that have not proved tractable to a purely scientific Enlightenment approach. Meanwhile, the romanticism and psychologizing of the spirituality movement help ease stress at least temporarily, even if they don't solve the business problem.

Although the new spirituality programs cannot always define spirituality, they know when it's "blocked": low morale, poor productivity and creativity, and lack of teamwork are sure signs of spiritual imbalance. Spirituality promises both exalting inner healing and a seamless connection to business effectiveness.

Science Offers New, Multiple Paradigms

People resonate to claims that they need "new tools" to help them master the many daunting technological and social innovations of the day. New science paradigms suggest that intuitive and systems approaches carry powerful capacity for problem solving (an approach Carl Sagan derisively called "the flight from reason"). These new mental paradigms—which start with such concepts as chaos theory, quantum physics, and genetics—are particularly appealing in their ability to model, if not predict, the uncontrollable. Fractals (those elemental patterns that create order when iterated millions of times) offer a population feeling overwhelmingly disjointed and chaotic a paradigm that is deeply reassuring. There is order in this chaos, an order that can be tapped. In this new paradigm, linear science is not abandoned but rather connected to nonrational, elemental associative powers of the brain.

Postmodern Paradigms and Religious Experimentation

At its heart, postmodern thought abandons the old science of assuming one correct answer in favor of multiple, simultaneously entertained ways of knowing. In the past, religious belief might have implied the abandonment of reason (C. P. Snow's "two cultures" framework). Today, many people are quite comfortable with the idea that both science and religion contain a truth, that multiple intelligences and multiple interpretations are not only possible, they're essential. Today's spiritual person knows that both Ecclesiastes and chaos theory plausibly describe the rhythmic aspect of the seasons. The new blend of science and religion in the spirituality movement, its association of progress and sacredness, establishes a particularly congenial religious format for the postmodern mind.

Multiple, ultimately relativistic frames of reference fit well in an economic environment that is marked by uncertainty and the need to adapt quickly. They also fit well with the essential pluralism, innovation, and want-it-all behavior of the boomers. Postmodernism invites individuals to try out multiple worldviews and even multiple identities, to be exchanged at will like a new pair of shoes.

The Rise of the Business Guru

The past few decades have seen a dramatic rise in use of consultants (knowledge experts) inside the corporation. Between 1987 (the crash of the U.S. stock market, the era of insider trading abuses and other scandals) and 1992, U.S. corporations doubled their spending on consultants, to the tune of $14 billion annually. By one estimate, upwards of thirty-one thousand gurus now hawk their wares in the marketplace.[4]

Their buzzwords suggest a changing focus over time. In the early 1980s, most experts advised on "management science"; but people such as Tom Peters and Robert Waterman and James McGregor Burns in the 1970s were touting the need for "a whole new corporate mindset," "transformation," and "synergy." By the end of the 1980s, a number of business best-sellers picked up the intuitive theme to transform management from a science into an "art" that required not just pragmatism but passion. Soon, the business knowledge industry split into two camps, each conferring celebrity status on its special, best-selling experts. The rising interest in business gurus with expertise in spirituality occurred just as the guru culture of corporate consulting on synergistic, organizational dynamics was taking off in the early 1990s. (For the latter, think Peter Senge, Gary Hamel, or Rosabeth Moss Kanter.) The themes came together in the many books on the "soul" of a business entity.

Contours of Today's Spiritual Quest

Although these trends have contributed to today's spirituality in the workplace, adapting religion for business purposes is not new. Ben Franklin's Poor Richard repackaged Calvinism and directly applied it to business success. Charles Dickens and the Rev. Horatio Alger both created secular narratives of young men adopting Protestant discipline, good personal habits, helpfulness, and ambition for worldly improvement. The Rev. Norman Vincent Peale's *Power of Positive Thinking* was a direct descendant of this type of popularization.

In each of these works, some divine ordering of the conditions for worldly success was accessed through qualities of character and piety. Today's movement has once again coupled the longing to succeed with the longing to lead a good and meaningful life. The labels and content, however, have changed radically. Mainstream church authorities do not generally represent this coupling. Personalized, secular spirituality does.

Secular Spirituality

Today's so-called secular spirituality is not about secularism in the normal sense of the term (meaning rational, modern scientific thinking), but rather about a spirituality that is not governed by the ecclesiastic elite of a specific confessional Judeo-Christian religious tradition.[5] *Secular spirituality* is a term that the Dalai Lama uses, for example, to describe Buddhist practices and generalized beliefs that are accessible to all people, without the strict religious order of Tibetan Buddhism in its institutional form. In fact, today's spirituality is to be found equally in the mystical and the mundane, the scientific and the irrational, the therapeutic and the pedagogical, the personal and the universal.

Many spirituality programs explicitly advocate the importance of having a developed personal religion but refrain from endorsing a particular dogma or theistic stance. Few of the popular programs are allied with any ecclesiastical institution.

Essentially, the new secular programs are presenting spiritual alternatives to the church, but not necessarily to people's faith. Participation by nonconservative Christians is significant. Many report that these new books and seminars help them make connections between their belief system and what they do at work. One Episcopal interviewee said:

> My company made us participate in an off-site leadership workshop run by someone who was basically teaching Covey. And we went through a lot of the spiritual exercises, shared stories about some of the hardest times at work, our dreams, you know, that sort of thing. I didn't see this as anti-Christian. It just made a lot of sense about how I could be stronger about bringing my whole

self to my life, including to my work. If I'm more balanced and aware of my priorities, if I can draw on that
inner self, I'm able to be a better Christian when things
get crazy at work.

The secular spirituality programs do not explicitly exclude Christians or atheists, as long as they support humanistic values. Indeed,
they target *everyone*, and in many cases *everything*. Says one new-
spirituality devotee in real estate: "Businesspeople have got to realize this spiritual thing is key. I mean, they have to know how to
bring their whole selves to the marketplace. It's going to transform
business."

What Do They Mean By Spirituality?

In essence, all of these programs seem to understand spirituality as
access to the sacred force that impels life. Whether they are talking about creativity, inner power, core identity, the soul's code, or
systems logic in nature, these programs seek to heighten personal
awareness of life-generating, creative forces that inspire awe, rev-
erence, and extraordinary power. Conversely, they imply a moral/
religious opposition to life-destroying habits, states of mind, or business actions.

A conservative or mainstream Christian may immediately turn
to the equivalent of the Nicene Creed to name this force and object
to the suggestion of any other name. But the general religious profile of Americans is more eclectic and syncretic in its religious
understanding. A good number who embrace parts of the spirituality programs have no trouble with the vagueness of the terms; it
allows them to customize the new spiritual messages to their own
deeper beliefs. Indeed, many stress that their spirituality is not the
same as their religion. It operates on a different level.

Most spirituality-and-business programs try to avoid sectarian
controversies. Reflecting the root meaning of the Latin word for

breath (*spiritus*), spirituality is often meant to indicate essential core of life, intense awareness of being alive, or the faculty of intuition.[6] Some authors associate spirituality with religious concepts such as the Holy Spirit; others do not name its origin. Stephen Covey defines spirituality as "your core, your center, your commitment to your values system. It's a very private area of life and a supremely important one. It draws upon the sources that inspire and uplift you and tie you to the timeless truths of all humanity."[7] Peter Block, in *Stewardship: Choosing Service over Self-Interest,* says: "Spirituality is the process of living out a set of deeply held personal values, of honoring forces or a presence greater than ourselves. It expresses our desire to find meaning in, and to treat as an offering, what we do. . . . There is a longing in each of us to invest our energy in things that matter."[8]

Block's definition is more precise than most. It reflects several themes that run through the entire spirituality-and-work movement: the inner self, forces greater than the individual, and a search for significance in what we do in everyday life, including acts of benevolence or moments of success.

Make no mistake: none of these programs advocates unbridled hedonism, pure selfishness, excessive materialism, devil worship, or any of the other negative stereotypes critics have launched against them. Even the most blatant prosperity titles in the evangelical market turn out to be talking about prosperity *and* the "real riches in life," which rest on worship and helping others solve their problems. None, however, try to replicate an ethic of total selflessness, suffering, and sacrifice such as to be found in some traditional Christian theologies modeled on a suffering Jesus.

Our basic definition of the new spirituality as access to the sacred force that impels life helps us understand the content, purpose, and measures of success in the current programs. Connection to the sacred is essential, as is connection to the patterns or powers that impel creative acts. This holds true at a personal as well as an organizational level. Spiritual success is about awareness and experience of the sacred, not about imposing a political stand or membership in a religious institution. So, too, it is measured in life-affirming outcomes: peace of mind, an empowered organization, stronger community relations, creativity, new products, a profitable balance sheet. Even the most obvious measurement of success—whether the spirituality program or book manages to entertain and stimulate the audience it is hired to "train"—is itself a positive, affirming notion. A book is offered as an act of friendship, not as imposition of dogma. A corporation sponsors a program not only to improve performance but also to affirm that it values the employee's "inner self."

Why Spirituality? Four Felt Needs

As our general definition of the new spirituality suggests, this movement is a contemporary expression of age-old, common concerns about the nature and purpose of life, transcendence, universal principles, material well being, and moral purpose as these all manifest themselves in practical life.

But why this particular form? Exactly what is the excitement about? Even though today's pilgrims are embarking on widely diverse paths to religious awareness, and interviewees described different patterns of integration, a core of dissatisfaction and expected payback forms their ideas about the nature of spirituality and what it should address in their lives. Many wish to save their souls from the false values and dehumanization of the business culture. All look to spirituality as a way to be more effective. We call this core the four "felt needs," which make up related but distinct goals in the businessperson's spiritual quest[9]:

1. Emergent awareness of the sacred self (soul)
2. Harmony with an ultimate order (balance)
3. Connectedness with community (sacred community)
4. Religiously consistent morality (faith-based business ethics)

Not every businessperson and corporation weights all four types of spiritual focus equally, and no single economic tension drives the spiritual quest. Lighter examples in the new movement often fail not simply for intellectualism but because they have underestimated one of the four needs, in terms of either access or application. For example, many of the feel-good programs about-self esteem quickly lose spiritual force because they fail to address the community or the ethical aspects of today's spiritual quest. Sober, ethical programs may lack needed power because they neglect to cultivate the connection between ethics and personal engagement in ethics, for which one needs to develop knowledge of the sacred self, and connection to community.

Isolating the four underlying elements can help clergy and businesspeople conceptually locate all the disparate aspects of the spirituality movement as they circumnavigate the spiritual universe of faith and work.

Emergent Awareness of the Sacred Self (Soul)

No longing seems more widespread than the search for recovery of personal significance. As jobs, marriages, and identities change with the speed of a cybermessage, people experience extreme fragmentation of identity. They are told they have to "reinvent themselves." Media whose lifeblood is novelty bombard people with new products to change their image. Businesses celebrate models of super-hero stamina and activity. The fallout is hard on self-worth and self-identity. As one man told us, "I have these different hats that I wear, and each tells me to do a different thing. When you get involved at work, you can find yourself a stranger to yourself. Suddenly you just want to find the 'real me.'"

Like this man, many seek relief from confusion by reconnecting with what they variously term their inner self, authentic self, inner spirit, or soul. People feel they have lost their soul in spite of worldly success, or as a result of business stress and failure. In fact, one recent book spelled out the connection quite clearly in its title: *Losing Your*

Job—Reclaiming Your Soul: Stories of Resilience, Renewal, and Hope. As the sentimental language indicates, such a quest involves heart *and* mind; it must be emotive and savvy to be authentic.

Connection to the real self is particularly problematic in today's corporate culture, which sends highly ambiguous or contradictory signals about identity. Henry Ford lamented that all he wanted was a set of hands, and instead he got a whole person. But at least that set of hands could go home at night and put the job aside to become a real person. Workers today are expected to bring their "whole self" to work, to be "all that they can be," to "think outside the box," to draw on their creativity for problem solving. That's a lot to ask. Fed up with the moral and creative failures of Enlightenment reasoning, but not sure who the real self is, they desperately seek new tools.

The spirituality movement seeks to offer these tools. Most of the new programs sell the optimistic belief that tapping into one's spirituality allows access to an "inner power" that is inspiring and adaptable at work. Empowerment, it turns out, is an important feature of the businessperson's search for soul, a new kind of Protestant compulsion for personal improvement and effectiveness. Also, like earlier forms of Protestantism, this power is suspected of being intimately connected to one's relationship with the divine, reminiscent of Christian notions of calling or secular vocation.

The reality, however, may be less rewarding. As Richard Sennett notes in *The Corrosion of Character,* the corporate message of empowerment frequently occurs within highly controlled parameters. "Empowered" managers may actually be helpless to prevent an action directly threatening their group's performance—a layoff, a cutback, or a merger—despite repeated company demands to exercise personal responsibility. Being yourself, as urged, can be *disempowering* from a career standpoint when it conflicts with the goals of those at the top of the corporation.

These mixed signals about identity and self-worth are everywhere in business. Even a seemingly trivial issue such as office space becomes a self-contradictory source of self-definition. Workers today, for example, are likely to have their own office space, set off by walls or cubicles or located in their homes, an arrangement that is often claimed to represent a higher valuing of individuality and autonomy. In reality, however, employees may be forbidden to exercise personal choice or self-expression in decorating their cubicle wall and be "on call twenty-four-seven" with no time for personal activities. Similarly, personal development programs that seem to encourage a new, authentic self may prove to be highly repressive if that self likes to smoke and overeat—or pray on the job.

In short, the worker is caught up in a bewildering cycle of encouragement and denial of the authentic self. A world so dominated by illusion and contradiction prompts disillusion. Employees learn to disguise the "real me" even from themselves. Relentless conditions of competition trap them into a mode that does not fit their understanding of what it means to be an unconditional object of God's love.

Such confusion only sparks an even deeper spiritual interest: the greater the perception of personal inadequacy, the more intense the search to recover personal sacredness. This recovery, however, sees connection with the self as an exercise not in self-denial (as some religious mystics would believe) but rather the very Protestant value of self-improvement. Even Buddhist exercises to lose the self are turned into a technique for gaining personal power. Whatever the theologism, the felt need is for another self more valuable, more interesting, more effective, closer to immortality—a happier self than that which keeps track of the numbers.

Others embark on spirituality for purposes of self-discovery, feeling they must cultivate a better sense of what a significant life and identity are really about. One interviewee said, "The best times at work, when I really feel that I am living out a vocation in business, are when I've been in a situation that has worked out well and I have genuinely contributed to that outcome by contributing my self."

Again, this goal is usually hoped to be compatible with continuing to work in a profit-making business setting. In the 1960s, the formula for self-expression was "turn on, tune in, drop out." Today's spiritual formula is more likely to be "turn on, tune in, turn on, turn on, turn on. . . . " As one man told us, "I spent ten years single-mindedly pursuing success at my company, and all the time I felt I was a good person. But increasingly, I just feel empty." Those who do take time out are likely to do so in carefully circumscribed moments, oftentimes only to jump back into the economic fray without spiritual carryover.[10]

Although spirituality programs describe the core self as sacred, this search for the sacred self tends to be only loosely associated with religion. More likely, this type of spirituality is recognized in feelings of self-expression, and in happiness and accomplishment at work (hence the easy exchange of spiritual interest for interest in the secrets to success). Remarked one interviewee, "I just feel that I should be doing something that is more personally satisfying in work. I believe God gives each person a unique talent, and that my talent is business. But the way business is today, it's over the top. I want to find a way to be in business without losing that sense that I am really contributing to something." Generally speaking, such people are not seeking to discover sacredness in a self totally independent of God. Far from it. Many interviewees linked their sense of self-expression and personal contribution at work to their belief in God's personal love for every individual, the God of their Christian belief. Not all felt that God had a plan to work his purposes through their business lives, but many had experienced some sense of God's support or presence, however indirect, at occasional moments in their careers. Indeed, Gallup reported that more than 45 percent of respondents who were religious claimed to have some awareness of God on the job. The felt need is for *awakening* these punctuated moments of transcendence more frequently.

Three goals are important here: experiencing personal sacredness and connection to God, building understanding of the nature of the human condition, and finding practical ways of applying such knowledge. One interviewee alluded to this combination in saying that she felt it was particularly important not to become "a lesser person" as she grew in her corporate role. Such longings play out in the prayer groups and spirituality programs in practices and readings that affirm individuals with regard to the deepest part of their being, beyond time.

Harmony with an Ultimate Order (Balance)

If the current search for spirituality is experiential and individualistic, it is not entirely self-centered, despite the strong participation of the "me generation." Today's spirituality derives much of its energy from a conviction that everything has a place in a higher order than that circumscribed by the self. This order presents a standard for harmony, growth, effectiveness, and ultimate purpose. Certain notions, such as service or cosmic harmony, constitute the spiritual mediation. Robert Greenleaf's influential management book *Spiritual Leadership* uses the notion of service, modeled on the life of Jesus, as the cornerstone of economic productivity and personal leadership.[11] Spirituality is about discovering this harmony and aligning oneself with it. The terms most often used are "perspective" and "balance."

Although cosmologies vary widely—from new science to methodical religious disciplines for life—the practical discussion of sacred harmony usually gets down to the search for order (even in chaos), holism, and ecological integrity. One program tried to express all three in its title, "The Three D's to Spirituality: Diet, Discipline, and Deity."

Loss of spiritual perspective is imbalance. It takes many forms: extreme careerism, overreliance on human ability to control the universe, narrow goals, crass commercialism, short-term views leading to destruction of natural resources, the hubris of success, the despair of failure. Recovering a sacral perspective, then, is a way of preventing oneself from getting too caught up in a corporate mindset that throws the individual out of balance, a state neither personally rewarding nor ultimately effective.

Few interviewees presented their cosmological views in the detail of a catechism, although many were attracted to the various popularized accounts of systems thinking, new science, and holistic mental approaches. They were more likely to express their search for balance and perspective in emotive, nonlinear statements connecting themselves to a world order (including the natural world) that is inherently sacred. For example, one interviewee spoke of the need to "get back on track," an effort aided by church attendance. Another sought spiritual renewal in nature and saw nature as intimately connected to God. This in turn invited consideration of stewarding the environment wisely in business and the need to have "seasons" of intense effort and relaxation.

One man felt that his church was imposing a false order on society by failing to acknowledge new scientific discoveries that debunked certain assumptions about the animal world. These older views, he claimed, fed historical prejudices on gender and sexual mores. He abandoned his church and childhood religion and embarked on a personal spiritual search that led him to believe that he had discovered a cosmic order in which diversity was tolerated. It had given him a great sense of confidence, actually leading him back to being able to accept a bare-bones Christian doctrine of love and grace.

Spirituality gives us a balancing mechanism in alignment with larger meaning by offering the insight to understand and prioritize activities or goals. By reenacting the mental states associated with larger truths about connectedness and divine power (sacred perspective), one approximates sacredness. When people told how religion and spirituality influenced their lives, they often remarked on these two functions. Rarely is the search for harmony only about an overworked schedule. It also involves redefining basic religious assumptions to conform with the individual's understanding of how the world works.

One woman told us she had signed up for a spirituality seminar to equip herself to make the right choices on career decisions she was facing that would affect her family life. She discussed her need for stress management techniques as a route to personal and professional happiness: "I really get carried away with work. I need to put my priorities in balance, and I think that a deeper spiritual life will help me do that. You can't wait until it's all over to decide what's really important. My religious belief helps me keep the important things in mind."

Another person, attending a secular program on new science and spirituality, felt that it made great sense within his Christian orientation:

> There is an order, and we don't understand half of it. Just when the rational, linear order asserts itself, there is a breakdown into chaos, and that forms a reorganizing principle of its own. You know, the cigarette smoke thing. This is magic to me. It is God's hand in the universe. Who else could have created such life-giving patterns? I'm fascinated about this in and of itself, but I also think it has analogies to my life. When you let a little chaos into your life, a little unplanned time, a little stepping back, the most amazing things happen.

This person's search was primarily about finding mental techniques for "stepping back" in ways that replicated this pattern and connected these notions to God. Remarked another: "There is no being a Christian without recognizing that you are here not for your purposes but for God's. For me, there is a connection here to ecology. You cannot help but see that we need to operate in harmony with nature if we are to be in harmony with God's plan. My spirituality deepens my motivation to do something in this arena."

Some interviewees actually turned away from new science and back to the monastic exercises of early Christianity to recover an overtly religious state of consciousness and recharge the batteries. Others sought communal reinforcement of this perspective through church attendance or prayer groups. New Internet sites to serve these spiritual exercises, such as Beliefnet.com and Faith.com, are multiplying rapidly.

Given the heavy emphasis on the experiential and the self-discovered even in disciplined and methodical approaches, the search for harmony (like recovery of the sacred self) finds satisfaction in an emergent awareness of a sacral reality. The chief desire is for a process of connection with this sacred perspective, more than for a static presentation of an airtight cosmology. Such experiential and personalized religion is not what most laypeople have associated with mainstream Sunday religion.

What may sit most uneasily for some ecclesiastics is how the new spirituality uses the study of cosmic order to model and benchmark activities in business to promote profitability. Whereas older biblical economic laws frequently concentrated on methods of restricting profit (usury) or redistributing goods to the community, today's spirituality is expected to produce a business-enhancing payback, even though it is about more than financial payback. Whereas a religious viewpoint might demand fixed hierarchical prioritization of these goals, today's spirituality sees them *systemically, in a process of interrelatedness.* Such relativism defies conventional religious hierarchies. As one person claimed, "God can be in a bank account or not. It depends."

Social Connectedness (Sacredness of Community)

Both devout Christians with strong church affiliation and unaffiliated seekers expressed a felt need for deeper connection to community. After all, this is a generation that, if it did not grow up with Mister Rogers, gratefully had its children watch him. As Rogers, the unusual ordained minister and bank director, said when featured on the cover of *Esquire's* "Heroes" edition, "The older I get, the more convinced I am that the space between communicating human beings can be hallowed ground."[12] *Esquire's* informed and surpris-

ingly reverential treatment of Fred Rogers speaks to how far the celebration of spiritual connectedness has pervaded the culture.

Interviewees and spirituality books alike express the need for
community in many ways. They want to give something back, to
belong to something larger than themselves, to avoid exploiting
others, to be part of a team. These motivations all turn on rejecting unbridled greed and self-interest, but the need for connectedness is not seen as contradictory to capitalism. Whereas the church's
discussion of community frequently poses an indictment of capitalism, the new spirituality programs link community to spiritual states
of mind, cross-cultural connectedness, and respect for others. They
are not hesitant to point out the corporate-enhancing value of such
high-minded goals.

Some have argued that the new spirituality is so enthralled with
performance enhancement and self-fulfillment that eleemosynary
religious notions of community and action on behalf of the disadvantaged cannot possibly be taken seriously. The picture is less
clear than that.

Both the secular and religiously affiliated programs stress the
importance of relationships, appealing to the desire to be personally valued and belong. Many offer an exercise that is some variation of the question, "Who do you think will come to your funeral,
and what would you want them to say about you?" As Ronald
Green notes in *Religion and Moral Reason*, most religious traditions
value community, need for respect, the cause larger than yourself,
and obligation to the poor.[13] Many religious authorities frame these
concerns as an eleemosynary question of duty and obedience. The
newer spirituality programs view community through a more instrumental and therapeutic lens: healthy, harmonious communities are
a sign of personal wellness and planetary health (not to mention
the backbone of a first-class corporation).

The experiential and pragmatic bias of the spiritual quest seems
to be a significant factor here. It defines who makes up community

and how spirituality can be applied to community. The most urgent problems of community that many businesspeople experience are right in the next cubicle. Overworked and constantly traveling, they become isolated from local civic needs, long-term friendships, and activities. Today's free-agent culture, unstable ownership structure, and widening income gap only exacerbate the businessperson's sense of isolation and shame. The personal orientation of the new spirituality is understood as a way to help address these shortcomings, not perpetuate them. This channels spirituality into a quest for empathy with others, membership in a moral community, and participation in just actions. Spirituality seekers want to experience the special sense of accomplishment that occurs in cooperation, fair competition (another form of relation), and teamwork.

Christian teachings offer a rich perspective on these longings but often in a way that restricts their application to situations working against profit or outside the realm of business. Community is about those outside the corporate umbrella, or the lowest-paid workers, as witnessed by the widespread faith-based demand for an end to sweatshop labor. Such language is limited, however, in its ability to engage the businessperson's longings for better spiritual expression of cooperative, synergistic relationships among *all* people. Nor does it acknowledge the widespread desire to change the many forms of abuse and injustice that occur in communities *inside* a company. This distinction is most acute in liberal mainstream churches; it is less so in evangelical business circles, where both religious life and corporate life tend to be measured through relational acts.[14]

On the other hand, business often celebrates community values in such self-interested terms as to render the notion absurd, contingent as it is on artificially constructed ownership patterns and economic strategies. One day you are going all out to interact with a dynamic team working on a new product and the next day the company has pulled out of that business and the group disbands. Under such short-term conditions, relationships are increasingly defined in a primarily contractual and inherently hierarchical way:

shareholders, consumers, competitors, the employed and the unemployed, management, hourly workers, suppliers, distributors. Even the public is defined as a corporate stakeholder, with a certain cost-benefit value implied. These conditions can severely limit ideas giving something back while creating respectful community inside the organization.

Despite these difficulties, even the cynics among our business interviewees tended to look for meaningful community activity by searching for ways to revise their business approach. They cited new job training programs at the entry level, modification of the corporate culture, improved working conditions, diversity efforts, mentoring, supplier relations, volunteerism, and ecologically friendly product improvements as examples. This variety adds up to serious competition for the social service interests of the businessperson; it presents a clear alternative to faith-based authority. Why not support the secular social cause and avoid dogmatic sectarian demands?

Indeed, mainstream Protestantism has been particularly cacophonous on community; perhaps it must blame itself for the lack of social conscience it perceives in the business community. Though hardly the first to criticize Protestantism's alleged social blindness, R. H. Tawney was perhaps its most eloquent critic. He attributed it to the extreme individualistic bias of Luther's doctrine, a belief that he claimed had "emptied" Christianity of its social content. Tawney claimed that extreme anxiety about the state of one's soul—a hallmark of today's spirituality interest in the inner self—became such a preoccupation that few external reference points penetrated this religious focus.

The inheritance of this tradition, coupled with the rational humanism of the Enlightenment, may indeed have set the scene for a society with values but no social ideals. Many have argued persuasively that this well-meaning individualism has created a shocking and ironic psychological inability to suspend personal self-interest for the sake of the group unless there is highly rational assurance of better survival. Current welfare debates reflect this state of helplessness:

How to reliably discern the relative benefits of proposed social programs when the scale, diverse recipients, and bureaucratization of social action are so difficult to assess?

In the absence of clarity, spirituality's strong legitimization of a preoccupation with the state of one's inner life may be repeating the pattern of Protestantism. Today's business and religion programs often attempt to relieve this anxiety with Hooveresque associations between the happy bottom line and the happy community.

Confusion over the religious representation of community and the interest in spirituality at work was echoed in interviewees' uncertainty about the spiritual weight of their community values. Said a venture capitalist:

> I've been pretty active in community work over the years—first I protested the war, then I worked at a soup kitchen, and I was treasurer at a local hospice organization. And this gives me great satisfaction. I just don't feel I'm right inside unless part of my life is about helping others. I guess that's religious. Yes. Of course that's religious in some sense.
>
> But [these volunteer activities] are very separate from my work. It's all charity. Then at work, I help people and then I'm rewarded. So it's different. I feel that at some point you have to belong to something that doesn't have a price tag on it. The problem is, I don't see a lot of this feeling spilling over into my work. This shouldn't have to be against who you are as a businessperson, it should be an addition.

To the sophisticated theologian or ethicist, such have-it-all optimism may seem hopelessly naïve and unprepared to sustain people through the uncomfortable commitments and murky tradeoffs involved in acting on community feelings productively. One of the chief criticisms of the new spirituality is optimism and therapeutic instrumentalization of community feeling.

These weaknesses are real. Few organized social action efforts seem to be evolving from the new spirituality. But, in our opinion, this does not mean there is not strong *interest* in community. Rather, neither the liberal church's approach nor the new spirituality movement has found a way of collectively engaging the true value placed on community expressed by the spiritual seekers. Clearly, current expressions of community have yet to achieve as deep a power as traditional religious descriptions of divinely-sanctioned communities. Traditional formulations, however, are not fulfilling people's new longings for connection between personal spirituality and obligation to a globalized, diverse population—outside and inside a corporation or specific religious community.

Religiously Consistent Morality (Christian Business Ethics)

According to Daniel Yankelovich, noted social analyst and cofounder with Cyrus Vance of the Public Agenda Foundation, the number one issue spurring the new search for spiritual growth is declining confidence in the ethics of business leaders. Polls reveal that almost 87 percent of the public think there has been a decline in social morality; 90 percent see a threat to the family and a decline in family values. After a decade of highly public scrutiny of the personal habits and financial rewards of business leaders and politicians, many worry that the nation's leaders are out of touch with the fundamental values of average Americans. Looking around their own workplaces and communities, people decry what they perceive as a general decline in personal ethics. A widening income gap offers evidence of extreme favoritism in the system of rewards.

Interviewees put the felt need in simple terms: there has been an ethical breakdown. Common standards of decency have turned chaotic, in no small part because of business ingenuity in tapping the volatile combination of money, marketing, and titillation. An active press has increased awareness of the moral breakdown of leadership, covering messy divorces and billionaire spending habits in salacious detail. Freedom of speech seems to be selectively upheld to support the least dignifying aspects of social life. Meanwhile, social basics are neglected: child support, health, and safety. Such widespread distortion of American democratic impulses has triggered what amounts to an ethical nervous breakdown among the American public.

The decline in confidence in business ethics is not new; it has been in a steady drop-and-hold pattern since the late 1960s. The reaction to this decline, however, has dramatically changed. In the 1970s and 1980s, the public supported a range of governmental remedies to ethical abuses in the marketplace: EEO, tighter EPA laws, tighter product liability laws, the Foreign Corrupt Practices Act of 1977, the Criminal Sentencing Guidelines of 1991. The last five years or so have seen a substantial shift in confidence away from seeking further government solutions. But alternative remedies have not been notable for raising the general standards of business ethics.

Many businesspeople share the public's moral angst over business values. It is dismaying to hear even experienced, savvy managers confiding a belief that those who make it to the top of a company have to be capable of abusing others' interests in favor of their own.

Appalled at the many examples of corporate indecency and a culture without scruples, people feel the need for a personal recovery of moral grounding and membership in a moral community. The two are rightly coupled to spirituality. Even in its most existential forms, the spiritual is by nature the avenue to a moral life. As theologian James Gustafson put it, "the whole of our being, existing in the measure of faith that is ours, makes moral decisions."

The many calls for integrity and connectedness are finding a public audience because the public needs to regain a sense that ethics counts, that there is a negative meaning to any act of dishonesty, promise breaking, injustice, and craven self-interest. To paraphrase Iris Murdoch, the presence of such violence and banality in business morality does damage to the inner life.

People want to feel good about the place they work in, to feel that their corporation stands for something they can look back on and be proud of. Those who put it in religious terms say, "I'd like to know what it means to be a good Christian businessperson." The expressive bias of this observation does not focus the search for religiously consistent ethics on prohibitive rules of conduct, but rather on the possibility of experiencing creative, honest action in the marketplace. Thus the need for ethical fortitude is channeled into reinvesting in business life with standards of contribution, controlled generosity, and virtues such as honesty and the courage to make retribution for mistakes.

Spiritual revelation and revolutionary progress once again are evident in respondents' discussion of the fourth felt need. They spoke of a moral urgency to look at business "with new eyes," "different paradigms," and "reorientation of priorities." They were not looking to "get out" so much as to do things differently. They frequently mentioned socially progressive companies such as Tom's of Maine, Timberland, or Malden Mills as exciting models. Part of the draw went beyond social responsibility; the leaders of these companies had gone on record as having religious or spiritual interests that they carried to their work.

The new spirituality has brought a therapeutic, holistic response to the fourth felt need. High ethical standards are posed as logical extension of self-expressive, self-improving goals rather than sheer reasoned moral paradigms. A better self is a morally higher self. Simply obeying the laws is not enough. One must improve business ethics through spiritual self-transformation. Some of the religious programs personalize the ethical by discussing acquisition of *discernment*. The Woodstock Business Conference program, for example, includes a full program exploring Jesuit notions of discernment and how they might apply to ethical decisions at work. Others encourage the formation of prayer partnerships, whose participants hold each other accountable to high ethical standards at work.

The Response of the New Spirituality

In 1910, Emile Coué published a slogan for healing: "Every day, in every way, I am getting better and better."[15] Almost one hundred years later, advocates of the new spirituality sing a similar refrain. As we have seen, current spiritual interest suggests that many businesspeople are searching for deeper knowledge and expression of their inner self, seeking connection to transcendent states of mind and patterns of life. They want to live a life of meaning, they want to be more effective at problem solving, they need connection to other people; through it all they optimistically assume that in discovering this sacred, authentic self, they will find that it can be a rather noble self. The new spirituality seems drawn to notions of attitude over obedience, to existential morality (Paul Tillich's "listening love") over doctrinal law. Simple axioms (do unto others) and biographical testimonies have dominated the conversation. Such approaches do not give guidance on how the many paradoxical moral notions of Christianity would be seriously integrated into satisfying the four felt needs.

Some critics of the new movement have concluded this is just an optimistic (even selfish) desire to have it all, to get rich and feel good about it. We are slightly less cynical. By interpreting this interest as the expression of deeply felt needs, we have tried to emphasize at the outset the spiritual and economic potential of this movement, rather than its shortcomings.

The new spirituality offerings have been knowledgeable in responding to the four felt needs. Much of their popularity can be attributed to the fact that the needs are urgent, and that self-empowering, personally experienced religious activity has long been neglected by the churches. No doubt, many forms of the new spirituality are highly romanticized. With Deepak Chopra, the package includes a self that is slimmer, stress-free, and possibly ageless. Their language hovers between the evocative and exotic. It promises the means to control the scientific and emotional frontier, to harness the unknown. Nothing is without purpose. All is according to plan. Synchronicity is everywhere. As Ralph Waldo Emerson's friend Margaret Fuller once exhorted, accept the universe.

This is not a pessimistic or morbid religious psychology. At its best, the new spirituality associates the transcendent with an ethic of creation, joy, heightened self-esteem, and usefulness. Thus do Twelve-Step programs draw on a connection between healing and the knowledge that the essential person is not in total isolation but in relation with a higher power. This in turn leads to functionality in life. So too, for Covey and others, time management is of ultimate concern because it regulates one's ability to save one's soul.

Do these programs work? Many adherents pick and choose what they feel works for them. As for pretechnological people who bang on a drum during an eclipse, it is enough that the moon comes back.

Despite the absence of empirical proof of effectiveness, it would be foolish to underestimate the force of the new spirituality simply because it does not match the intellectualism of ecclesiastical forms of religion or academic philosophy. Its power to put nonmaterial, dignifying, and empowering religious notions on the mental map of businesspeople is undeniable—and far more penetrating of the business culture than most mainstream religious activities. Its lack of formal allegiances makes it adaptable and accessible to a constantly changing business population. The gurus are charismatic and (so far) surprisingly free of scandal, compared to the televangelism of the 1980s; but without a bureaucratic support system, it is not clear how far their authority can be supported. Covey's business expansion into the Franklin Planner and his social initiatives have been met with some cynicism and charges of trivialization of his message.

Clearly, in terms of effective response to the four felt needs, the new spirituality is currently at the head of the religious pack. But is this spirituality capable of coalescing the will to create humane capitalism when confronted with truly opposing points of view? The very conditions of the new spirituality's attraction pose real limits to the ability of this movement to address complex social problems, including impulses of greed and evil. So long as the spirituality program is the CEO's latest interest, there is little substantive opposition inside a company. Rarely are prophetic conclusions extended into the controversial arena of free public discussion.

Business clearly needs new ways of creating common goals that reward investment in community, equitable access to economic power, and human dignity. Will the transforming worldviews and mental exercises prove any more fruitful than a narrow, free-market orientation in accomplishing this task? Will spirituality transform how businesses respond to exploitative, meaning-sapping forms of capitalist endeavor? Will the personalized and experiential approach to community yield sufficient wisdom and political power to have a positive effect on such systemic problems as equitable trade and human rights issues? Many today criticize spirituality as inadequate to the problems of injustice, famine, world conflict, and economic and ecological disasters.

As Wendy Kaminer commented, the new spirituality movement is essentially about a promise of bliss. No one is evil, only less evolved.[16] The new economics simply requires new adaptation.

It is precisely this voluntary, therapeutic facet that most attracts people to the spiritual shopping mall and most bothers many thoughtful theologians. Religions, as Craig Dykstra has pointed out, make claims on their believers.[17] They assert an authority beyond human will and reasoning that demands commitment from individuals to see that life is lived a certain way. The "required" aspect of religion is precisely what secular spirituality avoids. In this free market, exercising choice concerning the soul's expression does not institutionalize its teaching into social or political demands.

These programs are frequently based on assurances that life is basically OK. Many Christian ethicists are not happy with this starting point, noting that life is *not* basically OK for a great portion of the world (including those in the highest corporate positions). Indeed, our review of the spirituality literature revealed few references to anything approaching a powerful definition of evil, despite the many expressions of empathy with people who feel lost, hurt, or threatened. It is unclear how traditional, institutionalized religion can successfully enter this arena without trivializing itself.

We can view the new spirituality movement in two ways. Empirically and conceptually, there are grounds for viewing it as a moral nightmare, naïve and unprepared for hard times. But we can also see it as a positive response to new longings to recover the sacred and at the same time be equipped to handle today's intense economic questions. Traditional religion has not seemed to offer a path to fulfillment of these longings. The new spirituality fills the gap left behind. It is not just changing the face of business; it is changing the face of American religion.

The new spirituality, then, is a legitimate contribution, but one with genuine limits. Its view of business life is undoubtedly richer than one with no spirituality. Its view of life as a whole, however, seems to be poorer, constricted as it is by a nonnegotiable ambition to create utility for the corporation in whatever form. Connection to worldviews independent from business and embedded in rich expression of the human condition are also essential for the survival of the soul.

Quite likely, a second stage of the spirituality movement is in the making, to compensate for the thin areas and sustain attention to complex issues. People are already searching to expand their spiritual quest to learn about more traditional expressions of religion, as evidenced by a number of religious Web sites experiencing extensive use. Some, like Belief.net, continue a strong lay and experiential orientation, targeting people interested in acquainting themselves with the various wisdom traditions that have given guidance in understanding the human condition. Others, like Faith.com, which links viewers to more than 170 groups, offer a new clearinghouse for denominational activity.

Will such inquiries segue back to the context of business? Will accrual of noncommittal religious knowledge stimulate a new vitality in the churches? The contours of the new spirituality movement suggest that unless churches demonstrate keen connection to the major economic and social forces businesspeople are facing, unless they understand and honor the four felt needs, they will offer little competition for the businessperson's soul.

Reflection

- As noted in this chapter, many people feel a split between who they are as spiritual beings and who they are at work. How important is it to you to be able to bring your authentic self and your religious values to your work?

- How well are you managing this task? (Think of a concrete example of how your faith affected your work: which of the four felt needs were active or being suppressed in this incident?)

- How much disconnect do you see between the way you and others approach business, and the way you approach spirituality or religion?

- Does the phrase "spiritual but not religious" help you negotiate the reservations you may feel about drawing too close a connection between religious values and business life? Why or why not?

Action

- Engage in prayer and meditation to evoke sacred awareness.

- With an attentive ear, listen for signs of the new spirituality and the four felt needs (sacred self, harmony and balance, community, ethics) in your own workplace (and church, if you attend). How are these expressions changing the way people work together, compete, and formulate the purposes of the organization?

- If you haven't already formed a study group to discuss faith and work, use this listening test to begin to search out a group of people who would be interested in pursuing questions of spirituality, ethics, religion, and business.

2

Between Worlds

Attempts to Integrate Religion and Business

You can't argue that religion has a role in business.
They're totally different. Sure my inner values over-
lap, because that's who I am, but that's not religion.
—*Christian businessperson*

One of the most important tests of a religion is its ability to
enable believers to lead a life in accordance with its basic
tenets. As the opening epigraph indicates, for the businessperson
of Christian faith there are few coherent paths to integrating the
religion of the New Testament and the activities of a modern business life. Opposing purposes, contrasting ideologies, and fundamentally different time frames can leave Christians with few
connections between the religion they know on Sunday or privately at home, and the demands of the workplace. For these people, the horizon of Christianity—what Susan Langer would call
"religious envisagement"—keeps slipping away as they move into
the business realm. Some happily let it go, citing separation of

church and public life. Others long for some way to strengthen the connections but find little help in their notions of religion.

As noted in the last chapter, the new spirituality has come up with a number of ways to integrate concerns of the soul and concerns of the corporation, ranging from universalization of its language to a focus on empowerment and personalized religious experience. We see the success of this personalized approach in the common distinction that many businesspeople assert: "I'm spiritual but not religious at work."[1] In saying this, they are not necessarily rejecting the fundamental truths of Christianity; rather, they see no connection between what they understand to be religion and their own daily lives.

The new spirituality programs are not much help in this area. Either they do not address problems of institutionalized religion or they offer conceptions of Christ that trivialize the religious message. Strong institutional separation of the church and government (which sets the law governing the corporation) completes the spiritual schizophrenia. Religion on Sunday, spirituality on Monday.

How Businesspeople Cope

How does one become "one person" as a Christian? How does religion become active in the portion of daily life that occupies the most time, namely, work? In our interviews for this book, as well as those conducted for the earlier *Believers in Business*, we discovered that businesspeople have developed a range of coping strategies designed to help them retain their faith and yet keep it separate from some or all parts of their business. It is important to understand what these patterns can offer and how they can also limit a strong conception of integrating faith and work.

A broader problem connected to integration is the vagueness of the term *religion*. People understand it many ways, with few vocabularies to communicate the differences, and they make few distinctions in the terminology they actually use. In fact, many of the people we interviewed could not offer a precise explication of what type of religious experience or activity they meant when they said that "faith," "religion," or "spirituality" was a force in their business lives.

Not surprisingly, their coping strategies reflected this ambiguity as they tried to bring some sense to their twin desire to limit how religion is practiced in the workplace and yet retain their private identity as a practicing Christian. Three aspects of religion constitute the rough parameters of the territory through which we are traveling: (1) a religion's *institutional mechanisms*; (2) its *message* (rules and revelations); and (3) religious *experience* (state of consciousness), which some people call faith or spirituality. Putting religion into daily practice may involve one area only, or some combination of all three facets. For example, one person's sense of religion in business may be about following the ethical rules presented in biblical or church messages; another's may be about summoning up the experience of religious consciousness through meditation, worship, ritual, or prayer. Still others may feel that religion in business is about entering into some relation with official institutions of the church—attending church, or contributing corporate time and money to a faith-based social service charity, or inviting a minister to lead a management group in prayer.

Our integration model (Figure 2.1) lays out the spectrum of coping strategies used by Christian businesspeople and clergy. At the two extremes are the Secularists, who do not expect integration, and the Resacralizers, who expect full integration. Neither approach presents a viable model for a person of Christian faith in the modern corporation. Between these two is a messier set of coping strategies—the Cynics, Justifiers, Generalists, Atomists, and Percolators—who variously expect everything from sporadic to partial integration. These strategies, too, bump up against severe limitations of religion as a relevant force. In this section, we look at what these coping strategies mean to businesspeople. In the next section, we see what they mean for clergy.

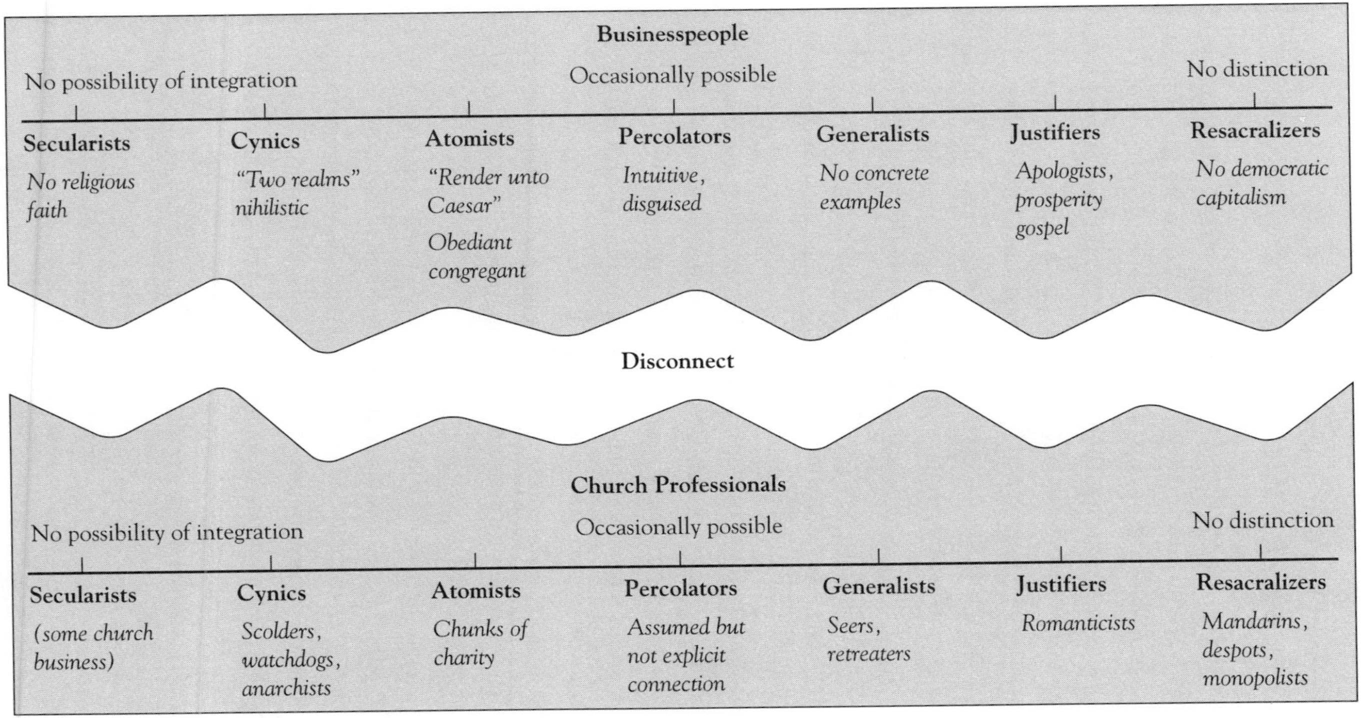

Businesspeople

No possibility of integration			Occasionally possible			No distinction
Secularists	Cynics	Atomists	Percolators	Generalists	Justifiers	Resacralizers
No religious faith	*"Two realms" nihilistic*	*"Render unto Caesar"* *Obedient congregant*	*Intuitive, disguised*	*No concrete examples*	*Apologists, prosperity gospel*	*No democratic capitalism*

Disconnect

Church Professionals

No possibility of integration			Occasionally possible			No distinction
Secularists	Cynics	Atomists	Percolators	Generalists	Justifiers	Resacralizers
(some church business)	*Scolders, watchdogs, anarchists*	*Chunks of charity*	*Assumed but not explicit connection*	*Seers, retreaters*	*Romanticists*	*Mandarins, despots, monopolists*

Figure 2.1. Integration Model for Faith and Business: Seven Christian Coping Strategies.

Secularists: "You Can Believe What You Want, But Don't Bring It to Work"

Integration is not an issue for Secularists because religion is a not an issue. A typical Secularist might say, "People are free to believe whatever they want, and worship whatever God they want. But when they want to bring their religion to work, that's where I draw the line." The Secularist is as likely to be an agnostic or atheist as a Christian who believes in radical separation of the realms.

Ironically, this expectation of a totally secular mental and ethical business environment seems to invite great tolerance and agreement between agnostics and believers of different faiths. It allows them to share humane convictions about the proper ethics of business without messing things up. As the popularity of Buddhist practice shows, they may even participate in the same kind of mental exercise to evoke certain states of consciousness associated with spirituality and nonrational mental states, seeking to enhance their creative imagination or aesthetic appreciation. Psychological wholeness, human dignity, and the welfare of society may be very important values for the Secularist. While this strategy is obviously effective at carving out common moral ground in a diverse business population, it has a serious flaw. The Secularist view denies any possibility of bringing faith to bear on these ethical concerns.

For a person of faith, this is a harsh price. Either one must adopt a view that business is a necessary evil wholly outside Christian values and purpose or that there are no ways in which the blessings of faith would outweigh the dangers of misplaced religious zeal. Essentially defeatist, the Secularists confuse freedom of religious expression with no religious expression. Religious worldview, to use Clifford Geertz's term, presents no interpretive role in the Secularist's conduct of business.

Resacralizers: "To Walk with the Lord at Every Step"

The absolutism of the Secularists is balanced on the other end of the scale by the absolutism of the Resacralizers, people who envision an economic life fully governed by their religion, with no distinction between sacred and secular in the business culture. To use Peter Berger's term, the Resacralizers seek to restore the sacred canopy over the corporation, subjecting its every activity to a religiously based authority. As was true in the world of the monk of the Middle Ages, all modes of economic choice would be subordinated to the interpreted will of God.

The Resacralizer's framework suggests a blessed state of utopia. What could be better than to seek total adherence to one's religion in all aspects of life? To walk with the Lord at every step in the marketplace? To recreate sacred states of consciousness through regular prayer and ritual? To serve the world with a biblically based ethic?

But such expectations of total religious integrity in business are hardly so benign in the light of history. Whose religion would dominate? Resacralization requires reintroducing religious culture into the workplace and some form of religiously based authority over institutional decisions. This strategy implies permission for a designated religious authority to make privileged claims on businesspeople at work, or for businesspeople to carry more religious authority than the church. The dangers are well known from history. Economic profiling by religious status has historically invited numerous forms of institutionalized intolerance and persecution, from the pillage and horrors of the Conquest to the anti-Semitic economic measures of Hitler's Germany.

The difficulties of Resacralization are many. The Bible did not lay out a blueprint for modern postindustrial capitalism, nor was Jesus on an explicitly economic agenda. His thoughts on the little children did not extend to injunctions against child labor. Even if one takes the Bible quite literally, most of the conditions of modern capitalism are not addressed in the sacred book.

In practice, the Resacralizers compose a very small group. They are most likely to be found in orthodox sects and cults; some monastic groups; or small, privately held businesses located deep in the Bible belt where religious diversity and secularization are still a relatively weak force in the culture. Resacralizers who favor communal economic arrangements have yet to produce an inclusive, sustainable competitive model of wealth production on a large scale. Nor have they found a social model that sustains the nuclear family as having equal religious status to monastic or state-run organization of the household. These failures and loss of diversity pose serious difficulties for those who would seek a seamless connection between their Christianity and their business.

Cynics: "You Can't Be True to Your Beliefs in the Business World"

Cynics may profess private belief in God but feel there is no possibility for truly Christian values, Christian consciousness, or Christian culture in the workplace. Like Secularists, they see no room for religion in any form in the workplace: "I try to be true to myself," a Cynic might say, "but we all know that's not really possible in the business world."

Essentially, Cynics adopt a strategy of nihilism. They give up on business as a potentially ethical institution, and they may have given up on religion for the same reasons. Given this extreme disillusion, the Cynic's business ethics may be less compatible with Christian values than the Secularist's. A typical Cynic remarks: "Sure I'd like to work in an ethical corporation, where high standards were rewarded. But in my experience, that's a delusion. Business rewards the selfish and the ruthless."

The Cynic's reasons for taking a skeptical, self-interested view are legion. Many are knee-jerk skeptics about the corrupting forces of money, which they associate with crass materialism, exploitation, and selfishness. From the standpoint of religious consciousness, they find little in the workplace with which to resonate. They understand religion to be about higher things and associate it with deeply private concerns about death and life (including sex)—but not money.

Cynics tend to frame ethical issues in business primarily as a question of necessity. For Cynics, the term *business ethics* is an oxymoron. You do what you have to do to get the job done, within vaguely drawn prohibitions against killing (or destroying the market). Cynics may feel their identity as Christians partially shaped their character, but they do not see any connection between the Christianity they know from church and what they do in business.

The Cynic's mental framework is not just reactive; it actively distances business and religion. The Cynic constantly strives to exclude religious sentiment from explaining why things work or are appropriate in the workplace. Here's a typical cynical comment: "We always try to follow the Golden Rule in our company, not because we are necessarily religious, but because it makes good business sense. I don't think you can really claim to bring your religion into business. Let's face it, you'd never make it. All you can do is try to be a good person, but don't expect the people on top to share your values."

Personal disillusion with religion or business often fuels the Cynic's rejection of integration. Cynics may be estranged from the church of their youth, be disturbed by the management practices of the church, or have suffered a disturbing incident in their business career that takes on definitive power. Business is indeed ungodly. They cope by separating their business expectations from religious values associated with high ethical standards, which is far more efficient than wrestling with a world where both evil and good exist simultaneously. One executive in the media, who had seen a number of extremely aggressive deals in his career and who was prospering along with his company's growth, expressed his understanding of faith and work this way: "These people [business leaders] do some very good things, but when it gets down to it, that's not what Christianity is about. Not at all. You don't get to the top in business unless you are willing to put your own interests first. I would be disturbed if people actually seriously tried to bring their religion into work. When you make a business decision, it should be rational, not some touchy-feely thing. That would be totally irresponsible, to draw on faith for business decisions."

This remark illustrates how a Cynic's coping strategy relies on the undifferentiated expectation that to be religious an action must be dominated by all three elements of religion: culture and symbol, ethics, and religious state of consciousness.

Justifiers: "I Just Try to Do What Jesus Would Do"

Justifiers hold a mental idea of a nearly complete integration of faith and business at a foundational level. As one Justifier said, " I just try to do what Jesus would do. God is the chairman of our board."

Justifiers expect substantial coherency, and they cope with fundamental differences between capitalist and Christian frameworks by constructing a worldview in which no significant contradictions exist. They explain poverty, for example, as regrettable but ultimately inescapable—not a critique of one's personal choices to OK a layoff. Typically, Justifiers offer shamelessly untested testimony of religion's "effectiveness." Say a religious person acts on what he or she believes is a religiously based impulse. Say the outcome is economically successful. How is that to be interpreted? Justifiers have a simple answer: religion "works" in the marketplace. Executive X gets spiritual, feels calmer, and stops being so abusive to employees. Productivity increases. Ergo, religion is not just compatible with business; it is the key to business success.

Although refreshingly integrating, the logical extensions of this view are highly disturbing. Are the material rewards of business always signs of God's favor and approval over how the Justifiers have conducted themselves? A number of platitudes connecting ethical standards and prosperity are used to reinforce this assumption: do good to do well in the marketplace; the Golden Rule is the highest principle of capitalism; be honest with your customers and they'll stay loyal. Biblical promises of prosperity to God's people may also enter in, summed up by the title of one evangelical business book: God Wants You to Be Rich.

The truth is, most of the platitudes are harmlessly benevolent summaries of good business practice. The What Would Jesus Do (WWJD) movement is similarly well intended. Contrary to the view of the religious Cynic, the Justifier is not necessarily thumping a gospel of all-out greed and hypocrisy. The classic Protestant work ethic—hard work, methodical self-discipline, delayed gratification, and signs of election in economic prosperity—is as likely to mark a Justifier's business ethic as a get-rich-quick value system. It's just that God is essentially benevolent and loves the best. He is in the details, and any detail of life that promotes one's sense of ethics and prosperity must be a sign of God's presence. A timely, long-awaited phone call from a banker? The Justifier assures you God must be shining on the business. God is not just good; he is in partnership.

Thus the real sense of accomplishment and contribution businesspeople derive from parts of their work becomes suffused with religious meaning. As Princeton professor Robert Wuthnow has noted, the rise of a service economy has blurred earlier distinctions between work for pay and service. The Justifier framework reflects the melding of doing good by others and doing well from it.

Similarly, the Justifier may be particularly drawn to forums that resacralize the arena of business relationships. Their prayer meetings and support groups reflect this goal, combining moments of prayer, confession, and celebration of religious devotion with discussions of business success.

At its best, the Justifier model is a platform for accountability to an ethic of fair exchange, service, and vocation. But as Tawney noted in his discussion of Protestantism, it can also cultivate extreme anxiety about the state of the soul. Coping, one looks for signs of inner grace in the fact of external prosperity. Causality gets turned around: riches must be a justification that one is a person of faith. Conversely, poverty suggests moral degeneracy and laziness.

Most of these assumptions exist in a half-life of unexpressed prejudice and appeals to necessity. Tension about questionable treatment of others for the sake of the business, or about moments of underperformance, are masked by the Justifier's single-minded focus on alleging God's support.

How *does* a Justifier mentality sort out moral problems? Not surprisingly, sentimentalized statements on witnessing and the market itself become two sources of guidance. The Justifier enhances the market's authority by explicitly assigning Godlike attributes to the principles and accomplishments of business. Using metaphors of Jesus or God as a businessperson—the "What Would Jesus Do?" mind-set—aids in this assimilation.

In practice, of course, the Justifier strategy is usually more nuanced. When pressed, very few reduce their understanding of grace to the size of their bank account. They agree that the benefits of capitalism are not equitably distributed. But at a deeply operative level, achievement (particularly one's own, because it is so well intended) confirms the divine ordering of the world that they see in Christian doctrine. For this reason, religious attacks on the system feel extremely provocative to Justifiers. Success at what price? At whose expense? Such questions usually prompt an attack: What do you want to do, kill the golden goose?

Always looking at the bright side of business, Justifiers tend to get stuck when it comes to acknowledging the presence of pain in people's lives. Is there a religious reason to be disturbed by compensation patterns favoring the few rich while the poor get poorer? Yes, but how else to attract the growth and innovation of the best and brightest to your company? Without that there would be even greater poverty. Cried one devout venture capitalist: "Who is to say what is really Christian when it comes to determining how much people will make? I never worried about those things. I just concentrated on doing my job well and the rewards came. Does that make me a bad person?"

The attraction of this stance is very strong, particularly if one is trying to sell others on the idea of good ethics in business. Like many of the so-called secular spirituality programs, the Justifier view posits business as an outlet for personalized religious expression. It concocts a romantic reenchantment of the business world at a generalized level, backed up by moral justification of material rewards. Justifiers explain all success (except the most obvious exploitation) as examples of how Jesus ultimately provides the key to the right way to do things. As in the secular spirituality programs, here empiricism is not terribly important.

Generalists: "My Faith Has to Operate at All Times"

Generalists vehemently assert the power of faith but limit the arena of concrete examples of faith to settings outside of business. Personal religious testimony, prayer sessions in the company of other businesspeople, or family matters are the concrete beacons of faith. A classic example came from this interviewee: "My faith has to operate at all times. That includes work. Certainly it's relevant. I have a deep faith. I have never cheated on my wife."

The Generalist's associative leaps, in connection with the topic of faith and work, can at times be startling, as in the example just offered, which leaps from discussing faith at work to faithfulness in marriage. But there is a definite pattern to this approach. Like the Justifiers, Generalists sustain two strong personal convictions by which they define their professional identity: capitalism and Christianity. They do not try to systematically locate the influence of one on the other. This strategy facilitates sidestepping the hard questions; they never get asked.

A few comments from our interviews explain the tenor and depth of the Generalist response. The word *just*, which they use often, underscores the limitations they place on potentially integrating faith and work, despite their optimism: "I just feel that my religion is important to me in everything I do. I don't try to think about it all the time. It's just there." And another: "I basically think that the really successful person in business is pretty selfish. I find that appalling. But I don't think you have to be that way. The important thing is to keep a perspective. You just have to keep your belief in God. That will take you through it."

Such remarks, simple as they sound, often represent deeply believed faith in Christianity. What is lacking is a vocabulary of concrete behavior that would suggest a need for transforming certain aspects of business beyond attitude. The Generalist, to use Max Weber's term, has an ethics of ideal but not of action, as these two comments show: "I've always felt my religion was important in daily life, but I don't try to get tangled up in theology every time I have [to make] a decision. I've felt if you just follow the Golden Rule, you'll have all you need in the workplace." And "You can't wear your religion on your sleeve. It's who you are that counts. I've always tried to be decent, and I guess that goes back to my religious belief. And I feel it's very important to do something for others. I have worked for years with a tutorial service for inner-city kids."

The last comment may explain why some people adopt a Generalist view of religious integration. To cope with the conditions of pluralism, the Generalist in business does not remain totally silent but sticks to nonbusiness examples such as charity, home life, or other presumably safe topics. In this they echo the nonengagement of many churches in questions of business decision making.

Generalists tend to see a dead end only when their intuition tells them something is wrong, or if they have a psychological breakdown in the face of bad fortune. Generalist businesspeople may say they want "something more" on faith and work; but when confronted with hard questions about, say, pressure to adopt a materialistic lifestyle that causes one to neglect one's family for work, Generalists retreat to platitudes about "just" keeping things in perspective. "The secret," intoned one sage interviewee, "is balance."

Generalists walk a tightrope. The faith that supports their business thinking is a thinly drawn thread, as in this classic example (the only concrete example the interviewee could give): "I think your faith comes out in little ways. I don't try to pinpoint it, I just know it's important to me. Well, OK, here's an example of my faith being a force at work. Take my secretary. She had a problem with her fiancé, and one day she was crying quietly at her desk. I was very busy, but I stopped everything and we had a conversation about her thoughts about marriage. I feel that if you are sensitive to people, that's a sign of what God is asking you to do."

The Generalist's sense of overall piety is so strong it can mask or divert attention from uncomfortable details. They cannot afford to look down at the turmoil of conflicting demands. With no framework to help them think through the religious challenges of business, their faith is a thin tightrope above the demands of daily life. One Generalist proudly told us that she refused to carry benefits coverage for abortion; in fact, she had no health insurance benefits for employees. A manager in a financial services firm spoke at length about socially responsible investing as a sign of Christian practices. When asked to explain what was explicitly Christian about these investments and how it affected his own business practices, he could only answer, "Well I don't invest in tobacco stocks."

It is no wonder that the Generalist represents a large category of believers among those we interviewed. By looking the other way on most of their specific business practices, they have developed a good coping mechanism for feeling right with the world and fulfilling felt obligations to bear witness to their faith. No wonder the Generalist appears to be a hypocrite to outsiders; nothing invites suspicion more swiftly than a claim to perfection.

Atomists: "Render Unto Caesar"

Atomists represent the pessimistic alternative to the optimistic Generalists. These are the people who have religious faith but feel that the two realms are better kept separate, with only occasional intrusion.

Atomists try to preserve religion and its fit with the business culture by subjecting both to a kind of mental compartmentalization. Language, thought process, culture, goals—they presume all these things to look quite different from a business or a faith perspective. Yet they are not necessarily hypocrites, any more than is Jesus' elliptical admonition to "render to Caesar the things that are Caesar's, and to God the things that are God's." One Atomist interviewee remarked sadly: "I have come to believe that I can bring my faith to work, but not my religion."

As this remark indicates, Atomists may even compartmentalize the various aspects of religion, giving it different terms, depending on how private or public their context. Faith, for example, is about private belief. It shapes character and basic ethics, and perhaps it also suggests a cosmological ordering that creates a conceptual anchor for problem solving. These aspects of religion, however, operate nonverbally or in a deliberately disguised fashion. Religion, by contrast, is equated with institutionalized forms, the church or denominational nonprofits. These aspects seem entirely inappropriate as direct authority over business and its culture. The terminology can make Atomists sound more cynical or antireligious than they really are. The Atomist who is categorically against religion in the workplace may never mention that he or she privately feels a deep personal reliance on faith, ethics, or spirituality in everyday affairs at work.

We also found that Atomist strategies were particularly evident among those whose religious traditions conceived of charity and good deeds as "spiritual points" in the game of life. Contributions and social service activities outside of work or philanthropic giving by their companies were sufficient evidence of an operative faith. The corporation's profit-related activities remain off limits.

The Atomist's mental ordering of religion and business is made up of many separate pieces and roles, of which religion is only one. It is a natural product of modernity, which has imposed extreme pressure toward specialization and fragmentation since the Industrial Revolution. These forces are so strong that even today's supposedly holistic programs about balance become subject to atomistic strategies. Life is divided into scientifically sorted chunks of time spent in each role, which only promotes more atomization (three hours as parent, eight hours as manager, one hour as churchgoer, and so on). On this model, the Atomist may view church attendance as a key indicator of faith and think of this activity as the core example of religion. One "fuels up" on Sunday by participating in ritual, taking time out from work, and evoking other-worldly frames of consciousness. But there is no perceived need for tangible carryover here. Any expectation of integrating religion and work is already bounded by definitions of religion that reinforce separation of the realms and multiple roles in life.

Contrary to C. P. Snow's nightmare scenario of two cultures at war in our society, people today resist total capitulation to either science or religion. They acknowledge a certain degree of spillover or simultaneous reference to various ways of knowing, even if they cannot envision total coherency. The current popularity of holistic spirituality programs among businesspeople is good evidence of this desire to overcome atomization.

Still, the Atomist approach has many attractions. At its best, it reinforces the preciousness of faith by keeping it separate, supposedly free of contamination from secular forms of thinking or mundane motives such as profit. It avoids imposing sectarianism in the workplace. Unfortunately, this framework can also construct a spiritual dead end. By being conceptually so separated from the mundane, it is almost impossible to draw a link between specific religious notions and the business setting. The Atomist is defined by the whole picture, but the pieces do not relate very well. As a result, one may develop multiple and conflicting personalities—being a person at work of whom one would be ashamed in church. Some dissatisfied Atomists describe this pattern as "leaving one's religion behind in the pews" or "not seeing the connection between Sunday and Monday." Faith is fundamentally different from vocational concerns and activities.

One variation of the Atomist strategy is the Obedient Congregant. Religious faith is seen as an act of literal obedience to church or biblical authorities, but only where the rules are made explicit. Depending on the denomination, the source of biblical rules might be personal interpretation, or it might be mediated through an official religious authority such as the Vatican. Given the general expectation of pluralism in American business, Obedient Congregants tend to restrict their integration strategies to their own personal activities and do not try to impose these rules corporationwide. This model roughly seeks to establish the kind of ecclesiastical or biblical authority over the economy that operated in medieval and Calvinist communities (typical of the Resacralizers), but without an expectation of a cultural revolution within society. Integration is thus achieved in sporadic, compartmentalized acts. This Obedient Congregant's story is a good example of these dynamics: "We were a carrier of information services, and one of our customers was dedicated to providing information to teenagers about safe sex. Technically, we don't get involved in the content of what we carry, but the cardinal's office approached us, objecting to this service. It was basically my call, and I quietly found a reason why this account could not be opened. I did not try to make this a corporate policy. There would be no chance of that, and it's not my place to carry my religion that far."

In this case, other members of the same denomination objected to the decision, and eventually an agreement about freedom of access to this service was reluctantly agreed upon by the cardinal's office.

This outcome illustrates two key problems. The first is the problem of permission and honesty: the Obedient Congregant does not have permission to impose the church's stand on the corporation and therefore must engage in a "cover up" of the sort mentioned above. The second is the lack of applied religious understanding. If the Obedient Congregant looks to the church or the Bible for specific interpretation of the rules in the new business context, he or she finds insufficient guidance. The rules have not caught up with the marketplace, or the attention of the church is at such a macropolitical level as to be inapplicable to a specific business situation. Without further resources for guidance from the church, and with no vocabulary to translate the religious worldview into business-acceptable language, the Obedient Congregant cuts off religious thinking at this point, turning to secularized standards for guidance. Take this interviewee's discussion of his church's view of the dignity of work and the living-wage question:

> I totally agree with the Bishops' Pastoral letter when they said we need to reemphasize the connection between work and the possibility of human dignity. Living wage is a separate issue, and I'm not sure how it relates. So far, the church has aligned with a few unions on this, but we are largely not in a business that is unionized. There are many first-entry wage earners who work part-time, and minimum wage is lot of money to them. It's a difficult issue. *Fortunately, I don't have to think about it in my business*—we pay so high above the minimum wage that living wage does not come up.

The self-imposed limitations of this approach are obvious from the italicized comment above.

As one congregant who specifically rejected the Obedient Congregant strategy remarked, "The nature of work is dynamic, flexible, and free-flowing, not static or rigid." He then went on to speak about new notions of business, finding more that is of use in secular discussion of love, wonder, humility, and compassion as leadership qualities than in the rigid rules of the church.

Percolators: "My Religion Just Kind of Percolates Up"

Percolators sit between the Atomists and the Generalists, expecting occasional, concrete instances where religion "percolates up" into one's consciousness and problem solving. The mode of connection may be an ethical rule, a sense of God's help in sustaining a moral stand, a particular obligation to a certain constituency, or even an occasional appearance in the company of business peers to participate in church-related activities. One interviewee's description of his own hesitancy to have religion penetrate the realm of management concerns was the source of our term for this approach: "I am deeply devout, or at least I try to be, and my religion means a great deal to me. Not the church; my religion. But I don't expect to call on my religion in my daily life. I don't think that's appropriate. I know it just kind of percolates up."

Percolators are afraid of imposing religion in an inappropriate setting, such as the workplace. The values of tolerance, equal opportunity, and freedom from discrimination are the cornerstone of a diverse workforce. Why push it? Vocalizing religious belief may be an abuse of one's power if it implies pressure on others to suppress their own form of belief. Unlike Justifiers and Resacralizers, who would resuscitate a Christian identity for the corporate culture, Percolators seek a highly disguised form of religious expression. This approach has been the chief strategy of liberal Protestant laity in the last thirty years—a religion that is privately meaningful and publicly irrelevant, to quote Peter Berger.

To remain relevant but disguised, the Percolator's faith must penetrate consciousness and behavior in indirect, highly subtle ways— so subtle it seems to be hardly recognizable even to the Percolators themselves in day-to-day life. The man who describes his faith as percolating up is one example. A woman who was in charge of a social responsibility program in her corporation relates a different faith journey that arrives at the same conclusion: "I am religious in some sense, but after seeing and experiencing the intolerance that the church preaches, I really can't be very open to the idea of faith in my daily life. And yet I know that I have certain basic religious beliefs that I would not abandon, or [that] would be very important to me, say, if I were dying. Meanwhile, I can act on my social conscience in real ways in my business life, ways the church has never done."

She assumes capitalism to be a system that rewards investment in good things, whether it's a new product, employee training, or corporate citizenship. Social aspects of Christianity thus percolate up in the social responsibility activities of her company without the baggage of religious rationale per se. As both of these people's comments indicate, a Percolator strategy helps the businessperson handle concerns over the church's effectiveness in action, as well as concerns about sectarian conflict inside an organization were religion to be more overt. Indeed, among our interviewees, this type of strategy—typified as "religion is about social concern"—was most frequently expressed by liberal Protestants in upper-middle-class suburban congregations.

Percolators think about the ethics of business in one of two ways. They may favor secularized, utilitarian terms, such as participating in a community-building activity on the grounds that it builds goodwill in the marketplace. Or they may make an intuitive judgment that responds to what "feels right to me in terms of my personal values," such as refusing to participate in a shady deal even though it appears no one will know.

Percolators assume that these problem-solving approaches are mysteriously influenced by the percolation process, primarily through its effect on character. Those who are satisfied with this model may actively resist further reflection on faith and work as being suspiciously inauthentic or trivializing of a truly religious experience. Those who are dissatisfied with this model may regard it as a necessary fall-back strategy, believing that the church has never participated in society without cultivating intolerance and conflict.

A Disheartening Pattern

We saw a disheartening pattern emerging from these coping strategies: each approach invites a kind of dead-end thinking by posing limiting constraints on one's ability to entertain sustained attention to inherent conflict in the foundational values of one's corporation and religion. With no language with which to explore faith or to create shared understanding in the Christian community, these models fail to offer the kind of active guidance and transformative power that would make Christianity a distinctive, supportive force in people's lives as businesspeople.

In practice, most people adopt a mixed bag of coping strategies to avoid the excesses or inadequacies of each approach. They may, however, simply be moving from one dead end to another without building a deeper connection between faith and the challenges of work. Some of the limitations of these coping models are obvious: few bridging mechanisms between sacred and secular contexts, rules without practical application guidelines, little understanding of religious or spiritual meaning in the activities of work, and the danger of unnoticed carryover (such as heavy-handed proselytizing) that may not be a legitimate application of religious thought in the workplace. Given these limitations, it is understandable that many Christians long for alternative forms of religious expression to support their daily struggles—especially since the church frequently reinforces the separation of business and Christianity in its own models for thinking about integration.

Coping Strategies for Clergy

As you can see in Figure 2.1, the church has evolved a number of familiar roles that either match the business group or effect even greater mental separation of business and religion in its three aspects. Not surprisingly, the Secularists are unrepresented in the clergy, save for a few examples where a church becomes purely a business owner and abrogates all decision making and cultural symbols to secular authority.

Cynics

We found good representation of the nihilistic view of the Cynic among the clergy. These include the Scolders, the Watchdogs, and the Anarchists—church representatives whose only stand toward capitalism is against it. Cynics among the clergy assume that the values of the realms of religion and business are hopelessly irreconcilable. Integration is not possible because, however well-intentioned or personally devout a business person may be, capitalism is seen as an irredeemably unjust economic framework. Participation in its zero-sum purposes is portrayed as an exercise against the poor.

Ironically, a Cynic in the church may unintentionally be contributing to a lower standard of business behavior by perpetuating an ultimately nihilistic mental framework. Just as Cynics fail to take into account the motives and accomplishments of people inside the business system, businesspeople shrug off the church as a source of guidance—while still hoping for a deeply personalized spirituality or belief system to kick in at the right moments in their own honest careers.

Atomists

The religious Atomists are persuaded that redemption is best bought with chunks of business time and money devoted to charitable deeds, maintenance of church activity, and so on. These clergy may welcome the businessperson as head of the finance committee or chief donor to the building fund, but other aspects of the congregant's professional identity are sealed off from church acknowledgment. This group includes clergy who regularly frequent the soup kitchen to communicate with the poor and displaced but never venture to sit at the table with a business leader in a corporate setting. Interestingly, this Atomist approach prevents clergy from fully entertaining the possibility of integrating faith in their own management responsibilities. Content to relegate religious possibility to ritual, teaching, and social action outside the support of business, they may perpetuate uncomfortably poor management and accountability in the running of the church.

Atomists are also an interesting example of how these coping strategies can be well intended but limiting in practice. One of the nation's most popular housing programs for the poor engages businesspeople and corporate donors in actually constructing homes with their "sweat equity." By all counts a wonderful experience, the program nonetheless atomizes its own literature to deemphasize its conservative religious roots when appealing to companies. Nor could we find significant examples of businesses that had participated in this program changing their own lending habits or other activities on housing. They tended to describe the activity as "team-building" and doing good, a "gift" to their employees that gave back to the community.

As this example illustrates, the Atomist view permits some integration of religious social action and corporate commitment, but it essentially fails to sustain this religious mission once the specific project is over.

Generalists

Seers and Retreaters are two types of religious Generalist. The seer focuses on a bold new vision of effectiveness, moral courage, and social justice in the marketplace, glossing over complex social or financial factors by emphasizing a utopian outcome achieved through single-issue action.

The Jubilee movement has suffered such a simplification in some religious circles. The prophetic call to forgive debt in developing countries attempts to change an aspect of capitalism without destroying it. But the failure to address (if not solve) real problems of theft and brutality that accompany illegal use of these loans in a number of countries itself raises difficult questions about the subsequent use to which the freed-up money will be put. Even if one places the blame for lack of accountability mechanisms on the lending nations, the problems of implementation and potential to finance theft cannot be glossed over.

But financial accountability and regard for the law are not typical topics of Christian relevance. In the absence of concrete mechanisms for engaging in such debates, Seers bridge the gap with rhetorical and polemical filler. Certain aspects of capitalism, such as preservation of competitive markets, are particularly vulnerable to oversight. The Seers are also fond of idealized conceptions of the progressive corporation, the new model of "caring capitalism." They hold up generalized, romantic visions of the Body Shop or Ben and Jerry's for admiration and awards, while omitting the mundane and mixed motives that are part and parcel of these businesses. Profit, it seems, happens automatically to those who are caring.

Religious Retreaters see religious integration occurring in settings and roles outside the workplace. The church may sponsor a retreat, for example, in which businesspeople are encouraged to draw on their faith to address their marriage relations and leave work behind for a few days. Clearly, this activity may have some effect on a businessperson's ability to lead responsibly, but it does not offer a model of *direct religious integration*. Other examples are the faith-based journals and seminars designed to assist businesspeople in their effort to integrate faith and work but fail to engage in any topic beyond sex, family, or encouraging testimonials to one's experience of God's love or profession of personal affiliation with Christianity.

Justifiers

The most notable church-based Justifier is the preacher of the prosperity gospel. Promising material blessings to the true believer and laden with sentimental examples of how a religious view "paid off," the religious Justifier constructs an essentially self-serving rationale for the link between Christianity and profit. The bounty of this approach has been fairly widely realized by (but not limited to) certain televangelists.

Resacralizers

Religious Resacralizers adopt an approach of benign despotism over the marketplace, largely based on alternative notions of distributive justice. They advocate redistribution or monopoly to short-circuit market mechanisms. They suggest a number of ways to override a competitive context: forced contribution to workplace ideals, such as living wage; barriers to market entry through exclusive contracts to promote development; or church-mandated investment in products and services for customers who cannot cover the cost of production and capital.

This resacralization of purpose, however, cannot be implemented without accompanying resacralization of power. Haphazard, voluntary measures are unlikely to be competitively sustainable over the long run unless they are universalized into law or reframed into a not-for-profit contribution. Resacralizers take on the role of bureaucratic despot asserting a claim of religious authority, much like the Mandarins of ancient China. Rather than becoming a political voice, which seems totally appropriate, extreme Resacralizers seek to establish a specific religious interpretation as political power players. The church becomes a significant arbiter of national economic choices. Anything less is portrayed as not caring for whatever group they claim to represent.

By accepting the Resacralizer's new standard for strategic choice, the marketplace is indeed transformed. It becomes less market-driven. But the arbiter of choice in the absence of market mechanisms must be endowed with statist power, a condition in which there is less accountability for poor results as long as the rules are followed. In a pluralistic democracy, no single religious group is likely to achieve such power. Resacralizers must therefore either adopt market-friendly strategies in which social responsibility is sold on its market power (as is the case with many of the social investment funds) or acquire political power. In the first case, the resacralizing purpose is effectively secularized. In the second, the separation of church and state is violated, to the unease of many people, for political and economic reasons. Both issues are fully apparent in the current debate over government funding of faith-based charities.

For these reasons, the Resacralizer integration strategy has been undergoing a number of interesting modifications to accommodate democratic and market mechanisms. One of the most promising may be relocating faith-based economic development efforts to a not-for-profit venue. Job development, low-income housing, and health services are all efforts that redefine the systemic rules at both the entry level of the economy and at the top level (in terms of redistribution in the form of charitable donations). New concepts such as social entrepreneurship are an exciting possibility for reframing the questions of poverty so as to retreat from the model of church despotism but not the problems of justice in the economy.

On the other hand, these strategies rarely deal with the religious meaning of their secondary effects. Once economic activity becomes competitive, will it no longer be faith-based? Should the protectionist measures continue, they will raise other problems about justice. Take low-income housing, for example. Much subsidized development approved by the church produces housing at prices very nearly market rate by the time the projects are completed—*if* they are completed at all. Is the subsidy of the developer truly just?

We heard many in academia and the church assume some sort of *ex cathedra* authority over the economy and businesspeople. Given their position in not-for-profit institutions among colleagues who tend to share an anti-capitalist ideology, they can become overconfident about the authority they carry. To the outsider businessperson, these calls can appear naïve or even hypocritical, a foolish disregard for nourishing the goose that lays the golden egg. The problem here is not their questioning of capitalism, but the absence of a diverse voice with differing interests to consider and debate fully informed, strategic alternatives.

Thinking About New Integration Strategies

Each coping strategy we have presented in this chapter entertains some possibility of integrating religious faith and as such is useful. But each also has a certain dead-end quality that prevents it from being a robust connection between faith and the difficult complexities of business as people experience it. They fail to draw a line in the sand that holds up to pressure but still affords an avenue for wealth creation. Even more disturbing, the institutional religious strategies particularly seem to trigger retreat. Businesspeople think about spirituality and work with unnuanced confusion between personal faith, conviction, and claims of institutional dominance that lead to sectarian conflict.

These coping strategies tend toward a state of moral and intellectual entropy. Notions of integration are so encumbered by dualistic parameters opposing business and Christian religion that they create closed systems in which faith can play only a limited role. Rather than being an energizing force, religion comes quickly to a state of quiet, shut down by anticipated irrelevancy or inappropriateness to business life. Many of the more recent faith-based programs to give substantive support to believers in business may find themselves replicating these foundational notions with similar results. This would account in part for the failure of many of them to take hold significantly.

We were also struck by how the business and religious professionals mirrored each other's strategies, despite their differing economic ideologies. The patterns do indeed run deep. Both groups are turning capitalism and Christianity into an either-or proposition, an exclusive choice between two distinct realms or between free enterprise and an economic model that suppresses secular-driven conditions supporting free enterprise. (In classic terms, these would include legitimizing a profit motive, free access to the resources of production, and free exchange.)

Spirituality and Christian faith require more than being naïvely "nice" or well-intentioned. In our definition of spirituality, they suggest several other benchmarks:

- An engagement with life-destroying forces, whether generated by wage scales, product choices, or personal relationships at work

- Religious consciousness, which does not mean praying all the time but finding space in working life for the punctuated moments of transcendence that represent knowing God

- Justice—a passion notably lacking or watered down for many businesspeople today

Current notions about religion and business cause many people to cut out of this deeper engagement long before there is substantive transformation of their workplace. Given the thin conceptual framework even in their own churches and the radical differences of the realms, this is understandable but not helpful. Either they shortchange business or they shortchange religion.

Clearly, we need a new strategy that offers Christians a richer possibility of integrating their faith with their business life. Just as the secular spirituality movement has opened up radical new ways of thinking about business problem solving, so too Christian communities must develop conceptions of religion as a powerful resource in business thinking.

The coping strategies described here constitute a fruitful beginning for starting that critique. The church professional and the businessperson should scrutinize personal coping strategies to understand how deeply they drive or limit the religious meaning *of* work and the impact of religion *on* work. More powerful concepts for knowing God in one's life must evolve not despite the sharp contrast between the realms but because of them. A good place to start is with a gap that was noticed in all the strategies, between personalized and experiential aspects of faith on the one hand and the full range of business ethics that most business people confront on the other.

This gap is unlikely to be addressed unless churches devise a new relational format with the business community so as to draw on business experience in the initial stage of the conceptual effort.

If a new model is to be developed, it seems imperative that representatives of both communities engage in that development together. As we quickly discovered, however, deep-seated conflicts of worldview, culture, and authority between the church and business professionals reinforce a tendency to avoid conducting a spiritual journey about professional responsibility *in concert*. Our interviews revealed that despite growing interest among laypeople in the business-work connection, there is little church-business dialogue at the moment. Discouraging as this is, a superficial coping strategy to keep religion alive but in its box is no better. Rather, we must understand why it is that the separation has been so severe, and what is driving it today.

Reflection

- Review the seven main coping strategies for integrating business and religion. Which one describes you best?

- What are the advantages and limitations of this view in your experience of who you are at work and how well you feel anchored to your core values?

- Which are the most common strategies you have observed among businesspeople and clergy? What do you make of their position?

- Were you to shift strategies, what would look different in your business behavior or the actions of your company?

Action

- Invite a small group of businesspeople and at least two clergy to a meal to discuss the coping strategies. (You may copy Figure 2.1 and distribute it at this gathering.)

- Ask the group to describe the types they most frequently observe, and the effects they see on business behavior.

- How do these strategies compare to the way you observe business colleagues discussing or practicing so-called secular spirituality?

- If destructive stereotypes are shutting down the inquiry, call a time-out and share this observation. Note what the group is observing, and revisit these observations after reading Chapters Five, Six, and Seven.

3

Not Our Modus Operandi

The Church's Response to Business

> *I do not try to interfere with their business. I wouldn't have the expertise, even if I thought it was right to advise them. But I am very close personally to several businesspeople in my congregation.*
>
> —*Protestant clergyman*

Jack, a manager at a large company, is a lapsed Catholic. He looks at the church's social policies with dismay but feels a strong personal connection to the religion. He values being a good person at work, by which he means being considerate, honest, and if at all possible, generous. He told us his story.

He has to make a choice: to decide whether or not the company should continue offering its current policy of paying for certain disabilities. It is generous, treating any disability as a total disability, and the successful claimant receives total benefits for life. New economic circumstances and changing claimant patterns have rendered the policy an ongoing financial loss for the company. Moreover, many people with disabilities are still able to work, but not at their previous jobs. It seems ethically preposterous to demand that the company fund their leisure for life, although by legal rights this is the contract.

In reviewing whether to reformulate this type of policy, Jack summons up a panoply of utilitarian arguments to decide whether it is morally and financially right to end or modify this offering. He reasons that the claims will hurt many other people by eating up so much of the company's revenue. Insurance costs will go up in other categories, and jobs will be lost. What is more, the policy encourages people to lie. Corporations seeking to lay off workers have been known to tell their employees to claim total disability as a way of continuing an income, and they even find doctors who reinforce these claims.

Secular utilitarianism, humanistically applied, mediates the problem, taking into account the various constituencies affected. But as Jack comes to his conclusion, a second level of meaning intrudes itself, one that has to be called "religiously based." He finds himself thinking about human dignity, about "defending and opening up the possibilities of life," as John Paul II advocated in *Centesimus annus*. Jack has always liked that phrase, and it frequently occurs to him like a mantra.

The disability program under scrutiny does not open up the possibilities of life. It degrades the claimant, in his view, and threatens the livelihood of employees and shareholders. But simply ending all such policies because they are likely to be unprofitable is also unacceptable: some people truly need permanent, total disability. Can his company choose to offer it, or will the decision fall to the state?

He might resolve this problem with a tough-minded look at the numbers, finding a pricing structure for such insurance policies that makes them available (but only to people in exceptionally generous companies or who personally have the wealth to finance them). Instead, Jack forms a task force of doctors, insurance executives, and customers. After several years, a number of innovative practices emerge to ease the cost of this kind of insurance. Legislation to approve graduated degrees of disability payment is submitted, thereby allowing partial claims payments and opportunity to demand that claimants seek some sort of work. Additionally, the company works closely with one of the leading rehabilitation hospitals in its area to develop new therapies and hardware to allow disabled people more mobility.

A cynic would say religion has nothing to do with these outcomes. The whole program makes more money for the company. Jack says it is a combination of good business sense (secularized ethic) and something deeper that has to do with how he values human life, a view he traces to his religion and feels he must not neglect.

The irony is, Jack barely recognized this process of faith in his own work life until our interview. He is so used to seeing his church as being hostile to business in his industry and to its extensive family policies on child care and birth control that he has erected a secular filter for his conscience. A business decision might be personally meaningful, but it is basically a secular matter.

Jack is not alone. Ambivalent about his church's social and economic policies, comfortable with the ethical mechanisms of enlightened rationality, he fails to explore the connection between faith and work. Yet he believes it is there in his heart, and at times he longs for a career in which he can closely access the dynamics of religion and spirituality: a sense of larger meaning; and awareness of a world larger than business, of community, of right and wrong—the things that define humanity and define a Christian identity. These hallmarks of religious concern become felt needs in his life. They are not fully articulated and not necessarily a cause of despair, for the businessperson is essentially optimistic. But when Stephen Covey suddenly presents a pattern for work effectiveness that echoes the desire for balance and humanity that Jack seeks, or when author Meg Wheatley suggests there is a new explanation about the order of the universe that happens to support many of the values he most admires, and when both programs suggest to this stressed-out manager that it is not only possible but essential to think about these things as part of one's business role, the idea is powerfully attractive. He buys into their programs for pursuing these ends. What similar support do Jack and fellow businesspeople get from the church? Not nearly enough.

Robert Wuthnow's extensive social surveys of data from a large sample of alleged Christians of all denominations underscores the gap in understanding between business and religion that we saw in the last chapter. In his words, "People are not drawing connections between spirituality and their daily lives. They are preoccupied with their own economic needs, and they do not feel that the churches are ministering to the needs."[1]

The new spirituality, on the other hand, *is* responding to those needs. As Al MacDonald, businessperson, board member, and founder of Trinity Forum (a lay organization for top executives), commented: "The churches simply aren't doing enough in this area. If they were making even half an effort, we'd be out of business. Instead, people are flocking to our retreats."

The Church's Traditional Response to Business

What are the churches and ecclesiastical institutions doing? How do they construct their own terms of engagement with economic life?

During the 1990s, two main trends surfaced in liberal churches: focusing on the public voice of religion, and promoting volunteerism in a postwelfare society. The past few years, as Martin Marty notes, have seen a sudden increase in academic attention to religion in public life.[2] Much of this good work is about a generalized "civil religion" that offers a common base of conviction about social values.[3] The other main stream of academic activity regarding public religion has concentrated on the study of what religious institutions (or, in the current coinage, "faith-based institutions") are and should be doing in respect to public welfare. Both of these fields of concentration have tended to overlook that halfway world between public and private: the corporation.

Even though the church has long scrutinized economic systems and investment principles, these studies have either been devoid of specific business content or presented such an outdated view of business concerns as to be unrecognizable in the context of the twenty-first century. How can churches reconnect to their specific tradition? The diversity of lay and academic religious views on economic life expands, ranging from liberation theology to neoconservativism, Christian prosperity gospels and new forms of social investing, therapeutic twelve-step models of spiritual healing, and general seminars on leadership. What model of guidance and authority should the church adopt?

The church's traditional response to pragmatic economic concerns has taken three major forms: (1) ideological statement, (2) social action, and (3) relationships.

Ideological Statement

No religious document in recent history has arguably been more widely circulated than the 1986 pastoral letter of the U.S. National Conference of Catholic Bishops, "Economic Justice for All: Letter on Catholic Social Teaching and the U.S. Economy." Notable for its inclusiveness of diverse views among the bishops in discussing and adopting this document, it is a good example of a religious ideological statement. The document lays out a detailed statement of the principles by which Catholics should approach modern economic life. Chief among these are dignity of persons, solidarity with the poor, and subsidiarity (a principle of spreading the work and responsibility to those in the church best qualified to do the task).

Churches have always been comfortable with such abstractions. Not surprisingly, they frequently seek to address serious economic and social concerns of the day through carefully argued ideological statements. If there's a problem, then theorize about it—preferably in normative terms. (For example, what *should* be the criterion for defining and measuring a Christian's duty toward the coming of the Kingdom of God, with regard to the poor?) Some of these arguments are written as clarifications of a former theological point; others are posed as "commandments," normative rules about what to do in certain situations.

Such tracts are circulated to parishes or academic institutions in the hope of planting a seed. Thus in September 1999 both the Roman Catholic and United Methodist churches signaled their increased interest in faith and work by issuing sample Labor Day messages. These statements, institutionally aligned with organized labor groups, emphasized Christian responsibilities to promote justice in the marketplace by fighting for "those who go to work day in and day out, earning little as they humbly toil."[4]

As a problem-solving framework, this response has received the highest endorsement of the church's elite: the theology schools and denominational ecclesiastics. For this group, *doing* something means writing a position paper and *discussing* it. Examples abound, from the many descriptions of ethical business behavior coming out of Jesuit-affiliated business schools, to the Roman Catholic pastoral letters and the economic position papers of Protestant denominations.

For many in the church, sermons and position papers constitute a sound response. The unstated assumption is that the road to relevance is already well traveled once a theologically appropriate stand has been articulated—even if the final destination has not yet been reached. The depth of this bias is apparent when we consider the abundance of theological argumentation over why a new language that bridges the moral landscape of religion and pluralistic society needs to be developed, and then compare it with the absence of living examples of the language in practice.

Social Action

Direct engagement in social action is another key religious response to the issues of faith and business. We interviewed a number of clergy for this book who cited social action as the primary evidence of their concern about being relevant to business. Indeed, business was the focal point of their message as they sought to encourage congregants to care about taking responsibility for addressing society's ills; but business was relevant only insofar as it could be regarded as the source of the injustice, not its cure. Faith demanded a position over and against business activity and all it seemed to represent.

The comments of one liberal Protestant cleric in the Boston area are typical. When we asked whether he and his congregation were doing anything in the area of integrating work and faith, he responded enthusiastically: "Yes. We are very concerned about economic justice. Our church was one of the first in our denomination to boycott businesses in South Africa." Said another, "We are daily ministering to those left out of the economic system, and trying to get the businesspeople in our congregation who have more to get more involved."

It is not that these sentiments are inappropriate, but they leave a residue of other assumptions. They depict business as a negative force to be fought, and they direct congregants' economic attention to realms outside the arena businesspeople actually experience. Responses like these demonstrate how the church erects a certain backdrop that frames its tendency to engage in activity related to the economic system, but not to the people in it. A logical conclusion would be that Christian social action is either a negating activity (directed toward stopping business) or, if positive (as in getting business people involved in social action), one to be deflected toward nonbusiness activities such as nonmarket mechanisms for providing food, shelter, or health services. None of this prepares the church to address economic life as businesspeople and their colleagues experience it.

One faith-based social service organization, for example, claimed to be primarily about economic justice. It turned out that 90 percent of its resources were being poured into youth programs to combat drugs. When we asked how this offered business a chance to engage in economic justice, they explained that they really meant business could contribute money to correct for the abuses of systemic injustice. Their youth programs were rightly seen as addressing root problems that were partially a function of the economic system, and that would prevent participation in the mainstream economy down the road. But how can businesspeople be expected to make some direct connection from this position to their own work and the actual problems over which they have some power in their professional lives?

Relationships

In the second response, the church engages with the economic system rather than the people in its mainstream. Response number three goes to the other extreme, engaging with the people who happen to be in business but not the activities and roles they assume at work. A number of clergy assessed their impact on congregants' search to deepen their faith and work by the status of their friendship. Recall the words of one pastor, given in the epigraph that opens this chapter; that person continued by saying ". . . I am very close personally to several businesspeople in my congregation. Some of them have been through a lot personally. We have a good relationship."

They formed those relationships primarily from exercising official pastoral duties (weddings, funerals), participating mutually in the church's rituals, seeking out personal or family counseling, and in a few cases through receiving a kind of personal sponsorship with a leading business congregant. The pastor would be invited to accompany the business leaders on golf trips or travel to the Holy Land. These acts of friendship encouraged both to share their perspectives on life and were tangible ways in which the clergyperson was a part of the business congregant's life.

Other pastors cited moments when they helped a businessperson through a family crisis, job loss, or other dark time. The affection and insight into each other's character remained long after, manifesting itself in the businessperson's being open to special requests for funds for a church need or in returning the support and counsel when the pastor hit a rough spot. Such relationships were undeniably important to both the congregant and the pastor; both reported them as indicators of a healthy respect on each side, despite largely unvoiced reservations about one another's economic assumptions.

What's Really Going On Here?

Each of these responses has been strongly legitimized in the traditions of the institutional church. Clergy and theologians described them as a good indication that the church is "doing something" in terms of involvement in questions of faith and work. It is important, therefore, to reexamine what the churches are *doing* to understand what they are *accomplishing,* for there appear to be significant inherent limitations to the actual insights and changes these responses effect among business laity.

The first response, not surprisingly, reflects the language and temperamental preferences of the people generating them. The theoretical orientation of an ideological statement, and the nonbusiness setting in which responses two and three occur, suggest a tendency to favor approaches that are oriented to the community of church professionals and academics. It is not unusual for a pastor expounding on a theological tract to paraphrase at the same depersonalized, macro level.

Clergy are versed in theological distinctions about a religion that lays total claim to your soul but does not demand full-time praying. They draw concrete examples from domestic or psychological experience but analogies to a business milieu are only partially apparent. This indirect approach can simply be too subtle for the pragmatic mind, too broad to enter the narrow passageway of commerce. The businessperson typically has a far lower affection for theological rhetoric and argumentation. A number of people told us they had participated in adult Bible class sessions in which they were eager to review a pastoral letter or passage on economic issues but found that the discussion quickly petered out when it came to critiquing actual practice. Either the participants were temperamentally indisposed to extended textual probing or the pastor's knowledge skills ran out shortly after the abstractions were fully defined.

Conversely, a platitude or contemporary parable that would turn off the pastor or theologian as too sappy and naïve might strike a deep chord among businesspeople and be repeated to peers. Excitement over a theoretical religious argument per se was much less frequent.

Several reports of experience in interpreting such a tract confirmed a basic distancing effect in focusing on theological argument. If the businessperson agreed that the concept was important, the means of carrying out these positions in practice were rarely discussed. (A good example would be the concept of solidarity.) The result: no understanding of real-world application. In other cases, if the businessperson disagreed with applications being suggested (such as an interpretation of solidarity that is grounded in liberation theology), he or she found ways to avoid a confrontation that might jeopardize the relationship with the priest. This resembles the reaction of many American Catholics toward the church's position on birth control: don't discuss it with your priest. The resulting distanced relationship has been well documented regarding gender and sexual matters, but it has been much less discussed regarding businesspeople and the church's economic positions.

Meaningful engagement in theological ideology requires overcoming problems of language and a transition from general to specific guidance; it also requires legitimation in the form of a willing listener.

Several pastors expressed frustration about incidents in which a top-level executive in the congregation bullied them with a categorical attack on a social justice position of the denomination (such as South Africa, or layoffs). The businessperson would brook no response, and the pastors felt it was both futile and needlessly risky to respond to such close-mindedness. Result: no meaningful discussion or follow-up to the church's position.

In this instance, a strong culture of conflict avoidance within the congregation, supported by religious norms expecting community harmony within a congregation, caused both professional groups to avoid taking advantage of any opportunity for deeper exploration of theological positions and what they would say to a Christian in the marketplace. Clearly, then, the first response of the church (write a position paper clarifying the theology) makes a certain sense if only because it is not likely to seriously damage lay relations in the way that discussing views on specific business contexts closer to home would do.

For pastors whose jobs are held at the pleasure of their congregations, such harmony is not a trivial issue. The social action mode (response two) suffered similar diminution of effect on businesspeople when subjected to deep scrutiny, even as it found reinforcement among the clergy's peers and authorities. The social action being advocated was often so limited—or, if radical, directed so distantly from the local community of the congregation—that it prompted discussion about using church resources rather than the businessperson's professional spiritual compass. In one church, a project using church resources to subsidize a new kind of housing created great controversy over whether this was appropriate use of funds. Congregants became engaged (and divided) on whether the church should be involved in this type of activity.

What did *not* occur was reexamination of the lending structure of the community banks. Why? Because business congregants, several of whom were prominent bankers and real estate agents, felt confident that there were no serious discriminatory practices that would obligate radical review and change. Whether or not they were correct, the result of this nonattention was that they were not stimulated to consider *any* possible ways in which banking and lending procedures might have better served these neighborhoods—at least not from a religious standpoint. When one of their colleagues, a devout Episcopalian, later considered whether to fund more ATM machines in this neighborhood, he staunchly refused to see it as a possibility for prophetic religious action. Once again, the specific form and focus of the church's response fails to provoke business congregants to turn their efforts to transform business in ways that promote a just, life-supporting society for all.

Similarly, assessing the businessperson-pastor relationship (response three) proved in many cases to impose serious constraints on any frank consideration of the church's relevance to the congregant's vocational roles and decisions. In feeling "close" to the businessperson-congregant as a person, clergy and congregant assumed perhaps more of a connection to the businessperson's working ethos than was true. In many cases, this assumption was never tested. Further questioning during our interviews revealed that the relationships were strengthened primarily in situations outside the businessperson's professional, decision-making activities—in moments of leisure, family time, or service at the church. The vocational spillover that each assumed to be important was extremely vague, safely protected from any test of each other's views through examining real practices for which the congregants had control and knowledge.

Clearly, there are surprise factors constraining each of these responses, which suggest a significant gap between the intended relevance and actual support that the church's standard modes of guidance offer. Given the many alternative sources of guidance on ethics, spirituality, and management on which businesspeople rely, or the often-voiced comment in our interviews that they preferred to "go it alone" rather than seek institutional input in understanding faith and work, it is important for church professionals to revisit how they respond to questions of economic and business decision making.

Learning from the Secular Spirituality Programs

The new spirituality movement enjoys overwhelmingly popular success in the business community, just as many factors are weakening the church's ability to be a distinctive voice in exploring spirituality, ethics, and work. What's going on? Can the church learn anything from the modes of response that these programs offer? After personally attending some of the programs, talking to participants and readers of the books related to those programs, and reading more than a hundred of them ourselves, we feel they are worth considering for their insight into how the church might change its patterns and strengthen its voice.[5]

Synthesis

The secular spirituality programs shift seamlessly from presentation of extremely distinctive spiritual traditions and practices to highly synthesized notions that presume a radical integration of all the world's great religions into one term (such as *cosmos*). This paradigm is frequently used to frame spirituality as being a supplemental form of wisdom rather than a competing one that claims exclusive dominance over the believer's life and thinking. These books make plausible connections between science and spirit; they also conflate the two. This conflation is as holistic and eclectic as it is intended to be empowering. The argument is postmodern: managers need to cultivate and discipline numerous levels of consciousness for a balanced life and effective leadership. As Robert Bellah has said in summing up postmodern thinking: "We will recognize that in both scientific and religious culture all we have finally are symbols." He notes that there is constant demand to translate between scientific and imaginative vocabularies.[6] This is the task that secular spirituality programs take up gladly.

Old Information Is New

The secular spirituality movement also owes its rise to the relative lack of religious and humanities education among the business population. Best-selling author Deepak Chopra, for example, amply salts his books with quotes from Vedic texts, Shakespeare, and Blake. The material is not only interesting; for many people, it is quite new. For the past thirty years, mainstream Protestant and Catholic churches have been losing membership among regular church attendees. Similarly, taboos on religious education in schools and a strategy of religious silence in the corporation throughout the 1970s and 1980s have cut off businesspeople from once-familiar forms of religious education. Novelty sells, and for many of the participants in these programs Eastern religious frameworks, ancient cultural practices, and premodern forms of creative thinking are especially new and exotic intellectual territory.

Many of the programs and books are largely popularized presentations of the new science or a history of Western and Eastern thought. Postmodernism paves the way for incorporating two almost contradictory ways of coping with globalism: going tribal and going global. We saw several executive programs whose content was primarily a historical review of scientific discovery and the beliefs of premodern civilizations, all in the name of reenergizing the businessperson's connection to his or her soul—as well as any problem-solving powers that might occur. In these programs advocates rightly see that changes in science leading to a new worldview imply changes in our understanding of ourselves. Instead of fending off this information or concentrating on the potential horrors of new science gone wrong, these books embrace it as an exciting metaphor for asking the big questions about one's own place and power in the universe.

In contrast to this agenda of mental liberation, the bare basics of Christianity and the church's teaching may be assumed to be less interesting, an old story with regressive (or possibly oppressive) associations. More mature conceptions of Christian theology—historical modes of religious expression such as those recently celebrated by the popular Sister Wendy and Judeo-Christian religious history—are largely unknown, untaught in schools, and not bridged by a popularized language until quite recently.

Building Bridges

Most of the secular spirituality programs focus on creating new bridges from the newest and oldest learning back to a context of personal meaning and business management. As one spirituality book puts it, "Corporate mystics have a strong connection with their intuition and know how to use it where it counts."[7]

Some call this a bridge between soul and science, or between spirituality and business. The contexts to which they bridge tend to cluster heavily around self-empowerment, interpersonal relations, and organizational design, but these dynamics are shown to be evident in every aspect of corporation life, from the process of creating technological innovation among global industrial partners to the creative teamwork in developing a new ad campaign.

No Moral Absolutism

The point is important: most of these programs do not demand total allegiance, but rather only an investment in the price of admission and any follow-on products one might like to purchase. Membership is transitory, voluntary, and contractual—a seminar, a book purchased, shared with a friend or coworker but without pressure to "believe." Belief is not monitored, and people take away the bits and pieces they like. A corporate-sponsored event may impose enforced participation in certain rites, but these rites are deliberately packaged as a path to self-discovery and self-expression, teamwork, and new forms of problem solving—not as a challenge to adopt a particular confessional belief.[8] By not taking a stand of moral absolutism, these programs lower the stakes for acceptance. If some of the material turns out to be wrong or not to the consumer's liking, there is still the possibility of some legitimate take-away.

New ideas presented in this way are not so threatening and thus are likely to be entertained. Even better, the learning is explicitly brought back to its application to business. These programs are framed as being about business success, no matter how deeply they also delve into individual meaning, the psyche, the cosmos, or reasons to support ethical principles.

Given their user-friendly, supportive approach, it could rightly be asked, Are secular spirituality and business-friendly lay evangelicalism promoting the culture of greed that so bothers the mainstream church? If so, why would the church want to follow their techniques? The answer is beyond our knowing, despite much certainty on this from others. We see no evidence of a particular causality between secular spirituality and specific instances of greed. What is clear is that these books are reframing religious expression and its practical implications. They offer *some* preparation for integrating spiritual concerns whatever their other shortcomings.

Community

The starting point is in a self-expressive, personalized religious search. Kant said the most important question is "Who am I?" This question has taken on infinite meaning in the postmodern world of interchangeable identities. The mutability of self-identity makes appealing the promise of a new, more spiritual self; the intense pressures on personal inner strength make it urgent.

In the Christian tradition, this kind of happy fortitude was expressed more often in habits of clean living than in a mysterious search for inner harmony or workplace effectiveness through ethical conduct. For some church attendees we interviewed, finding in one's daily work a means of harmony with God's purpose was understood as a commandment to *stop* work. Said one person: "I just need to make space for the important things, like family. Religion helps me remember to make that space. You go to church to be reminded of the really important things in life. It's scary to say no to the job."

Other church attendees were not content to confine religion to family and the formal sacred spaces of the church's authority. They were receptive to programs that offered some avenue for spiritual or religious expression in their working roles.

For many businesspeople, the corporation is the closest thing to community that they have after family. Said one interviewee: "There are really great people in my company. I love those times when you have a project and you work together and you do the impossible. The *spirit* of that—if you could bottle it. Everyone has something to offer if you set it up right. When you work productively with people, you create tolerance. You begin to accept each other, warts and all. You get curious about who they are. You see them a little more clearly because you value each person's contribution. I find that very fulfilling."

The new spirituality frames community as something without boundaries, occurring inside and outside the corporation. It is a paradoxical concept in other ways as well, something an individual needs to belong to and cooperate with while also remaining a self-reliant pioneer. Some see this as evidence for a corporatist conspiracy, but there is also an inclusiveness here in which everybody can become fulfilled, good, and rich. (The echoes to nineteenth-century positivism are everywhere.)

A strong secondary strand in the movement is the search for new models of business that are responsive to community. A number of conferences featured the combined topics of personal spirituality and what are called socially responsible business models. A host of social critics have argued that the Protestant view, emphasizing individualism, self-improvement, and vocationalism, inevitably (if inadvertently) cuts off community values from their religious roots in a communal form of sacred institutional belonging. The new spirituality movement takes these same forms of religious expression and enlightened humanism and offers therapeutic tools to counter anticommunity tendencies. Troeltsch's observation of a fundamental dualism in Christianity between absolute individualism in one's relation to God and absolute universalism with respect to the ultimate equality of all persons is less paradoxical in the new spirituality movement. "Doing unto others" is but another facet of heightening personal spirituality through connection to universal truth.

Connections with the Earth

The earth, too, is a source of spirituality and communion, especially in the programs that offer information on premodern or non-Western religious practices. The new spirituality responds to the boomers' ecological interests. Its poetic and scientific concepts on ecology and holism stimulate a strong personal spiritual link to nature, from which connection to new powers is derived. Stones are passed around, helping connect the group to each other and to the earth. The ridges on one's fingertips are noted to be like the patterns the life-giving wind traces on sand (cited as a Navajo belief in one book on secular spirituality); observe them and know something about the origins of your makeup in relation to the universe. Candles are lit to focus concentration. Fire is braved, rapids are shot, and the warmth of the bowl containing one's soup is mindfully assimilated—fuel for connection with larger life forces.

Standing at the halfway point between postmodern rational understanding of psychological states and ancient magical connection to nature, such practices are not positioned as worship per se, but no one is too concerned with systemic theology here. Contemplation of chaos, for example, leads to contemplation of nature, feedback loops, *and* stewardship. Participation in the experiential discovery of these organic patterns is framed as a fertile activity rather than a self-denying one.

Even ethical goals enter through the passageway of "connection" with natural, spiritual forces and models of an authentic self. Expressions of gratitude and respect are abundantly pursued, as are probing exercises about one's deepest life-giving values. The package is exotic, but connections of this type are not new. The most respected, rational Enlightenment thinkers also prefaced their ethical conclusions with observations about human nature.

A Benign and Eclectic Worldview

Behind the cosmology and technique of these programs is a worldview that is essentially therapeutic and benign. (One should not give in to anger because it destroys one's sleep. The purpose of life is universal happiness.) If all this sounds utopian, it is. The romanticized, poetic, and highly pluralistic language also reflects this utopianism, presenting a vivid contrast to the scolding pessimism or territoriality that interviewees observed in some of their encounters with the church's views on business.

Inspiring Language

The drama of the new spirituality language is inescapable. Operating on consumer appeal rather than the pressure of guilt or institutional power, the new spirituality must build a strong element of entertainment and inspiration into the language, which is not unlike the close connection between drama and religion in pre-modern and early Christian worship practices. This language can sound messianic, traceable to its charismatic celebrity guruism and its claims to understand the future.

Not So New After All

All of these features also characterized the nineteenth-century positive thinkers, whose mind-body eclecticism was so carefully described by William James in *Varieties of Religious Experience*. Though the movement never resulted in institutional cooperation among the gurus and did not adequately impart a religious grounding to sustain adherents through the horrors of the first two decades of the twentieth century (think World War I and the excesses of the business trusts) we should not dismiss the strengths of such approaches. As James noted, their language was hardly bearable to the educated thinker; but he also observed that they carried powerful religious potential for more optimistic types. Among these he included the businessperson.

What Can We Learn?

The theology of the new spirituality movement has a number of obvious shortcomings (especially regarding its lack of attention to bad luck, systemic social forces, and evil in the world). Nonetheless, it has much to offer to those who want to learn more about revitalizing religion in daily life. This juxtaposition of soul and business, with its holistic patterns, contemporary focus, and deep pragmatism, holds great appeal for businesspeople who profess Christian and eclectic forms of faith. The appeal lies in how it dignifies the businessperson's role, in its authoritative claim that soul counts, in its ethic of inclusiveness, and in its claim that we can access soul rather than separate it off from the concerns of business.

Though overly romantic and sometimes resembling nothing so much as sci-fi literature, the language succeeds in exciting people, and it is accessible. Chopra's and Covey's books sell in million-dollar multiples, while Randy Komisar, Ken Wilber, and Lama Surya Das know the pleasure of being best-selling authors. Most important, this movement is not afraid of being contaminated by the business world. The books and programs frequently speak of the spiritual toll produced by managers who never listen, or of the person who goes home defeated and stressed because of overwork, difficulty in prioritizing, and lacking sense of accomplishment.

The danger of such personalized approaches, as Michael Walzer points out, is loss of social reinforcement for religious commitment, and a sense of distancing from one's own deepest convictions in the public arena of life. Secular spirituality modifies negotiated pluralism by assuming that one has an inherent possibility of integration and that its expression is evidenced through observation, mental discipline, and cognitive patterns, not dogma.

We would slightly modify this assessment. These books and programs do indeed tend to assume a baseline of human potential that is essentially optimistic. They do not, however, say that the status quo represents a successful fulfillment of this potential. Far from it. This is why, they argue, their programs are so needed. Emphasis on changed values here is clearly less radical than in mainstream Christianity; but in their indirect approach to ethics, these programs may be provoking renewed ethical resolve nonetheless. By posing psychological, spiritual, and economic benefits to systems paradigms for tolerance, conflict resolution, creativity, and ecological well-being, these movements do indeed prohibit many of the exploitative behaviors of laissez-faire capitalism or free-agent markets.

The essential utilitarianism of this approach and its appeal to those professing some personalized Christian faith underscores the fact that the secular spirituality movement is indeed not a religion, but a new *face* on religion in the form of a bridge between religion and daily activities. As such, the church should study it both for its successful bridging techniques and for suggestions of how it might offer authentic access to the sacred element of life. Theologian Craig Dykstra is correct in thinking that the church cannot simply imitate the secular spirituality movement wholesale to close the distanced relationship. It can, however, exploit the many positive attributes of the secular spirituality movement to revitalize communication and understanding of Christianity in a contemporary context that includes participation in business.

There are, however, many significant obstacles. The fundamental polarization between God and humans expressed in the Old and New Testaments is difficult to reconcile with the holism of the secular spirituality movement. Christian social ethics in the tradition of Reinhold Niebuhr (arguably the dominant form of liberal contemporary Christian ethics for the past forty-five years) emphasizes the cross, not the dharma. There is an enormous difference between finding oneself through suffering and self-denial and "letting go" and "going with the flow."

These problems aside, there are a number of important lessons for the church and laity to consider regarding how mainstream churches approach business—in what they say, what they affirm, and how they say it.

Understand the Appeal of Positivism

It is important to be aware of the optimistic, essentially tolerant impulses that draw people to this movement, and that mainstream presentation of religion often squelches these feelings. Associating "spirit" with self-acceptance, feeling for others, belief, and ethics in a way that emphasizes psychology over dogma is a natural stage for consideration of the "transcendent law of love," which James Gustafson has noted is the central imperative of Christian ethics.

Blending spiritual concerns with new science legitimations of reality should not be totally trivialized for being applied to business problems. These models are receptive to contemporary knowledge that appears to be essential to getting along in this brave new world. They suggest explanations for the natural order of things at a time when genetics and the mind-body relation are overturning definitions of human nature. By contrast, Christianity as presented by the Church can seem socially and cognitively regressive, bound to the social mores and agricultural economies of biblical times, spirit-killing, or simply not applicable to contemporary life.

Take the Soul of the Businessperson Seriously

The most important point about the secular spirituality movement is that it takes the soul of the businessperson seriously. The entry point for religious possibility is personalized rather than systemic, cutting through legitimate fear that religion requires adopting totalitarian ideas more associated with sectarianism than globalism. This movement constantly signals that it takes the context of business seriously as an arena for spiritual identity, faith, and community— as imperfect as every other arena in life, but far better than famine.

At its heart, the secular spirituality movement is about being part of the next era of business success without losing one's soul. When the church ridicules these programs and veers away from any positive association with business, it is dismissing those who feel real tension at work and acute longing for sacred integration of faith. Christians are seeking new models of faith and new meaning at work. They have probably read one of the new spirituality books or attended a seminar and felt its particular celebration of the spiritual helped them in their work.

Encourage Charitable Activity

Spirituality is a social act, not just a program of discipline and consciousness. Evidence shows that people engage more in charity when they are connected to a church. As the new spirituality groups mature and receive feedback, some have begun to move beyond interpersonal support, sacred text readings, and brief prayer rituals to less-personalized, more socially active roles.

An in-house religious network at a major Boston bank, for example, began by holding regular prayer meetings in a quiet place each month; it soon entered the mainstream of the company's corporate giving and support group programs. It became an official "support network group," alongside the gay and lesbian resource group, the single parent group, the two-parent parenting group, the Alcoholics Anonymous group, the diversity action group, and the cancer support group, to name only a few. Each of these groups are allotted control over a set amount of corporate contribution funds to not-for-profit and community organizations. The religious network teamed up with the gay and lesbian resource group to jointly contribute to an AIDS hospice program. They made a second alliance with the diversity resources group to fund a children's after-school education program in a poor inner-city neighborhood. Such efforts suggest that a new form of religiously based social action seems to be emerging inside the corporation, initiated by businesspeople.

Connecting to the Wisdom Literature

Virtually all of the secular spirituality movements are concerned with seeing the sacred in everyday life. The age-old disciplines on which they draw for accessing this sacredness (such as the notion of mindfulness, stressed by Jesuit and Buddhist traditions) have been largely absent from Western mainstream Christianity. For many Christian businesspeople, engaging in sacred ritual and language during a busy day awakens a religious orientation that is quite satisfying. Take, for example, a popular Torah-reading in New York City led by Rabbi Burton Visotzky. There is no agenda of integration. Participants are simply invited to share any reflections they may have on the reading—even from their own experiences, which do regularly include work. A number of Christians interested in the Old Testament attend, eager for more exposure to the biblical wisdom tradition.

When we asked a regular participant in a Christian business luncheon group what he got out of his monthly sessions, he replied, "I don't really know. I can't point to anything I hear about business practices or the Bible [at these sessions] that I haven't already known. But I find it so satisfying to attend. Where else can you hear the words of St. Paul in the middle of the day in the company of a group of very high-powered executives?"

No doubt the barbs against the new spirituality—Wendy Kaminer called it "spirituality Lite"—are frequently well deserved. Clearly, some people are simply looking for feel-good therapy. No doubt, too, that the new spirituality will get old fast unless it finds a new infusion of novel religious exoticism. But as two authors who have collectively lived and loved Boston's rich religious heritage for more than sixty years, and who have also observed the positive impact the secular spirituality movement has on businesspeople, we feel the church should be learning from this movement and modifying its own modes of contribution to the Christian's understanding of business. Simply scoffing at new spirituality in favor of high intellectualism or church-centered religiosity is, if nothing else, a waste of opportunity and the neglect of a deeply felt need in the congregation.

Reflection

- What examples of "living and defending human life" do you see in your own business experience? In business in general?

- Where do you see significant violations of this principle?

- Do you notice any religious worldview making a difference in these two outcomes? Why or why not?

- What do your observations say about the relevance of faith-based principles in your observation of business?

Action

- Write down key statements of values or obligations that reflect your ideals of business responsibility or the meaning of work.

- Diagnose your answers. Are any of them drawn from denominational statements, sermons, or other ecclesiastical writings? If not, why not?

- If so, how do you share this wisdom with people of other faiths (or no faith) in business?

- If you have read a secular book or heard a speech on business values or spirituality, what did you take away concerning business behavior?

- Compare what was most useful in your choice of wisdom texts, from a spiritual standpoint and from a practical standpoint. (As a preassignment, you can collect excerpts from the source materials and share them with the group at your meeting.)

- If you are in a study group, test how much difference you see between the way the businesspeople and ecclesiastics express religiously based business insight. If you see a difference, note and discuss the strengths and weaknesses of each.

4

Testing the Relationship

Mapping a Framework for Integrating Church and Business

I love Sunday. I love Monday. Then there's my faith,
and that's separate from both. What I don't really
understand is what relationship they have to each
other, or what it should be.

         —Lutheran businessperson

In suggesting that the Church find a new, more constructive mode of responsiveness to the businessperson's concerns, we are not suggesting that it abandon the foundational notions of Christianity that at times pose sharp tensions for Christian believers at work. Development of a new mode, however, progresses more rapidly if people are fully informed. In this chapter, we try to remove a few scales by way of a framework for critiquing the business-church relationship as it stands in your own congregation. There follow, in Part Two, several chapters on how typical patterns of thinking have tended to cut off possible carryover from church to business.

    In this chapter, we present a visual map of the worlds of church and business that illustrates how they interact. This map is not intended definitively to classify the business-church relationship in all Christian denominations; the diversity of responses is far too great to generalize in this way. Nonetheless, it is a useful tool for self-diagnosis of the church-business relationship as you perceive it. Ecclesiastical and business groups that have been introduced to this map consistently report that it causes them to revisit and revise their current strategies. We encourage you to test your own experience and efforts at integration against this framework, both individually and in a congregational study group.

Key Relational Realms of the Businessperson

Most businesspeople operate in five major relational realms, stretching on a continuum from the personal to the public (see Figure 4.1):

- The *individual person*

- The *family life* of the individual

- The *private sector* (the corporate world)

- The *public sector* (that public outside the corporation's employees and shareholders, but with the same regional and national affiliations as the company's facilities or market locations)

- The *world* (the public arena that may or may not have business dealings with the individual's corporation, but in which the individual has some sense of relationship through citizenship, communication, or other symbolic indication of mutuality)

In today's economy, these discrete realms are collapsing, as when people work at home and find dinnertime a mix of phone calls from the office and talk with the children. We have separated them here for clarity and sorted them by their relationship con-

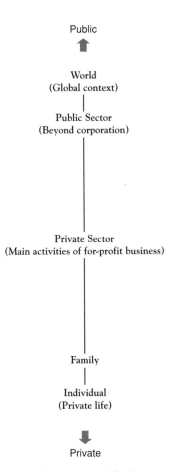

Figure 4.1. Key Relational Realms of the Businessperson (Without Details of the Corporation).

tent. But they represent more than relationship. Each realm plays an active part in shaping the businessperson's identity, cognitive playing field, and arena for exercising power and choice. These are personal realms of experience that dictate or imply roles, duties, actions, and formal organizational systems. These multiple aspects of the relational realms raise a more complex set of problems than does an interest group (stakeholder) definition of rights and duties toward constituencies.

Religion tends to address all of these aspects to some degree. For example, if you have a family, it is assumed you have some obligation to live in relation to family rather than as a completely free agent. Your role as parent demands sensitivity to the cognitive framework of children, and the duty to carry out responsibilities of care. The same holds true for citizenship or membership in a church, a corporation, a professional society, and so on. Mapping any system requires a certain amount of generalization. Real-world conditions for any one person may, of course, be radically less distinct and hierarchical than our visual schematic. In practice, the realms often overlap. Individuals move in and out of these roles daily. For some people, the realms themselves are highly atomized. Margaret's executive responsibilities and persona at work bear no resemblance to her role as parent, when she is at home with her family. Dan's impeccable appearance every fourth Tuesday as an elder and member of the financial committee of the church may be quite different from the Dan who regularly breaks promises to customers and suppliers or lies about his schedule to coworkers when he misses a meeting.

For many people in business, the process of negotiating these realms has become increasingly stressful. They are no longer a progression from private to public. In today's business culture, the boundaries among domestic, private, and civic life have all been invaded by corporate activity.[1] Although many in church have voiced concern over the increasing corporatization of life, there is also a tendency not to acknowledge these roles as an inherent part of a congregant's identity and therefore part of his or her Christian identity.

Corporations, on the other hand, have been all-too-quick to suggest ways for individuals to "manage" these realms, developing therapeutic techniques for dealing with the confusion and competing claims, from each area, for their time and affection. Family life, for example, is partially regulated and played out in corporate-sponsored family care programs. A businessperson's deepest emotional states and private thoughts (the individual of the first level) may be subject to semipublic company scrutiny (the corporate realm) within the therapeutic framework of a job application, genetic testing, or an employee development or team-building program. Civic participation is increasingly conducted through corporate volunteer programs. Indeed, professional career counselors now place fast-track executives on the right charitable boards for career advancement. Similarly, private friendships may turn primarily on workplace settings. Virtual community, telecommuting, and globalization are complicating the definition of *community* even further. Many executives today are more familiar with the setting and the people in a manufacturing site in Asia than in the neighborhood in which they live. Such changes in the structure of work underscore the state of extreme transition that typifies today's interconnection of the realms and the individual's understanding of what values and identities govern business role, private life, congregation, and larger community.

Blended roles and realms notwithstanding, Figure 4.1 serves to mark and distinguish a general drift of realms "outward" from the self, according to intimacy and proximity. They constitute a baseline of human experience from which to address religious as well as business concerns. Part of today's spirituality search, with its holistic emphasis, is an attempt to order and understand the meaning of this new configuration of personal roles in a business setting.

Traditional Functions and Roles of the Corporation (the Private Sector)

The businesspeople we interviewed expressed great concern over their sense that clergy do not really understand the internal world of business, including the different roles and functions individual managers must assume in their professional lives inside a corporation, whatever its size. In Figure 4.2, the shaded circle represents the inner workings of the private sector (this was the middle realm on Figure 4.1). It contains a bare-bones set of conventional functions and relationships that are essential to most managers' duties, whether they directly perform them or depend on these functions to do their own tasks.[2] The divisions are based on functional tasks and economic relations, again moving along a continuum roughly from the most personalized and proximate relationships (individual employees, employee relations, organizational systems, product or service creation) to a larger public (sales, marketing, business-to-business, corporation as public entity, community relations). None of these areas can be omitted from a business that expects to operate successfully over time.

This detail gives the private sector realm a deeper contextual richness that is not typically represented when many clergy and theologians stereotypically portray "business" or "the culture." In fact, without a richer descriptive of the business realm, no model for thinking about religion and business can grasp even the most obvious influences on the behavior and thinking of people in organizations.[3]

One of the Harvard Business School's most notable professors, C. Roland Christensen, revolutionized classic theories of management when he developed a set of highly particularized case studies of successful corporations. He used to remind new researchers to "check a manager's in-box," arguing that anyone who wanted to create a truly useful pedagogical tool for businesspeople had to capture the mental framework that an actual in-box provoked. In the same spirit, our set of categories maps a minimal reconstruction of the filters a faithful businessperson is likely to employ in acting on his or her expressions of faith "in this world." It should be understood that, as with Figure 4.1, the categories in the list we present here bleed into each other and are constantly changing in business.

- The realm of *employees* includes individuals alone and in relation to each other. Relating is both formal and informal. This realm

Figure 4.2. Traditional Functions and Roles of the Corporation (the Private Sector in Detail).

would include such varied activities as conversation between coworkers, formal boss-employee relations, a chat line, and many other group-marking activities.

- *Employee relations* is a subset of the first realm, representing the formal practices concerning employee conduct and welfare related to official policy and informal norms about how people are treated (including determination of salary, benefits, work conditions, and rules of behavior).

- *Organizational systems* are the structural systems that establish the formal patterns of responsibility, communication, decision making, and operations within a company.

- *Product or service creation* includes standard product or service development and delivery functions, such as research, innovation, creation of products, manufacturing, quality checks, and so on. Multiple products and markets must also be understood.

- *Sales* and *marketing* includes selling, distribution, pricing, warranties, and so on. These functions may include external and internal sales, contracts with multiple customers, and general consumer relations that answer to constituencies beyond immediate customers.

- *Business-to-business* implies contractual and personal interactions with other firms, such as suppliers, distributors, competitors, banks, outsider auditors, consultants, and so on.

- *External communications* includes product- and company-related representations to the public at large.

- The *corporation as public entity* involves its relationships with shareholders and formal political activities such as support of lobbying groups and legislation. This category also includes all financial accounting and control functions, which determine the company's financial representations to the public and are subject to public regulation.

- The *community relations* realm includes nonshareholder, non-lobbying "citizen activities" in the public arena, maintenance of facilities, and contribution (of money or of people) to not-for-profit causes and events.

When we look at this map, two factors are at once notable: First, although the term *private sector* describes ownership status, these functions and roles are not just about ownership. Second, the roles and functions are multiple. They often present conflicting tasks and responsibilities. Although outsiders tend to conceptualize business as a monolithic profit machine, the flesh-and-blood businessperson actually inhabits a nuanced and relational realm where he or she must focus simultaneously on money, power, people, products, information, and much more.

Businesspeople simply do not go about "making money" all day. They create services, relationships, symbols, and transactions of many sorts with people inside and outside the corporate arena. All of these areas of focus ultimately have a strong influence on the businessperson's sense of autonomy and responsibility, but not necessarily in direct proportion to their ultimate effect on the profits of the firm. They must be understood as being about more than profit.

Each category potentially poses myriad specific ethical, financial, and psychological choices for the businessperson and the corporation. In today's business environment, the boundaries of these functions and roles are often unstable, internally conflicted, and subject to differing priorities.

- A long-time competitor suddenly decides to source some of its components from your company. Now it is both your competitor and your customer.

- Employees are increasingly participating in stock ownership plans, which puts them both inside the corporation and on its edge, as shareholders who are members of a larger, more independent public.

- Internal restructuring may suddenly make your closest coworkers part of another division of the company, transforming them from team members to competitors for internal resources.

- Your company is acquired, and suddenly the financial target changes—along with the composition of employees with whom you and your customers work.

The categories in Figure 4.3 show points at which to map such activities as these. They roughly identify areas in which the businessperson lives and also might personally expect to find both difficulty and possibility for integrating faith, spirituality, and work. It is precisely to this reality that secular spirituality programs respond.

In real life, as noted, the categories are not as clean as the ones on our map. The map does, however, amount to a minimal checklist of areas that are essential to most managers' lives—and

Public

World
(Global context)

Public Sector
(Beyond corporation)

Community Relations
Corporation as Public Entity
External Communications
Business to Business
Sales, Marketing
Private Sector
Product or Service Creation
Organizational Systems
Employee Relations
Individual Employees

Family

Individual
(Private life)

Private

Figure 4.3. The Relational Realms of the Businessperson (with Detail; Overlay of Figures 4.1 and 4.2).

certainly to the running of a successful business. These can be a road map for moving beyond overgeneralized religious assessments of business or the partial coping strategies for integration that we discussed in Chapter Two. An interesting starting place for a dialogue on practical faith is to probe not how many of these functions and roles are shared by clergy and businesspeople but rather how each weights these roles in their field of concern.

Which ones are more likely to provoke feelings of religiously consistent duty or self-fulfillment?

Traditional Roles of the Church

What can the church do to help businesspeople integrate faith and work? In searching for answers to this question, we find it helpful to identify major categories of traditional church activity and authority above and apart from the concerns of any particular segment of the congregation. Figure 4.4 shows four major types of religious role, varying in their degree of passive and active participation in worldly affairs: preaching in some cases, healing, teaching, and acting. These roles are positioned in relation to the private-public continuum of the previous figures.

- *Priestly* includes sermons and other functions of the church, such as liturgical ritual and officiation as an ecclesiastical authority. On our map, it stands halfway up the scale to reflect the traditional public-and-private location of the priestly activity, and far to the left to reflect its essentially passive nature. Conducted publicly within the private confines of the church, or occasionally in larger public arenas, the priestly functions tend to serve individuals in a private or semipublic congregational context.
- *Healing*—pastoral care—is at the bottom middle of our map, next to the position occupied by the Individual and Family realms in Figure 4.1. This reflects the main location of such church pastoral activities as counseling, visitation of the sick, and the like. There are also notable occasions when the church seeks to participate in healing the entire community. Such activity falls in the category of "action" and just above "pastoral."
- *Teaching*—the rabbinic tradition of the church—is placed at the top of the framework near "World" (Figure 4.1) as a reflection of the universalization (as opposed to personalization) of most theological and doctrinal activities. It sits at the halfway point of

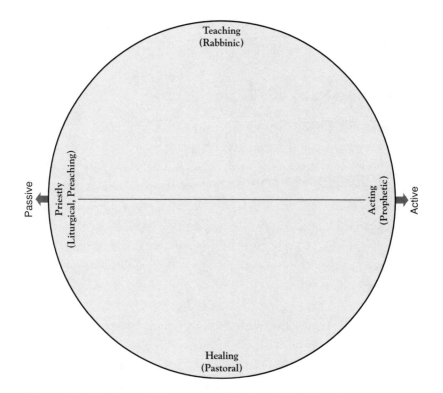

Figure 4.4. Traditional Functions and Roles of the Church.

active and passive. Teaching carries a stronger element of implied public action than performance of a liturgical ritual, which is a reenactment complete in and of itself, but it is not the same as executing the teachings.

- *Acting* is the most socially involved, historical, and least passive category of church-related activity, constituting as it does a living out of prophetic functions to transform this world in accordance with God's purposes and plan. Such activism is generally social in the Christian church, with the exception of hermitage models of daily life. Many theologians sit halfway between the teaching and acting positions.

One group of clergy, after seeing this map, wryly noted that they themselves had one other official function that they tried to ignore as much as we had: They, too, were managers! These clergy were absolutely right. For discussion purposes, however, it is useful to keep the complexities of the private sector intact but with the understanding that "management" is an alternative label for this circle, representing church or business management. This way, when we overlay Figures 4.1, 4.2, 4.3, and 4.4, the resulting diagram (Figure 4.5) presents a visual testing ground for the penetration of the traditional, sacred functions of the church and the realm of business and management. You can look at this overlay, however, as a depiction of the world of *both* professional groups (with only slight modification of "private sector" to read "nonprofit management activities" for the religious professions).

Mapping Integration: A New Way into the Problem

When we see the two realms overlaid in Figure 4.5, we can ask where and how a particular church seeks to penetrate the realm of the private sector with some form of the religious. Whether the sacred is experienced in action or as an assertion of a state of consciousness or cognitive difference is not of concern. The question for self-assessment is simply this: Where does the church, as you know it, and representing Christian religion, penetrate the private sector, and in what functional form?

By *penetration*, we mean that some activity of the church or lay group representing a faith-based organization effects a religious connection or provocative response inside the corporate realm that responds to the businessperson's vocational concerns. Effective integration reconnects these business activities to religious ethics or spiritual consciousness. As we explored the experiences of clergy and executives, including those who had participated in recent

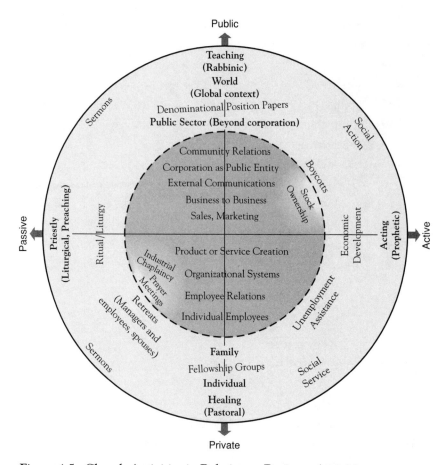

Figure 4.5. Church Activities in Relation to Business Activities.

church-sponsored activities on faith and work, the answer was alarmingly inadequate: not much at all.

Figure 4.5 maps some of the typical activities of the church that are intended to be directed toward business, as reported by interviewees and considered in focus groups directly contemplating this framework. Looking at this, two things stand out:

1. The shaded circle is nearly empty.
2. It is very difficult to find any deep penetration of the shaded circle that is not negative in message and content.

Let's take a look at each factor individually.

Sermons

Take, for example, sermons that touch on economic issues or some aspect of business life. Half-rabbinical, half-liturgical, they are relatively few and far between. What is there tends to skim off the rim of the private sector circle to focus on more generalized topics about business and the public (toward the top of the frame) or about personalized choices such as a meditation on misguided values concerning material wealth and status in the household (bottom of frame, near family). A sermon that suggests a faith perspective about the state of one's soul and private financial ambitions but does not cross over to the structure of life inside one's job or career may be very effective at redirecting a congregant's priorities away from money and status temporarily, but it does not provide help on where to go next as a businessperson. How does one actually draw on Christian ideals for the improvement of business itself?

Several clergy we spoke to said they occasionally addressed economic issues in sermons. These sermons, however, tended to address a business realm that was nonspecific, superficial, stereotyped, or about some mythical mogul's world. A term such as *globalization*, for example, was code for signaling that the church knew something about modern business without going into the messy details. Religious focus then passed right over the shaded circle of business activities in a global setting to target, instead, macroeconomic policies such as third world debt—a question that is of civic concern for a congregant, but one that does not enter the personal realm of business decision making to any significant degree. Similarly, positive appeals to help the poor were largely directed at an individual's private financial decisions on charitable giving, housing, or schools, while business activities were depicted as representing the antithesis of this felt duty.

Liturgy

Liturgy was deliberately reserved for places outside the workplace, until the recent explosion of prayer networks inside corporations, which, however, are primarily initiated by laity rather than the church and tend to shy away from extensive use of liturgy. (We did find strong resistance, especially among mainstream Protestants and non-Christians, to prayer groups inside a company.)

A number of businesspeople reported that they had begun to try to deepen their spiritual life by engaging in self-initiated prayer sessions or Bible readings alone in their office. Some of these disciplines were prompted by a secular spirituality session on meditation, which gave them a process for incorporating their own religious expression into these practices. Others made private leaps from the generalized content of secular spiritual programs sponsored by their company back to their own religious beliefs.

Business Group Prayer Sessions

Business group prayer meetings, during the week at breakfast or lunchtime, rest just at the edge of the shaded circle, in a public-private realm equivalent to where friends would be located (just above family, or just inside the circle in the "individual employees" position).

These sessions are generally individually directed, partially liturgical and partly pastoral. Believers who participate usually share religious rituals and offer healing and support to each other. Some prayer groups (notably, among evangelicals) penetrate the circle much further, sharing business problems in extremely confidential and frank ways. This is rare, however, and the obstacles to direct church sponsorship are many. However, this position on the "map" is probably the one undergoing the most attention and change.

Denominational Statements and Theological Positions

Denominational statements and theological positions on the economy—such as the bishops' pastoral letters, papal encyclicals, or an article in *Christian Century* or *Ecumenical Review* or *Missiology*— are broadly rabbinical for a wide, sometimes global audience and economic context. Universalized in context and generally directed at the systemic aspects of business (any and every business but no one in particular), they sit between "public sector" and "world."

As the content of these treatises moves closer to specific corporate activity, they tend to become negative: disinvest, stop producing product X, boycott company Y. Positive messages have been more general, as in a demand that companies must agree to be environmentally friendly or offer a living wage. Time and again, we asked what a living wage was. Ah, that's a deep question.

Disinvestment Initiatives

The disinvestment initiatives of the recent past were a good example of the negative emphasis on *not* doing business as the church began to penetrate the circle, while ignoring opportunities to engage in influencing the actual business being conducted. The churches' South Africa disinvestment initiatives, for example, placed their attention and energy on getting out of South Africa, but not on the contract conditions by which those businesses would be sold or dismantled. As Notre Dame theologian Oliver Williams and NYU business professor S. Prakesh Sethi have noted, a great number of avoidable harms were thus put into play.[4] Meanwhile, areas inside the shaded circle such as employment training, where businesspeople had more power and the need was acute, were largely left out of the church's disinvestment agenda.

So too, injunctions to stop producing certain products or advertising heavily overshadow church activities in giving advisory help on developing new, more responsible goods and services.

The church's current criticism of television programming and advertising follows this pattern. Positive injunctions to emphasize and celebrate family values are quite general, mostly influencing household choices too small to have deeply penetrated the market considerations of business. (Some churches, however, are now issuing "recommended" lists; there is an interesting, but as yet unprofitable, attempt by Odyssey channel to develop such entertainment. This station was formed by an ecumenical alliance of churches.) The passion, however, has been over the "shalt nots"—the recommendations to boycott certain programs or protest titillating ads.

Social Action

Church-based social action is frequently about food, health care, and shelter in ways that sidestep the economic dimension of these solutions.[5] Faith-based institutions that become activist in economic ventures often adopt a pattern that actively drives them outside the shaded circle in action and in results. Unrestrained by requirements to show a profit or any competitive strength, the faith-based social action effort may indeed deliver where no one else seems to be willing or able, but these efforts should not be confused with acts that penetrate the shaded circle. Such parameters fail to guide the businessperson's conception of service provision because they do not offer a bridge to financially viable models.

Social action efforts tend to rely on deep-pocket subsidies based on faith affiliation, or the suspension of normal accounting procedures and pricing structures. Not only is the process outside the rules of the shaded circle, but it may result in sending a message that the church (and by implication the Christian's business worldview) is above, or unconcerned about, these rules. By implication, normal indicators of business responsibility are reduced to morally trivial details. This is what happened when a church-sponsored housing project needed to raise emergency donations after it failed to use its scarce funds to purchase insurance. When the project was destroyed in a fire, it was not thought appropriate to hold people accountable for taking such unnecessary risks with the investment. Nor did the group itself disclose the costs of its management techniques in the group's claim to have created a viable paradigm for low-income housing that was deserving of corporate support.

The New Era Fund was another good example of the "business rule suspension" tendency of faith-based economic initiatives. This investment mechanism touted highly unrealistic investment expectations, backed by claims of benevolent, anonymous investors who could produce amazing returns annually. Both the buyers and the sellers failed to see that it was nothing more than a Ponzi scheme. A number of faith-based institutions invested their endowments in New Era and lost everything. Others that had profited in the first years of the scheme voluntarily shared those profits with those that suffered great losses. As an act of Christian solidarity, the episode stands as heroic. Less commendable, and certainly instructive, is the interesting way in which everyone seemed to consent to the idea that it was *appropriate* to suspend expectations of normal standards of risk and disclosure in making these investments for the sake of a good cause.

Social Services

Similarly, mission-sponsored housing projects that provide needed social services frequently create an economics that works outside any standard business parameters. As a vehicle for engaging businesspeople in a greater concern and understanding for the poor, they succeed. As a model for economic activities of religiously-concerned businesspeople, however, they fail. If all business operated this way, where would the sugar daddies come from?

Especially prevalent in the church's economic action arena is a tendency to go for a monopolistic position. Such activity serves many important purposes that are aligned with Christian values, but it should not be mistaken for a constructive, prophetic change in either the economic system or the decision-making framework of the congregant who goes back into the corporation. In many cases they encourage bad business practices and uncompetitive products.

The point here is not to deliver a final vote on the desirability of the church's current social action, but rather to ask how the current actions and the assumptions behind them are helpful to the individuals who have to make decisions while metaphorically sitting inside the shaded circle. It is interesting to try to map this effect. Does the faith-based social action pull religion into the shaded circle, or pull the congregant out of it? Which position on the map is likely to provide guidance and support for the person of faith who wants to shape his or her business's purpose according to the prophetic vision of society that Christian doctrine offers?

Church-Sponsored Programs Offering Employment Assistance

Church-sponsored programs offering employment assistance are another good example of the tendency of the church not to penetrate the circle. Several such services supported congregants and community when people were out of jobs, but all church support disappeared once the person was back at work! In some cases, even the job search and training support was consigned to a congregant without any further engagement from clergy or denomination. In one such effort, which lasted more than three years, a layperson was asked to run the program. She continued with permission from the church to use its space but witnessed *no personal* engagement of church officials in the actual program. Clergy from the participating churches said this type of activity was "out of their realm."

This last remark underscores the state of the business-church relationship. It is not that the church sees no obligation to engage in economic questions, but rather that it displays a remarkable reluctance to engage (directly or indirectly) in the pragmatics of capitalist economic activity. As a resource to congregants wrestling with the daily problems of business, this is hardly substantial.

Church-Sponsored Executive Retreats

Given their name, church-sponsored executive retreats are one area where one might expect more integration of religious and business concerns. These events are specifically geared toward the business-person and intended to be an opportunity for spiritual renewal and reflection about life inside the shaded circle. A number of inter-viewees reported having attended retreats repeatedly during their lives, with varying degrees of satisfaction. The content of many of these programs, however, tended to concentrate on family topics: marital relations, parental anxieties, sexual problems, and personal stress. Others concentrated on renewed testimony of personal faith and its effect on the emotions.

These retreats are relevant to the businessperson in that they try to draw on the faith tradition to help correct problems that stem directly from his or her business activities. In many cases, they have succeeded in conveying the need for rebalancing, per-spective, and love. But what of their effect on life inside the shaded circle? Where does the retreat generate reconnection? The church's message may not extend further than a recommendation to get out of work life more often! Again, the penetration is very shallow, if at all.

Industrial Chaplaincy

Industrial chaplaincy also deserves special attention because it rep-resents a deliberate, concrete penetration of traditional religious functions into the corporation. Halfway between the priestly and pastoral realms, industrial chaplains meet with employees on site or off site, at corporate expense. Many of their activities are associated with employee assistance programs (EAPs) such as alcohol or drug counseling. At other times, the chaplains do more generalized coun-seling, prayer, and support.

The chaplains enter the company on condition of noninter-vention, which in practice seems to have prevented them from being a source of perspective (moral and spiritual) on larger policy-related issues such as choice of product, sales practices, or organizational systems. There also appeared to be some confusion of agenda. When pressed, at least one influential chaplain organization explicitly felt its role was to bring businesspeople to Jesus rather than to bring Jesus to the workings of businesspeople—a contradiction of their policy against no proselytizing in the workplace.

Please Step Outside . . .

As you can see, many of the personally relevant faith-based activities for businesspeople are an invitation to step *outside* the shaded circle: to be closer to a spouse, to be a more effective parent, to participate in volunteer and civic work, and to take time to contemplate and strengthen a spiritual perspective through church attendance. In many cases, this invitation is urgently needed, as Americans work longer and longer hours and corporations provide services that profoundly shape the norms of family, friends, and civic duty.

Nonetheless, concentrating spiritual attention on getting out of the circle should not be confused with facilitating how businesspeople should bring their faith more actively into their working lives. Although it can be robustly debated whether the churches should or should not try to penetrate the shaded circle, and what limits or guidelines should be observed, we found no reason to be complacent that many are doing a good job at even "being there" in spirit.

Perhaps the most ironic observation came from the same group of clergy who noted that they, too, had a vocational responsibility for the shaded circle of the management-business realm. In thinking about this, one Episcopal priest exclaimed, "We operate there too. But we're no better at bringing our Christianity into that circle than the businessperson!"

Reflection

- Familiarize yourself with the terms used on the integration map (Figure 4.5). Now reflect on where you see the church in its four functions penetrating the shaded circle of business activity. What do you conclude?

- Were there to be more penetration, directly or through support of business people of faith, what would you expect to change about business and your own activities in business?

- What would you expect to change regarding the church and your own activities in it were there to be more penetration of religion in your business life?

Action

- Find one example of a new faith-based effort that has affected business. Study it and locate it on the integration map. Is the activity centered on positive change, or negative? How might it be made a stronger, more positive influence on business change?

- If you are a member of a church, ask if you might discuss with your pastor or deaconate (or equivalent group) where the church's own management ethos sits on the map, and how they see faith having an impact on church management. Are there common gaps and opportunities between this map and your own integration map?

PART II

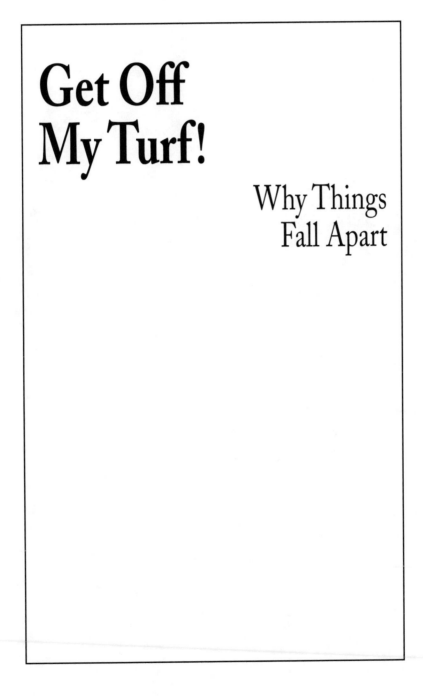

Get Off My Turf!

Why Things Fall Apart

5

You Just Don't Understand

Communication Gaps Between Church and Business

After twenty-five years as a CPA, I felt it was time to do something more meaningful to me. I'm not against business, but I sure do question a lot that goes on there, especially in terms of priorities. I'd like to find a place where people are more important than profit. My church? Very important. Reminds me about the real priorities. No help at all about business.

—Christian businessperson

What is it about contemporary business and the church that is making the proposition of integrating faith and business so elusive? Many in the church and in business entertain a desire for Christian beliefs to be a stronger resource in businesspeople's lives. Why, then, is there so little evidence of either business or the church drawing on the church's professionals for guidance in this area? The church's penetration of the business realm is not just a question of intent or interest. It is a question of relationship with the business community inside its congregations. What is affecting this relationship today, such that even those fond of their church would not think of it as helpful in integrating faith and work?

As we explored this question in extensive interviews and a survey of twenty top seminaries in the United States, we began to see a pattern. Two deeply conflicting worldviews have such profound effects that the two groups can barely speak the same language. The attitudes of the clergy and the businessperson, however ambivalent they may be about their own institutions in private, essentially fall into two camps: the naysayers and the yea-sayers of capitalism. Where the latter sees value creation and possibility, the former sees destruction and exploitation. Although we found representatives of both groups in both camps, the bulk of the yea-sayers are in business, and the clergy are overwhelmingly naysayers. Few felt their views were as unnuanced as these categories suggest; but we would argue that the two "camps" represent a complex of views and behaviors that are indeed recognizable and in need of being recognized by Christians seeking to integrate their beliefs and their work.

In this and the following two chapters, we take a thorough look at the evidence of these attitudes, and at the assumptions and behaviors on which they are built. Our goal is not to construct a political position on capitalism, nor to establish the definitive statistical profile of American Christianity and its view on capitalism. It is to shed light on why the clergy and businesspeople are having such a difficult time moving forward on bringing religious concerns to the conduct of business. Business groups and religious institutions attempting to start programs in this area are not likely to be successful unless they begin to understand these dynamics and the process by which the two camps' common religious concerns have digressed and hardened into a distanced relationship.

When the naysayers and yea-sayers are confronted with anything connected to capitalism, they see totally different pictures—even if at first they seem to agree. In this they are like a bridegroom and his jealous mother on the topic of the new wife. Joe, the groom, is besotted. When he looks at Alice he sees a promise of happiness and fulfillment, a source of creation. Sure she has faults, but who doesn't? When his mother sees Alice, she sees destruction and exploitation of her family and her son. Alice's faults loom much larger. Needless to say, after a few frustrating and tense encounters Joe and his mother try not to talk about it.

Over the years Joe and his mother continue to add bricks to their worldview about Alice. Each event is another piece in the structure. The worldview in turn colors their processing of the next event. Eventually, the worldview is so strong it colors the words they use and the expectations they have not just about Alice but about their own relationship.

So, too, the yea-sayers and naysayers of capitalism in the church community have been constructing their own opposing worldviews and educating others in them. Now, when business congregants and clergy or academics look at the same phenomenon, each group sees a picture totally different from what the other group sees. Our goal here is to understand the extremely complex and often unnoticed bricks in the pattern and to reopen the dialogue.

Symptoms of the Disconnection

We found disturbingly unproductive dynamics in many areas. The two worldviews have affected language, behavior, and explanations of each other's behavior. These patterns are only partially noticeable to either camp, and in many cases they cut off needed exchange and joint consideration of the thorny issues of being a businessperson of faith.

"The Church Doesn't Get It"

Most businesspeople we spoke to—despite varying affection for the church and differing understanding of the church's authority—shared the opinion that the church was not doing much to help them gain a sense of spiritual strength or religious wholeness in their business lives. Their negativity was moderated by deep reluctance to criticize pastors or church officials whom they admired for other reasons. If anything, affection for the church on the part of those who remain closest to the clergy masked the depth of disaffection and dismissiveness that the Church's attitude toward business has provoked.

Some accepted the negative assessment as inevitable, others were disappointed, and a good many felt misunderstood or demonized by the Church. Their comments boiled down to a few points: "The clergy are the last people to go to for guidance on business." "They don't understand the issues." "They can't manage themselves, how could they advise others?" "They hate business." "They're jealous of people with money." "They want to criticize business but they have no problem with accepting its money." "It's not their role to comment on business." "We don't speak the same language."

The pattern was very much like our fictional Joe and his jealous mother. When we asked businesspeople formally to assess their relationship with the church, they often suppressed these observations. When we asked whether their reported lack of mutual contact on business issues was evidence of a distanced relationship, a number of them objected, replying that they felt close to their pastors and the larger church organization. Nonetheless, when asked whether and how they would look to these people for guidance on business matters, the answer was remarkably consistent: not really. Did they feel the church valued them as Christians living out its purposes in their business life? No way. The only exceptions were business leaders who had developed a personal friendship with a minister or priest and subsequently spent time together in a context in which business problems naturally came up in conversation. These were rare instances, and in nearly all cases they represented only top-tier executives who were leading members of the church (in terms of financial contribution). The pastor then became a kind of personal counselor to the congregant.

Many were at peace with the idea of going it alone on their quest to remain connected to their faith in their professional lives. (The lapsed churchgoers, as would be expected, were more critical.) By contrast, whenever we mentioned in casual conversation that we had spoken to executives who wouldn't go to their pastors or anyone else associated with their church about a matter of faith and business, interviewees would nod knowingly. We were regaled with accounts of the naysayers' impact. Why, the yea-sayers would ask, is the church so negative and hostile about us?

People who had been engaged in some joint effort to look at faith and work were not as negative. Even a small gesture of support or interest in their questions from the clergy, such as hosting our own focus groups, signaled that the congregants were valued, in religious terms, in their professional role, whether or not the clergy actually subscribed to the view of the yea-sayers. Nonetheless, many had difficulty pinpointing how these sessions helped or changed their thinking.

The distancing of American businesspeople from the church—perceived or unperceived—is a real phenomenon with real consequences. A good example of this is the senior executive who convened an adult class on business ethics at his church for more than two years. He felt very close to his pastor and especially valued the support received during a messy divorce. After some members of the congregation ostracized him, the pastor continued the close relationship. But when we asked the businessperson if this pastor ever attended the business ethics class during its two years in the basement of the church, he replied, "Never."

The executive didn't perceive this as a distanced relationship because *he himself* did not feel that business was an area of expertise for the pastor. He (the Christian business leader) was the expert in that particular realm. A good Protestant, the state of his soul regarding his conduct in business was his own affair. He didn't expect help from religious authorities. That's why he had convened the adult study group inside his church.

"I'm Not Interested in Business"

Clergy and theologians were less consistent than businesspeople in evaluating their record of assistance. Some felt they had made no impact, attributing the failure either to their own lack of interest or to systemic problems in the culture. Some offered rationalization that avoided any implication of being against the capitalism of their congregants' lives. They simply felt they had no business making an impact in this area. As one priest put it, "My concern is the excitement of the liturgy. I'm afraid that what people do in business is not of interest to me. I make no apologies."

Many others saw any singling out of congregants by professional affiliation as a form of favoritism. Some clergy suggested they were enormously active in faith and economic issues, but they had never tested whether this activity actually influenced parishioners in any positive way. They knew what they said, but not what they accomplished.

Most clergy responded with some variation of a congregational minister's comment that "this culture is so materialistic, it's very hard to change people's ideas." When we asked seminary students and faculty, "What, if anything, would you change in the way the church deals with business issues and business thinking?" the overwhelming response—by a margin of ten times the second most frequent answer—was some variation of "change the way businesspeople think."

Most clergy expressed a desire to be a more effective influence on business and to help individuals experience the fullness of faith. Thoughtful and open to thinking about the problem, they simply had never addressed it systematically. They weren't sure where to start beyond the ways mentioned in Chapter Three: drafting a paper, joining a reform movement, or being a better friend.

What's Causing This Distance?

The more people we spoke to, the clearer it became that cultural factors were playing a very strong part. Disparities between clergy and businesspeople on economic worldview, variation in area of professional expertise, conflict of authority, fear of cooption or corruption should the church enter the business arena, difference of language, and the conditions of pluralism were all factors. Even the effects of generally different temperaments—the can-do businessperson versus the think-about-it clergy—could be seen in the preferences each group had for certain types of problem solving and analytical approach. Sometimes these factors marginalized the church from the economic mainstream in which businesspeople operate.

An example of an attempt to breach the business-church divide illustrates the main cultural fault lines along which the current distanced relationship is arrayed. The near-buffoonery of this well-intended event, and its escalation of negative stereotypes in the media, illustrates how quickly intelligent dialogue breaks down in this area.

With the impending panic over year 2000 (Y2K) problems in 1999 suggesting pandemonium in the works, the American Bankers Association (ABA) thought it reasonable to draft a sample sermon on the problem for distribution to the clergy. Two key considerations prompted the paper: a perception that some clergy were misinformed about Y2K and were using the problem to fan fears of disaster, and the fact of clergy being so trusted in their communities that they would be the perfect vehicle for calming fears about Y2K.

The ABA allegedly offered the homily not as a script but as a working sheet of factual and theological points for the minister to adapt in a sermon. ABA spokesman John Hall called the effort "a sincere outreach effort," explaining that the document was not disseminated in a mass mailing but was meant to be "a very personal exchange between a banker and his minister."[1]

The ecclesiastical reaction to this effort, as reported in one local newspaper, was largely negative or indifferent. An Episcopal pastor saw it as an attempt to peddle influence in a sacred place; a Roman Catholic priest felt that the effort was "a self-serving waste of time

. . . the love of money is the root of all evil. People who make their living out of messing with money just aren't on the right track." Only a Pentecostal minister was reported to have had a more receptive reaction, stating that he would like to see if it "spoke to the fear in people's hearts." By contrast, a banker reportedly felt the document did well to combine factual assurances about the FDIC's guarantees with a message of hope, eagerness, and faith in God. He thought the exercise was a well-intended effort to do something to prevent ignorant panic.

As a case study in enlisting religion and business in correcting a potential social problem related to the economy, the whole episode fell flat. The clergy felt the bankers' message was an "intrusion" on their authority; they were in no way prompted to address Y2K panic as a serious occasion for religious reflection of any sort. They either dismissed it out of hand or used the occasion to launch a religious condemnation of banking and business in general.

Business professionals and clergy have a difficult time accepting the idea of each other bridging the realms. They suspect these efforts involve an inappropriate use of authority and are most likely self-serving. They quickly tend to interpret any such attempt negatively. What is behind the knee-jerk assumption that elicits such distancing evaluation?

Living in Different Worlds

As the maps in Chapter Four illustrate, businesspeople and clergy live in two worlds. Between the two groups lie minefields seeded with attitudes about money, poverty, and the spirit of business— attitudes that can be summarized as those of the yea-sayers and naysayers of capitalism. Over and over, we heard two accusations: clergy accused businesspeople of "not caring" about the less fortunate; and businesspeople accused clergy of "not understanding" that their professional activities represented value creation, despite examples of greed.[2]

"Money Is Bad, Businesspeople Are Greedy"

The clergy tended to represent business as an aggregate concept, centered on money or profit—code words for excessive wealth and exploitation. They saw businesspeople as greedy and selfish;[3] they repeatedly mentioned money as business's primary concern (excessive salaries, consumption lifestyles, materialistic ambitions, the wage gap). Accumulation of wealth had especially negative associations of idolatry, sin, materialism, false values, wrong priorities, selfishness, and most of all injustice against the poor. They saw the religious possibilities for those with personal wealth as already tainted, their salvation contingent on giving the money away.

Comments about money usually led to comments about culture, which strongly influenced people's values. In fact, clergy used the term *culture* as a shorthand symbol for what they felt is the root of the problem: a value system centered on money. The culture, they told us, is a materialistic and hypercommercial place, worshiping money above all else. Heartless, it lays people off; it pays some too much and many too little; it is responsible for encouraging the worship of other false gods, as when entertainment businesses promote a taste for sex and violence to increase their profits.[4] All of this is interpreted as exemplifying that people will do anything for money.[5] The clergy often cited advertisements stressing wealth, greed, luxury, and nonessential consumer goods as indicators of a "business mentality" or "the values of business."

The association of business with profit, and profit with adverse religious meaning regarding money, was so automatic that the clergy tended to underestimate its force in coloring their views and distancing them from businesspeople. In our survey of twenty seminaries, students told us that they felt this attitude had changed. But we detected a false sense of confidence. As representatives of churches and seminary students elaborated on what they would like to say and explore about business and religion, their themes were overwhelmingly negative. They spoke of "making the church a louder and more critical voice," "naming large businesses' role in the economy with the consequent part in the responsibility for social injustices," and "helping them see the error of their ways." Some were indifferent ("I am not at all interested"). Even among those who were enthusiastic about possibly creating a forum or other occasion to explore faith and work, few suggested that they were eager to hear what businesspeople had to say about their impressions of the tension they faced at work. Feeling they had seen just about enough of what business really cares about—consumerism, selfishness, careerism, insensitivity—they prepared themselves for lecturing, not listening. Only one respondent in our survey—an evangelical seminarian—objected to this view, noting that the church tended to see the businessperson as outside the faith community with regard to the church itself.

The benign desire to emphasize positive, inclusive goals in the church's alleged new understanding of the economy—justice, faithfulness, solidarity, ministering to rich and poor alike, stewardship, responsibility to community—quickly turned negative when the ecclesiastics were asked to consider actual policy. In answer to the question, "What would you do to change business attitudes in relation to faith?" typical answers were "Give it some ethics," "Limit CEO incomes," "Change the system," "Feed the hungry, clothe the naked," "Make all dealings ethical and eliminate activities that hinder a person from being with their families or going to church."

Clergy had similar comments, explaining that they stemmed from a feeling that businesspeople "don't care" or have some sort of mental and moral inferiority. These were bricks in their worldview. Businesspeople either suffered from greed and inferior reasoning or were unknowingly captive to the values of the system. Clergy needed to teach them about the plight of the poor and the injustices of the market mentality.

It is easy to understand these views, which are exacerbated by the clergy's tendency to frame their mental models of business in terms of the state of the global economy.[6] Indeed, the current global wealth gap makes it is difficult not to feel urgently cynical about the widespread benefits of capitalism.[7] The assignment of blame for these conditions was, for the clergy, clearly based in "business interests." In their aggregate view of business, all businesspeople seemed touched by this sin.

Poverty is a key trigger for the clergy's mental representation of business. Despite the fact that businesses face a daunting range of issues laden with moral urgency and provocative of spiritual sensitivity—from interpersonal relations to the protocol for product safety—the church tended to cast the overwhelming majority of its religious and ethical messages about business in terms of caring (or not caring) for the needy. Public reports of layoffs, cases of racial discrimination, and overpriced products were mined for evidence of business selfishness and harm to the poor. This was in turn filtered into a negative message about businesspeople's general insensitivity to the poor. Human ignorance of unintended consequences, for example, was never given as an explanation. Nor did they give serious credence to the businessperson's frequently mentioned frustration over having to weigh short-term pains against long-term gains.

Clergy accused businesspeople of not caring; businesspeople accused clergy of willfully not understanding. No surprise, then, that businesspeople sometimes feel as if their own clergy fix them with the evil eye. "They think we're all tainted," said one; "they're afraid to address the real problems of business because they might be tainted by the contact." Another executive echoed, "They think money is dirty and yet the church needs it. So they leave the raising of the money to us and then want to use it for the church's purpose. I hate this hypocrisy. Where would they be if we didn't go out and earn the money?"

The plight of the poor was a felt problem for the clergy in all denominations, including evangelical pastors (though their first focus was the businessperson's personal relationship to Jesus, which they tended to envision as strengthening outside a business context).

Clergy felt obligated by their faith to be a special spokesperson for the poor and disenfranchised. It was a key reason they had become clergy. (According to comparative ethicist Ronald Green, caring for the needy is a shared, key aspect of all world religions.[8]) Clergy assumed it was their duty to hold believers accountable to this obligation, and this conception of duty heavily colored how they engaged on the topic of business. Many clergy had the good conscience to be outraged at the state in which large numbers of Americans are living today. Many made a direct leap from this concern to an all-out attack on the ethics of businesspeople. What they may not have fully realized was that many businesspeople also believed their professions were the key to alleviating the plight of the poor. It was the two groups' stands on capitalism, not their level of caring, that were the real point of difference.

Political ideologies also played a key role in shaping the clergy's conception of the causes of poverty and their view of businesspeople's concern about it. They saw the current political climate as a direct indicator of extreme selfishness and materialism; they attributed the source to business. The welfare reform bill and tax cuts during the 1980s and 1990s best represented the state of the business mentality regarding poverty, which disappointed them mightily. They attributed the legislation to "not caring" about the poor; they felt little motivation to take up the many other reasons why these bills were introduced as being religiously relevant questions.

The plight of the impoverished is naturally close to the church's perceived field of concern—so close that more complex views of economic injustice that would also focus on the advantaged or on non-business factors of poverty fall off their mental radar screen. Clergy considered statistics on beneficial outcomes of welfare reform relatively unimportant, if they considered them at all. Purportedly good news that welfare-to-work left some participants feeling they had more financial well-being were additional evidence that business didn't care; the statistics masked the *real* problem, the selfishness and indifference of the business mentality.

They were confirmed in their opinion by several other recent legislative issues, mentioning opposition to the living wage, universal health care, and universal parental leave. This liberal Protestant pastor's comment was typical: "The state of our society is shameful. There are people starving on the streets. People working four jobs to make ends meet. And businesspeople just look the other way. Why? They've bowed to the great God of the market and that's all they care about." The solution? "They have to deepen their faith and make it operative."

Few businesspeople actually disagreed with the religious duty to the poor, but there was tremendous variation in how they acted on this concern in regard to their business role. Some privatized their concern into charitable giving—in some cases creating their own foundations, in others happily ceding their charitable giving to the direction of the church. The latter practice may actually contribute to the distanced relationship in regard to business because it signals to the clergy that, in becoming the adviser on charity and poverty, they are legitimately the conscience of the businessperson on other economic discussions. Some business interviewees poured their help to the needy into imaginative new ways of creating jobs and training inside their businesses. Many mentioned that job provision in existing businesses was evidence of their concern and a tangible contribution.

Interestingly, the businessperson's view of poverty was both more complex in terms of the manifestations of poverty and less sensitive to the fact that some people are not able to make a living within the current economic system. (The two are probably related.) To business, poverty was a problem to be alleviated through business mechanisms, not exacerbated by them. Failures were attributed to problems of "the system," by which they meant government or fate: corrupt governments, poor educational systems, long-standing cronyism, racist attitudes, or government monopoly. The striking rise in living standards among developing countries with a high level of multinational activity, and the overall drop in the rate of world undernourishment, were examples of the increased ability of business mechanisms to be responsive to the needs of the poor.

Commented one banker: "Clergy fail to accept the fact that rising tides lift all boats. They only see the person at the top, who clearly does gain out of all proportion." Another: "What they fail to think about is how many people would *become* poor were we to abandon this system. So why can't they think about how to be a Christian *within* this system?"

We found similar disjunctions between insider and outsider worldviews on the issue of mercy. The congregants tended to give examples of forgiveness inside the workplace: offering nonperformers a second chance, giving a participant in a business deal the benefit of extra time. To the clergy, mercy in business was directed toward those *outside* the economic loop. The most frequent example was the forgiveness of debt in third-world countries, a Jubilee concept that has captured widespread ecclesiastical support. Others suggested that business needed to constrain competitive expectations out of mercy toward those who had not been able to cultivate good business skills earlier in life. Failure to support these conclusions prompted the familiar accusation of "not caring," attributable to greed.

What was going on? Could it be that each group's attitude about poverty was not just a question of ideology but a question of self-image? Both proclaimed a duty to the poor. The manager went on to conclude his duty was to manage an economic solution (his role in life), the clergy to represent the plight of the poor. Were they to see *themselves* more clearly in their stands, they might map out a space to act in concert over the problems of poverty, where the vocational talents of each were valued. For this to occur, however, the naysayers would have to agree on there being some value in the arguments of the yea-sayers of capitalism. The yea-sayers would have to make space for alternative perspectives on the problems they were addressing.

The *Geist* of Business

The charge that clergy do not understand is a marked contrast to the guruhood that businesspeople have conferred on the secular spirituality experts. Unlike their optimistic and sympathetic approach, the clergy's categorically dark depiction of businesspeople failed to match up with the businessperson's professional experience and sense of personal role. It went against congregants' religious belief in the uniqueness of every person. The reductionist aspect of the clergy's stand toward the poor confirmed the businessperson's view that the church was inappropriately critical. Scoffed one manager in our interviews, "You notice the church never complains about business ripping off the rich!"

As insiders, businesspeople see life inside the corporation as complex—associated not only with money and work, but with social relations, skills of every sort, and also with a variety of pressures. As Weber noted about capitalism, business is not just a collection of legal transactions; it has a *Geist,* or spirit, that comprises a rich cluster of ethical and cultural values, many of which have religious origins and require spiritual discipline.

To the laity we talked with, these nuances were obvious, as was the idea that business carried ethical *possibilities* as well as perils. Consider the fullness of vision in these three remarks from interviewees of different denominations:

- "Christianity is about this world. You look at business and you will find every aspect of human experience there. So any meaningful faith has to speak to the business world. . . . Life is not the monastery."

- "When you talk to businesspeople running big organizations, they recognize early on it's not just utilitarian-based. The best of them have very high ideals. So it's not hard for them to think about how to communicate these ideals, get others to share their vision."

- "I'm in a business that doesn't have the greatest reputation in the world for honesty and integrity. I think I owe a lot of our success as a company to being religious. It's very difficult living by the rule. It's had a real positive influence on me, on my company, on my life."

All of these remarks stress the human side of business, acknowledge profit, and qualify it. So, too, this comment from a speech by William C. Pollard, chairman of the ServiceMaster Company:

> As a businessperson, I want to excel at generating profits and creating value for shareholders. If I don't want to play by these rules, I don't belong in the ball game. But I also believe that the business firm I work in . . . has another purpose. It can be a community to help shape human character and behavior. It should be an open environment where the question of who God is and who we are and how we relate our faith to our work are issues for discussion, debate, and yes, even learning and understanding. The people of our firm are in fact the soul of the firm.[9]

Combined praise for profit and for such extra-profit notions as the religious, ethical, and social rewards of being in business can be difficult for clergy and academic theologians to hear. Some congregants, especially in liberal Protestant churches, actually recognized a close connection between the *Geist* of business and the church. They attributed the character and spirit of their own management to values they cultivated through their affiliation with their churches: "The church has tremendously positive influences on my life, which I take to my business every day. I think we all do. The way we run our companies is a reflection of who we are [in coming] from this place [the church]. I owe a lot of the things that I've learned here to the success of my business, because we pay our bills on time, we're ethical, we're honest. The quality issues, how you treat your people. It all starts from an education here [at church]."

The pastor of this person's church was exceptional in his positive portrayal of the businesspeople in his congregation. "These are good people," he told us. "I know many of the businesspeople well. And I think they have a lot on their plates every day that I know nothing about. They come to me more for family problems or to help out some project of the church. In my sermons, I try to bring them hope, remind them of God's love, and give them courage."

Similarly, a New England pastor who had been part of a large nondenominational church saw no saintliness in standing apart from the business world: "We have to accept some responsibility for the state of the culture. If we don't know what's really going on in our own members' minds [he was speaking of his business congregants], how can we expect to be a force in this world?"

By contrast, other clergy, also in suburban middle-to-upper-class congregations, felt quite differently. Over and over again, we heard despairing remarks. From a nondenominational evangelical pastor: "I really have never actually found Christianity to be compatible with business." An Episcopal priest's comment that "If you try to run a business on Christian principles, that business is going to fail." A Roman Catholic priest's feeling that businesspeople "have to be brought back to the church, and that's nearly impossible to do in the midst of their professional lives." As we listened further, it seemed as if businesspeople and clergy were standing on separate pinnacles. As one Unitarian minister told us, "Among my colleagues, praising capitalism is like praising child molesting."

"Just Do It" Versus "Let's Think About It"

A professor of theology and an ordained minister, Max Stackhouse is unusual in his profession for his ability to critique business and yet counterbalance criticism with the possibility of redemption. This attitude has drawn him to seek out new ways of reaching the business community rather than dismissing it. He finds reason enough not to declare business a territory where God cannot reach. Stackhouse has repeatedly argued that although corruptibility is an inherent condition of all human organizations, corporations have creative potential—even the possibility of grace—if they are justly ordered.[10] By his own admission, Stackhouse's suggestion that the corporation can potentially be an instrument of creative social change has encountered "considerable distance in theological circles." In faith-based social activism, this resistance can be especially acute. At the congregational level, given the predominantly dependent relationship of clergy on the wealth of the congregation, resistance is often less overt. This in turn leaves clergy feeling silenced and all the more convinced that businesspeople are insensitive.

To the businessperson, the blaming simply sounds off; the negativity seems not quite to the point. As one executive told us, the clergy "don't understand that we *do* care about the poor. I'm happy to give to charity. I take that obligation very seriously. But I also have a business to run." And another lamented (as we have already noted), "You know, I've never heard a minister castigate business for possibly cheating the rich. But to my mind, that is just as much a test of integrity. If everyone is my neighbor, why should I show favoritism to the poor?"

In this comment, the deep inheritance of Calvinism seems as fresh as ever. Tawney's comments are particularly poignant here: "The best that can be said of the social theory and practice of early Calvinism is that they were consistent. Most tyrannies have contented themselves with tormenting the poor. Calvinism had little pity for poverty; but it distrusted wealth, as it distrusted all influences that distract the aim or relax the fibers of the soul, and in the first flush of its youthful austerity, it did its best to make life unbearable for the rich."[11]

Many Calvinist values remain in the business culture, despite the divergent views of luxury today. Poverty, for example, still has associations with sinful sloth for some, particularly when considering racial issues and poverty.[12] More frequently, however, businesspeople saw poverty as a tangled, systemic problem over which they had only limited power. Wealth was simply its flip side, and both posed ambiguous questions for the sincere Christian.

In the liberal church especially, the attitude that poverty is a function of some deep personal sin has largely given way to sophisticated understanding of its social and cultural causes. Nonetheless, the churches have not totally lost their early, pre-Reformation ambivalence about the wealthy or about business prosperity. The critical challenge to the churches has not been the existence of the ambivalence; the Bible itself offers a paradoxical set of attitudes here. Rather, it is how open the churches are to *acknowledging* this ambivalence, which the businessperson has to face as part of the territory of personal accountability.

Take, for example, the question of efficiency. Businesspeople place great emphasis on efficiency and its related value of pragmatism. In its extreme free-market form, efficiency is seen as a moral corrective—a way of securing fair prices without government tyranny. For most interviewees, however, efficiency was simply associated with effectiveness and achievement—positive virtues, in a personalized sense. Solutions that are impractical or seriously undermine efficiency by being ineffective were seen as inappropriate, irresponsible, and a failure to avoid harm in the short or long run. Problems that are inherently not amenable to economic efficiency (such as care of the mentally ill) are better isolated from market competition, but in no case would *inefficiency* be regarded as good in a business transaction.

Businesspeople also see efficiency and pragmatism as essential ingredients in delivering service. Their presence or absence has moral value in and of itself, and also because efficiency is a product of other virtues: honest business practices, respect, taking responsibility to see that needs are met, effort, discipline, self-restraint, method, and ingenuity. An inefficient operation can make a businessperson seethe ("How can they treat a customer with such disrespect?"). A meeting that starts late speaks volumes and can also be interpreted as lack of respect (or worse: incompetence, and thus a breach of fiduciary duty).

To a cleric, on the other hand, being late for a meeting may simply be a sign of having had more important things to do. Clergy tend to associate efficiency with depersonalizing profit motivations. For example, they would cite emphasis on price inefficiency as an underlying force in promoting the businessperson's greed. Value on efficiency in church operations, then, would be suspect—an attitude widely evidenced in the indifference to poor management of many churches and nonprofits today.

Such differing attitudes, which reflect deep moral viewpoints, are a significant feature of the distanced relationship. One man told us a story that illustrates how these differences are apparent in even the most trivial details. This executive retired from his job as CEO of a $100 million company to attend divinity school. He hoped to realign his lifestyle and priorities but was not contemplating a life of the cloth. The transition was difficult. By his own admission, the theological community perceived him as too outspoken, too impatient, and superficially pragmatic. He seethed over the memory of registering for classes: "I don't understand inefficiency. It's an insult to people. We had to stand in line for three hours to register. Three hours. They knew how many people would attend, and yet there was no mechanism to register more quickly."

By contrast, many pastors and seminarians we interviewed felt that efficiency in operations was not a priority; in their view it often represented ruthlessness and insensitivity to people's emotional needs. Clergy mistrusted pragmatism. It played into their caricature of the shallowness and hard-heartedness of businesspeople.

Meanwhile, the business community hooted over the clergy's "fuzzy-mindedness." Though they attributed the church's antibusiness attitudes to this kind of ignorance, what they also meant was a propensity for reflection ("Quit thinking about it; just do it").

One problem is that many clergy simply fail to inspire or impress business congregants who are used to an extremely dynamic personality being in charge. As one businessperson explained, "The problem is the singer, not the song. What appears strong when done by Jesus just appears to be the act of an inherently weak person when it's coming from a pastor who can't tie his shoes." This lack of confidence made the clergy's ethical reflections on business seem alarming and overly critical, even when the content of the reflection was not completely negative.

Equally ineffective is the clergy's overcorrection toward the "happiness" gospel. In *Crisis of the Churches*,[13] Wuthnow noted that clergy tended to conceive of vocation as an important opportunity for authentic self-expression rather than emphasizing its opportunity for service or love. Thus pastors counseled people to get their motives straight about work, conduct themselves so as to be happy about themselves, and make others happy about themselves at work. This message *seems* positive, but in fact it limits religious possibility to attitudes about career, not to the institutional activities associated with attaining prosperity.

In many cases—both in Wuthnow's experience and in our interviews—clergy specifically juxtaposed the happiness of the right-minded faithful with false happiness in wealth and success. Most conceptions of religious happiness turned out to be subtractive in form: spending less time at work and more with family, needing less money, buying fewer consumer items. At no time were the potential contributions of business seen as a path to faithfulness or the happiness of faithfulness.[14]

These attitudes have a profound impact on the church's stature as a source of moral guidance. Clergy are trained to be openly reflective and questioning. But in the business world, questioning that does not lead to pragmatic conclusions is interpreted as antiproductive. Businesspeople—already sensitive to being stereotyped as greedy and blamed for situations beyond their personal control (such as the existence of world poverty)—feel entrapped by the mere presence of reflective questions. Said one congregant, in response to a questioning remark from the pulpit on wage inequity: "No businessperson can solve the inequities of wages in this country, but we are perfectly aware that we are supposed to feel very guilty about collecting a salary and profiting from this imperfect system." Said another, "You don't expect your pastor to pat you on the back all the time, but the level of criticism is ridiculous. You'd think every businessperson was Hitler! They just don't understand that businesspeople are just ordinary human beings trying to do a good job."

Tone and role are clearly contributing factors. One clergyman told us, "I'd like to take them [businesspeople] to the other side of town and make them live there for one week. Then they'd care." Like him, many clergy see their proper role as disciplinary and corrective, global in focus, representing major portions of heaven and earth. One mainline Protestant minister in a suburban church, when approached to participate in our study, was both welcoming and eager: "That's extremely important. I'd really like to participate. I'd really like to speak more on these issues to my congregation. I'd like to offset their materialism."

Scolding doesn't help. Congregants sometimes complained that the clergy had a tendency to moralize about everything: family relations, material purchases, behavior at school. Businesspeople—less gloomy than most clergy and not inclined to deliberately reflect on every issue—were doubly uneasy about the religious meaning of business because the question immediately provoked a negative moral judgment from the clergy. Not surprisingly, conservative Protestant and Catholic clergy who were not so uncomfortable with wealth per se seemed to be able to deliver their messages on poverty in ways that did not annihilate the businessperson in the process.

Businesspeople may be alarmed at business practices, but they do not accept the heavy guilt trip they perceive from many of their churches: "They just don't understand how complex these issues are. Many of the most highly compensated people have also offered the greatest number of jobs and services to the society. This is not all bad, but they (the churches) refuse to admit that anything good comes out of business." In some cases, they explicitly associated the blame with the propensity toward reflection: "You can spend your time gazing at your navel and telling everyone how wrong they are, or you can go out and *do* something."

Building or Tearing Down?

The differences in the yea and nay approaches may be partly explained by earlier religious cultures in both Protestantism and Catholicism that emphasized the preacher as the embodiment of the community's guilty conscience, there to remind the laity of its sins and wrong-mindedness. They may also be attributed to temperament.

William James suggested that certain personality types tended to be drawn to particular sorts of religious experience. He described businesspeople as inherently optimistic, which explained their involvement in the mind-cure spirituality movements of the day. The religions of healthy-mindedness, as James called them, tended to attract unreflective, pragmatic people, the kind who worry less about ultimate meaning and more about getting things done. The can-do attitude of this movement, later picked up by Bruce Barton and Norman Vincent Peale, appeals to businesspeople. It not only empowers but supports the general American ideology of self-reliance, opportunity, and freedom. Not surprisingly, the business community has been drawn to religious expression that exhibits their basic optimism and a self-empowering approach rather than advocacy of taking power away.

With this bias comes an accompanying one toward constructive goals. Problems are framed in terms of what can be accomplished, not what went wrong or why the goal should be abandoned for larger, less-tangible goals. Strength, decisiveness, and good humor are welcome virtues to businesspeople who would interpret such optimistic character traits as an effective and humane contrast to the violent arrogance that also typifies power in their world.

To the clergy, however, this business style can seem fake, shallow, or insensitive. As with our fictional mother-in-law on Alice's personality, they construct a negative explanation of what the businessperson sees as positive attributes. Said one pastor about a well-known business executive in the community: "He seems so good humored, but that's how he makes his money—by getting people to agree with him."

Intellectual elitism bordering on superiority creeps in. For clergy, religiously motivated human relations are often associated with quieter, more reflective styles. Being mild of manner and quiet of speech even when representing strong patriarchal notions of authority is a style usually associated with a fairly pessimistic focus, particularly suited to troubled moments, therapy, and such tasks as comforting the grieving or visiting the sick. So, too, many of the central concepts of Christian religion most emphasized in church ritual focus on what might be called pessimistic topics: death, suffering, sin, fear of punishment. As one liberal pastor put it in commenting on businesspeople's conceptions of religion, "I'm sorry, but this [Christianity] is not just some 'feel good' exercise." Another said, "They [businesspeople] say they want to be like Jesus, but I'm not sure they're ready to die on a cross."

Much of the language of traditional religion has been essentially pessimistic and focused on clarifying and identifying with *weakness*, stressing the fallen nature of humankind, moral weakness, dependency. But weakness is an uncomfortable concept for businesspeople. Even when they publicly confess weakness, it is often as a rhetorical foil, an expression of being humbled in the face of their own considerable strengths—as when the business student applicant who is asked to describe his or her greatest weakness, writes, "I am incapable of holding back. I cannot stop being a perfectionist and going out after whatever I'm doing 110 percent, all the time."

Such differences of style and temperament contribute to mutual demonizing, as well as shaping the first questions each asks. So the businessperson chooses market success as the starting point for an exploration of faith; the clergyperson chooses market failure.

Finally, in our interviews, conceptions of Jesus seemed sharply colored by such outlooks. The businessperson looking to model his or her behavior after Jesus portrays the son of God as supportive but decisive—rather like Barton's *The Man Nobody Knows* or Laurie Beth Jones's *Jesus CEO*. The clergy's Jesus, in contrast, represents an attitude of self-sacrifice divorced from worldly reward. This is the Jesus with whom they identified positively. (No one among the clergy reported a profitable business activity as the locus for such feelings of religious triumph.)

Is God in the Marketplace?

Place was also symbolic. Where is God in society? For the clergy, the social locus of God is firmly placed in the church—however balanced with views about the importance of the laity or the "living church." Some railed against the fact that the skyscraper (that is, business) was now taking up more of the cityscape than the steeple. For the businessperson, the locus of God may be primarily in the church, but it is also possible in the marketplace.

Failure to visualize God or God's work in the marketplace is another reason why clergy find it difficult to see the importance of addressing the needs of business. In our survey of seminarians, we asked, "How important do you feel it is for your curriculum to include ministry issues regarding businesses and businesspeople?" Answers were divided down the middle.

Those who thought it was important saw it that way only in relation to the business needs of the church ("Church members are in business of some kind"; "Each parish has building projects and investments") or to the sins of business ("To understand their mindset with money and power").

About 50 percent responded "not very important." They were reluctant to differentiate business as a discrete topic of sufficient religious complexity to warrant special attention; their responses ranged from "It is easily taken up in an ethics class" to "Social sin is prevalent in all society and the business community plays a role in it." Such responses help explain how clergy come to adopt a generalist, unnuanced view of business. Unaddressed, this framing would have clear effects on choice of curriculum and training of the clergy, with a bias toward materials with a macrosystemic view. Such is the framework that was prevalent in our interviews with clergy; it is also reported in Wuthnow.

In the congregation, the omission of the buisnessperson's struggles appears to be widespread. Many of our interviewees expressed similar impressions of the clergy at large. Pastors and businesspeople complained that there was active refusal on the church's part to deal with the issues of money, reflecting the culture of the formal church.

The Jesuit institutions seemed to offer the most "mixed" view of this-world avenues for Catholic teaching. When asked what themes they were familiar with regarding businesspeople as part of their religious community and the fabric of society, some of their answers (still less than half) cited the positive as well as the negative (macro or systemic) view. Positive religious contributions included "the holy use of money," "discernment," "the market as a worthy place to make one's profession," and "businesspeople are Christians, too." However, when asked if any specific biblical passages had informed their view of business, they either answered in the negative (60 percent) or uniformly cited negative pronouncements about profit and its temptations, especially about not serving two masters.

Why do many answers dwell on the business aspects of the church in response to a question about the importance of ministry to business? Once again, deeper attitudes about the simplicity and essential sinfulness of business seem to be contributing to this response. In assuming that business has no possibility for positive contribution to social justice or to living out faith, "ministry to business" simply does not register. Respondents move to the church's business instead. Such mental twists are an instructive example of how deeply the simplistic and negative bias against business can cause mental denial about addressing business as a Christian issue other than in a criticizing light.

Even the refusal to differentiate business as a legitimate topic for theological inquiry—an attitude sharply in contrast to that taken toward poverty—creates a platform from which the clergy launches personal attacks on the businessperson's character. Businesspeople don't count—a feeling many businesspeople discerned in describing how their clergy treated them in their roles as professionals.

The congregational structure itself tends to reinforce the silence and frustration. Dependent on the congregation for job security, the pastor quickly learns that nearly any substantive statement can provoke criticism from *someone*, and so he or she learns to stick to the safe, generalized topics.

What stimulates the businessperson's sense of faith and responsibility? To find out, we asked some interviewees to describe a situation or person in business that they admired. One interviewee recounted a story of a person he really admired. His is a very good representation of the essentially optimistic characterizations of the businessperson that we heard, and the focusing function of this optimism:

> The president at my firm had just received the news that a major product they'd been developing for a client had failed to perform. The client was canceling all further orders. The problem really wasn't our fault. The product development had been a headache from the start, and when the bugs began to show up after delivery, we discovered that some very complex computer components had not been up to the specs of the contract. We tried to work with the supplier, but it was clear that the source of the problem was not going to be quickly fixed. The supplier had other contracts, little time, and little inclination to fix the problem. The client had had it. The contract was broken.

This client was very abusive personally during the meeting. He was chewing out our president, right in front of his own people. We were appalled.

The president remained calm throughout. He tried suggesting a strategy for fixing the problem, and as the client got more abusive, he basically dropped it. The contract was canceled.

As soon as the client left, the president called the people in the office together and told them the news that the contract had been dropped. He then outlined the steps he was going to take the next day to evaluate the financial position this put the firm in, his strategic options, and how they were going to pursue another client. . . .

That guy, in my opinion, was truly strong. He did not in any way deserve the humiliation that client put on him. He just took it calmly. Then he thought about everyone else. That's what being a Christian is about.

The businessperson mentioned that he knew the boss was a Christian and took his religion seriously, but they had never discussed these things together. When pressed, he said that he thought the president's strength came out of his faith and out of his personality, but he was reluctant to see this incident as an example of religion at work. "He just knows how to keep his eyes on the important things."

The denial of religious meaning was interesting, again suggesting rigid boundaries between religion and business activity in people's minds. It also put the coping strategies we discussed in Chapter Two in a slightly different light.

Though character was a function of conviction, and thus a fruitful area for religious faith at work, businesspeople tended to disguise religious influence on specific decision making, perhaps even from themselves. In their worldview, a decision must be explained in rational terms of pragmatism and self-interest, even if people believe other factors are important. This particular disguising construct has real unintended consequences. It causes clergy to feel confirmed in their view that business does not care about religious values in work. When have they heard a businessperson professing otherwise? Only, perhaps, when a God-talking swindler wanted to cheat a naïve victim.

What is so striking about this story is its subtle rebalancing of emphasis in the teller's contemplation of typical religious themes: bad things happen even when you don't deserve them, honesty and humility are difficult and important, and placing others over one's own emotional needs is an essential responsibility. Ultimately, the firm's president had the characteristics of an optimistic saint: tranquil, as only those who wholly submit to the idea that God's will shall be done can be in the face of the enemy. The man seemed to be generating inner power from his calm suffering of the moment. Ultimately, strength to maintain a humane workplace even over profit, not weakness or martyrdom, are the hallmarks of this tale. (There is an implication, however, that such behavior combined with strategic skill is what creates profit-making business in the long run.) The man managed well; his religious values gave him this strength. Such a story held great inspirational meaning for the interviewee.

This self-reliant bias stood in sharp contrast to the hierarchical, often paternalistic culture of clergy. As one businessperson wondered aloud, while explaining her support of welfare reform in spite of her church's position: "What is the sign of goodwill toward one's neighbor? Deciding what is good for them? Or giving them the opportunity to decide for themselves?" She concluded, "The problem is, I think the church has this bias toward paternalistic solutions. When I don't agree, I get the feeling they think I don't care about the poor. That's not true and it's not fair. So I keep my mouth shut."

Again, we hear the silencing and distancing over basic assumptions about wealth and poverty. An interesting study by Joseph

Hough on attitudes among suburban, upwardly mobile, middle-class congregations suggests that such attitudes may even have the unintended effect of making business congregants feel they are in competition with the poor! For Hough's busy executives, church was expected to fulfill three main functions: to be a sanctuary from the pressures of daily work and family; to be a place that offered additional comfort (services such as visitation of the sick, counseling of the bereaved, and child education); and to be a source of moral inspiration and its application to the questions they face on a practical level. The last expectation was largely focused on character rather than issue.[15]

Keeping Their Distance

When clergy continue to appear to advocate solely for the poor, they become the businessperson's religious competitor. As Hough puts it, "They come to church to be served, not to be disciplined. They come to church to receive ministry, not to be ministers." Essentially, congregants expect a church to provide a place to which they feel they belong, offering simple and anecdotal wisdom with obvious pragmatic import, "something we can take home and use during the week." Among Hough's congregational group and our interviewees, the religious hunger of the businessperson was for personalized religion rather than discussion of the transformation of society. To many pastors, however, this seems a selfish stance.

The businessperson's inviolate bias toward empowerment within a temporal context is precisely what is so difficult for many in the church to accept from a theological standpoint (and so easy for the secular spirituality programs to exploit). Interestingly, there seem to be few attempts to prepare clergy to address their own discomfort with profit and images of secular strength. If anything, they learn to deny their own anger and scorn for business by diverting their religious attention to every aspect of the economy *but* business.

For example, seminaries seemed to offer little in the way of exposure to the character of the businessperson, the corporation, or the multiple tasks of business. Seminary economics courses focused more on liberation theology economics and specific global horror stories than on the rights and responsibilities of running modern capitalist institutions. In this scenario, Mobil is Nigeria. Shell is Brent Spar. Nike is sweatshops. Nestle is infant formula. Respondents reported few occasions when their seminaries exposed students or faculty to businesspeople, face-to-face, to exchange views.

Interestingly, both sides expressed deep support for the idea of bringing faith more fully into their lives. Clergy repeatedly expressed the view that it was important for religion to address "every aspect of this life, including work and money." Businesspeople asserted that they wanted "something more" out of their work than material wealth and power. Neither was able to move out of a Generalist or Percolator position toward a faith perspective that both informed and practiced a different approach to dealing with business pressures.

In adopting the strong biases of the yea and nay without occasion for an interchange of views, both groups retreat to a distance. In so doing, they suffer from what St. Augustine called "the inward curve"—a kind of thinking that suffers a turning in on its own direction, and away from God. The businessperson's emphasis on forward movement (production, pragmatism, and success), no matter how tied to Christian values of love, faith, hope, or service, keeps the economic actor's focus on those who are largely inside the economy. Frequently, their language is hopelessly caught up in a logic of efficiency, or highly sentimental, while clergy become strident when focused on such favorite topics as poverty or profit. Both need to moderate and explore their positions fully. Businesspeople need to be attentive to how systems that create success also create failure. Clergy need to pay sufficient attention to how specific measures to relieve suffering may also create suffering.

This is easy to suggest and difficult to accomplish, given so many differences of basic assumption, temperament, and style. The contrasting worldviews reported here work in many subtle and obvious ways to thwart the efforts of church and businesspersons to act as members of the same community on questions of integrating religious faith and business. Until these underlying worldviews are examined, no "argument" is likely to emerge to effect a change of attitude.

To deal with this distancing, the clergy and the businessperson turn in opposing directions, the former to social service groups and politics; the latter to secularized, therapeutic, or educational sources. Clearly, inadequate preparation to deal with the fact of differing worldviews is causing churches and seminaries to lose more opportunity to be of guidance on business than they are currently creating. A real-world example makes this clear.

A congregant in a New York City church, whom we'll call Fred, was a director of a major Fortune 100 corporation. He carefully constructed a seminar for his church on the issue of corporate layoffs. He laid out ten questions for the group's consideration, which he felt captured the difficult tradeoffs faced by the leadership of any corporation. None of the attendees, however, were in such a position. Most of them were consumers or middle-level managers. To his dismay, the questions were all perceived as fairly clear-cut. Anything to do with layoffs or high compensation was bad. As he tried to make his own struggle with these questions clear, he found the pastor chiming in with agreement every time a negative comment was directed at business. "They were totally negative," Fred told us. "They were completely unconvinced when I suggested that business actually cares about these things. I really wanted to hear what the church had to say about these tradeoffs, but what I got was just a lot of condemnation about executives' character."

It didn't take him long to form an ecumenical group of CEOs to discuss the social responsibility of business—without the presence of religious leaders. These people are actively trying to educate the next generation of business leaders as to a greater sense of social responsibility. Though they have largely met with failure, this group still meets and is still wrestling with the problem. So, too, many church-sponsored efforts to explore the role of faith at work start on a path that is almost guaranteed to run into a dead end. When asked about the concerns they felt would be most proper to help businesspeople approach their faith, clergy or seminarians would often begin with a rhetorical scenario reflecting great moral urgency and focus on the poor. This is probably the *worst* place to start as a basis of a dialogue: it triggers mutual condemnation without giving guidance. Framing the topic in this way leaves no room for coming to a shared definition of responsibility or goals, and it encourages the personal demonizing that makes it difficult for both parties to participate in a truly open inquiry.

Ironically, even when the clergy praise businesspeople, it tends to further this separation. In our study, the clergy's most frequent example of a businessperson's religious integration concerned financial contributions to church-related causes. Some business-people complained that this was the *only* role in which their church saw them.

Basic worldview and temperament create enormous obstacles to fostering shared understanding about religious faith and business. Rather than retreating from each other, the two groups need to develop a neutral ground on which to meet. But a number of other patterns of thinking and behaving only serve to enforce their positions on separate peaks, protected by their blind spot and distanced by a large gulf of misunderstanding. Next we take a look at how these fundamental differences of worldview generate and are reinforced by proprietary feelings about the "proper role" of ecclesiastics and business authorities. These notions create a turf battle over the authoritative source for proper understanding of how Christian beliefs should have an impact on business.

Reflection

- How many of the attributes of clergy and businesspeople described in this chapter have you personally observed?

- How many describe you?

- How deeply do you think these patterns color your thinking about religion and business? about how you are perceived by others?

Action

- Formulate a specific question for businesspeople and clergy about an aspect of business you find troubling. Try to frame it in such a way that it would prompt them to discuss their religious thinking and not just tell you what to do.

- Go test it out.

- Listen for the patterns described here. If you hear them, either stop and explore out loud what you hear, or keep track of them in a "parking lot" of issues for later discussion with a study group.

6

Turf Wars

Overcoming Negative
Stereotypes and
Notions of "Proper" Roles

*Why would I want to hear from a divinity school on
business issues? Look at how they run their own shop!*
—Christian businessperson

*This is my church, and I think that if I want to move
an altar rail, I should be able to make that decision
without interference.*
—Clergyperson

I t is said that true wisdom does not come until you walk in another's
shoes. Unfortunately, as we saw in Chapter Five, the people we
interviewed in both the laity and the clergy had a great deal of difficulty with this concept. Clergy confessed they would probably be a
failure at business. Business interviewees confided that God did not
give them the temperament or talents to be preachers. Neither
seemed unhappy about the situation.

Choice of Profession

In fact, when the ecclesiastical crowd contemplated business, they often found that the exercise confirmed them in their career choice. One class of divinity students we spoke to was wrestling with a business ethics case at a depth most of them had not encountered before. As they probed the many issues relevant to the problem, they repeatedly confessed surprise at their own naïveté. The trade-offs were much more difficult than they had thought—and more compelling. The material itself forced them to consider the multiple roles and motives that drive executives' decisions, and their struggle to balance conflicting values of service and self-interest.

Several students found the extended discussion of business pressures over the span of a semester to be unsettling. To their surprise, they found themselves gradually empathizing with the businessperson: you had to like some of those people; it was possible to identify with their goals. (Clergy felt the same way about individuals in the congregation even as they opposed the concept of business.) But this process of empathizing tore the fabric of their long-standing conception of business as a villainous, misdirected activity. They felt coopted, and their own religious culture offered little help in seeing a connection between this empathy and larger religious concepts. Despair was a common reaction. One theology student literally cried after class in frustration. She liked the class; she could relate to the people problems encountered in the material, and to the human emotions that played out on this economic landscape. "But," she cried, "I just really, deeply *hate* capitalism."

Her reaction was not unusual. In hating the song but learning to empathize with the singer, theological students and clergy often seemed to feel they were abandoning their "proper" role as supporter of the poor and disadvantaged. They conceived of business as embattled with the poor in a zero-sum game. They took it for granted: a stand with capitalism was a stand against the poor. Thin conceptions of business (solely in terms of systemic pursuit of excessive growth and wealth under unjust exploitative conditions) supported this position. Consideration of the human dimension of business, however, quickly muddied their view. The business cases presented the possibility of common ground and moral ambivalence, as does the experience of managing a church. They could not reconcile these conceptual models, and they often had trouble coping with the ambivalence.

Take, for example, the comment of a gas station owner who explained why he decided to keep his pumps open during a hurricane evacuation instead of leaving. With unsentimental plainness, he said, "I'm always there for my customers; they depend on me." When a group of seminarians discussed this incident, one of the first comments was cynical: "What price was he charging that day?" Others saw the entrepreneur's dedication as proof of a larger system's exploitative tendencies toward African American hourly laborers (this particular African American was the owner of a franchise). They either became angry and dismissive or retreated into highly abstract mental frameworks—anything to displace the notion of this person's business role affording an authentic source of identity, self-worth, or opportunity for living Christian values of community from Sunday into Monday. They could not withstand the pressure of trying to reconcile their negative views of business profit with their foundational views of Christianity.

Pragmatic executives see this gut-level refusal to engage in the problems of their world as a cop-out, especially since it comes packaged in moral censure. By contrast, the ecclesiastics found their own dismissiveness an effective reinforcement of their career choice to turn away from the transient to concentrate on higher things. Thus the choice of a religious profession buffered their fears of cooption to the point of removing any sense of duty to wrestle with the religious import of tough business trade-offs.

One group of students was considering a case drawn from a congregant's experience. A personnel director knows an employee has tested HIV-positive. She encounters the employee's fiancée at an office party. Does she have an obligation to make sure the fiancée knows of her future spouse's medical condition? Issues of confidentiality, legality, and the duty to prevent harm vie with each other. Legal guidelines also constrain the manager. The class pushed the issue hard to draw out the full implications of each grounded value, and the conflict soon became unbearable. But all discussion stopped among the moral experts-in-training when one student suddenly asserted, "Well, that's why I'd never go into business. I have to do what I feel is right, not what some company tells me to do."

As the other students picked up his distaste, self-righteousness descended on the classroom. In this example, the trigger for self-righteous reaction was conflict over confidentiality. More frequently, pressure to offer useful products and services at a profit triggered even more adamant rejection of the business profession as a whole.

The cultural tolerance of this reaction among the elite in the religious community feeds the inability of clergy to develop mature approaches to the real problems their parishioners face in business. Turning away from conflict, they fail to move beyond stating grounded religious values, toward the dynamics of applying them. Choice of profession—namely, to work in a faith-based institution—*excused* them from engaging in the hard questions ("Hey! It's not my territory. I would never create such a system").

The Dirty-Hands Syndrome

The classical notion of Christian theology that corruption is imbedded in riches was reinforced by real examples of corruption in business. Many conclude the taintedness is inevitable. Even Protestant asceticism has the same imbedded corruption, as Weber points out, in that it leads to capital accumulation and then backslides as one is corrupted by others' admiration of one's own wealth. John Wesley described it perfectly: "I fear, wherever riches have increased, the essence of religion has decreased in the same proportion. Therefore I do not see how it is possible in the nature of things, for any revival of true religion to continue long. For religion must necessarily produce both industry and frugality, and these cannot but produce riches. But as riches increase so will pride, anger, and love of the world in all its branches. . . . So although the form of religion remains, the spirit is swiftly vanishing away."[1]

Many of the seminarians we interviewed cited Wesley's simple solution: work as hard as possible to make as much money as possible to give away as much money as possible. Avoid personal wealth. His formula did not pretend to posit integration of the spiritual and the confrontation with wealth. Rather, it separated wealth from personal spiritual identity, a kind of dirty sidebar that could be cleaned by getting rid of it.

In Catholic monastic movements, the best minds were preserved for the religious, thereby avoiding the problem of personal wealth creation as a result of disciplined asceticism. The church, however, had no less trouble dealing with wealth and power than individuals. Thus we must see, as Weber noted, a cruel dialectic in the ethics of ascetic Protestantism and Catholicism that is with us today.

As Richard Weiss noted, the cruel dialectic of asceticism occupied the early Puritans: "The more their holy experiment thrived, the less holy it became."[2] In response, the church developed a number of measures, from the suggestion of self-imposed limits on personal income[3] to political action against capitalist institutions. The enduring legacy of this thinking is permanent guilt over the fact of wealth, even as people live out perpetual interest in becoming "better off" in some material way. The ambivalence remains active in our society today.[4] In movie after movie, the wealthy are the people we love to hate, but also the people we love to study and aspire to imitate. Businesspeople are ethically suspect, but their lifestyles are to die for. Large, profitable institutions are even more suspect, no matter how much we love the product.

Such ambivalence takes on more serious critique from the churches, though the criticisms may be based on no more information than popular media depictions of businesspeople. The first significant critique of business in America came from the social gospel movement in the nineteenth century, a movement precipitated by the tragic social consequences of rapid, unregulated industrialism and its need for new labor. Ironically, the movement was largely spearheaded by liberal Protestant clergy (especially in the Episcopal church), some of whom were pastors to the wealthiest families in the United States. Among their followers were many whose families had already made a fortune in a previous generation.[5] Ironically, the mainstream church first took the side of business against organized labor, moving only after several decades to a position of representing the laborer's need for organized representation. Failing to wrestle with the pressing question of new wealth generation, these pro-labor positions penetrated the shaded circle, but again in ways that did not lay the groundwork for anyone in a position of business power to discover an integrated religious life.

Not surprisingly, antibusiness social action models met with little interest among the businesspeople we interviewed. Like their nineteenth-century counterparts who were drawn to the positive thinkers, today's executives seek religious messages that equip them to compete with conscience in the marketplace. Class itself seems to be at issue. For those without an independent income or the guaranteed subsidy of a tenured professorship or pastoral seat, the need to generate wealth is a nonnegotiable part of being a responsible individual. Providing for others, "giving something back," is also an important obligation, but both purposes are considered ethical. There is, however, no New Testament model of a noble profit, never mind a noble profit in a nonagricultural economy. What would it look like? How big?

The naysayers of capitalism turn these questions of mixed business purpose into "What are the perils of wealth?" or "What wouldn't businesses do for the sake of a profit?" They see their role as critics, over and against the system. The yea-sayers create Justifier explanations and see themselves as guardians of an essentially positive mission: to create wealth for oneself and others. Neither response truly engages in critiquing business purpose from a religious standpoint without further thought. Both fail to inspire creative responses based on a sharper religious vision of business purpose in capitalism.

This pattern of disengagement from the questions of wealth creation, or ignorance of thick descriptions of business and the roles businesspeople assume, was reflected in the disparity we saw between students and clergy who said they desired to influence the attitudes and behavior of business and what they actually felt they should be able to contribute to the discussion.

The Prophetic Vision to Reform: On Whose Authority?

Seminarians we surveyed had a strong tendency to frame the notion of their influence on business in terms of broad theological concepts. When asked, "How would you influence the church's role or attitude toward large businesses?" a minority responded positively, from "Develop appropriate sermons" to "Integrate business and church life." More typical, however, was this response: "Call them into accountability for unfair practices and dehumanization of the workplace."

When asked how they would like to minister to the businesspeople in their own religious community, they gave a similar variety of responses:

Help them understand their responsibility to community

Listen

Develop contacts, have discussions

Help them combine their spirituality and economic life

Evangelize them, give spiritual guidance, help strengthen their relationship with God, hold bible study and prayer groups

Help them see the responsibility for the common good, treat them the same as any other person[6]

When asked how they would influence business, they responded:

Make it more personal

Make it more humane

Pay attention to morale

Make it more ethical

Emphasize better stewardship

Give more stakeholders a say

Be more philanthropic

Take a longer-term view

These answers are strikingly positive and similar to humane businesspeople's goals. Here, it seemed, was a common ground for dialogue. But as generalities turned to specifics, the message once again divided along yea and nay. The only specific suggestion came, tellingly, in connection with the church's traditional territory: stop working on Sundays.

The closer we brought the question to a request for specific religious concepts they had studied in relation to business, the less clear the answer. When asked, "Have you ever tried to apply any scripture passages to what you see is going on in the world of business?" nearly all said no or did not answer the question. When asked what their own religious tradition had to say about business, they gave many rather rambling answers about justice, community, prophetic action, and helping the poor. The Methodists and Roman Catholics had the clearest conceptual hooks. Methodists cited John Wesley's dictum. Catholics alluded to notions of solidarity and human dignity. In neither case did these answers indicate any penetration of the relational and behavioral aspects of business activity.

When we probed for particularized connection between faith and work, the response showed little depth or experience. When asked what business books or journals they studied, very few had any experience at all. When asked, "Have you discussed or been given any scripture passages to study with the explicit purpose of understanding God's message with respect to business or the responsibilities of the businesspeople?" respondents offered a range of passages that tended toward portraying bad business behavior.[7]

When we asked businesspeople the same question, they *frequently* offered "a handful" of biblical passages or lines from hymns that carried them through their business day. These tended to be reminders of God's relation to humankind, exhortations to work hard, and general prescriptions such as Micah 6.8: "What does the Lord require of you but to do justice and to love kindness and to walk humbly with your God?" Simple wisdom, much of it about attitude that they felt had direct application to their professional role.

Describing Each Other

These answers suggest that the religious community's general bias toward a larger, abstracted conception of business is learned early.[8] It does not seem to be particularly tied directly to biblical sources or liturgical ideas, but rather to contemporary theological notions acquired in seminary. The intellectual patterns have a number of consequences, especially on the process of role definition that in turn seems to contribute to the general distancing of clergy from the specifics of business. Bias toward large abstraction retards their ability to conceptualize business in concrete ways that encourage helpful guidance on activities that penetrate the businessperson's world. It also encourages stereotyping.

When the student or pastor is in control of constructing the portrayal of business and businesspeople, suddenly the issues become simple and clear, and the assessment of business generally negative. Moralizing replaces distancing, much of it centered on devaluing the businessperson's qualifications or moral authority to make religiously consistent judgments. To make the point, the stereotypes fly.

Frequently, the stereotypes come out in asides, except among the more polemical theologians, whom one would expect to engage in rhetorical caricatures. (It is not clear whether students are encouraged to critique these caricatures. Many seem to take them at face value as depictions of fact.)

For example, outside of the interview or survey situation, respondents were less self-conscious about their tolerance level toward business, and the same for the respondents in business toward clergy. A request for an interview frequently elicited a voluntary summary of the other profession. Clergy would become categorically nihilist about the morality of businesspeople, and businesspeople would become categorically nihilist about the accuracy and relevance of the church's views on economic life. For example, the *Houston Catholic Worker*, a publication dedicated to the tradition of labor advocate Dorothy Day, continues to portray capitalism in the most polemical terms, emphasizing with vivid rhetoric the exploitation and greed that is assumed to be driving economic activities. A visit to the organization's electronic newspaper turns up a series of articles that criticize the allegedly sinful state of capitalism, CEOs, and consumerism.

Businesspeople were frequently demonized and some of the business interviewees were extremely caustic in their stereotypes of the clergy, especially when they discussed their use of abstracted stereotypes of business and poverty: "[The church people] are just victims of fuzzy-minded thinking. The problems of poverty are so complicated. Haven't they noticed that socialism created its own special abuses of justice and failed to provide food for people?"

What is the solution? One interviewee said, "The church should be in there teaching people to care, reminding them of their responsibilities, but not butting in on politics. They don't know what they're talking about. And the way they defended Clinton just shows you how fuzzy-minded they've become. If that wasn't a case of sin, I don't know what was, but they were afraid of undermining the Democratic party. This is just wrong, when the church defends a sin for politics."

Here, too, a tendency toward generalization feeds the distancing. When businesspeople were confronted with obvious moral problems from a religious standpoint, such as the question of paying a living wage, they quickly retreated from religious perspectives to their more familiar role as assessor of economic facts and market outcomes. In discussing a regular prayer luncheon for businesspeople, the clergyperson in charge reflected that the most difficult task he assumed was trying to bring the conversation back to any religious authority once concrete business issues were raised. In other words, it was easy for the business community, almost unawares, to strip the inquiry of all religious tension, and the pastor felt unable to bring religion back into the picture.

The mutual stereotyping and its perpetration of distorted portrayals of the other's professional views have an obviously bad effect on the church-business dialogue. This also suggests that sheer ignorance of the others' world plays a major role in the distancing, a finding that Wuthnow has already noted in several of his studies. To cope with negative stereotypes of themselves, the church community similarly strips businesspeople of their professional identities once they enter the realm of the institutional church. Although this shedding of professional role can contribute to the ability of congregants to recharge the batteries from a spiritual standpoint, it is not helpful in turning the perspectives of the religion toward guidance on business events that are religiously or spiritually problematic.

The failure to acknowledge business roles as a realm of the sacred self has been keenly felt by businesspeople. In the absence of a better response from their church, they turn to secular spirituality programs and prosperity gospels. In these programs, both identities—Christian and businessperson—are posed as sources of sacred meaning. Many interviewees, however, were not optimistic about the Church's ability to help them recover the sacred self, primarily because they felt despised by their clergy, and possibly by lessons in the Bible. Many felt put down or used by their clergy. Said one, "I don't object to the church claiming its authority to tell me to be a donor; I object to them seeing me only as a donor."

To Be Like Jesus

These questions of role run deep, for their effect not only on the church community but on how people model their professional lives in imitation of sacred figures such as Jesus or the Buddha. The models often emphasize difference rather similarity within the community. As one religious group's paraphrase of "Ecclesia in America" (the Pope's proposal for a new way of life) put it, "We should live the life Jesus lived, a life of simplicity, poverty, responsibility for others, and renunciation of our own advantage." A Roman Catholic business interviewee responded to the same document by saying, "We should be good managers, stewards, disciplined but caring, and able to secure material welfare for all." A more liberal noncongregant Catholic manager responded, "We should be good persons. You need to feel you are making a personal contribution."

When we look for business role models within the Bible, it is easy to find adversarial examples where Jesus stands with the poor and asserts a system of justice unlike any economy on earth. It is easy to find atomization, wherein one is not against wealth accumulation per se any more than is Jesus, but the *activity* of wealth accumulation is firmly pushed off the religious map. The integrator model is far less observable except in fragments (Jesus standing with the tax collector and also with the poor). It is a role that African American pastors tend to assume more easily. As one remarked in reaction to this study, "What's wrong with wanting to help your congregation improve their income?"

A number of businesspeople saw in the sacred figures of the Bible good models of business leadership. One banker noted that the God of the Old Testament, who ordered society and provision of sustenance, shelter, and justice, was really "a banker." This symbolic assignment of a business role to God or Jesus enabled the personal integration process for a number of people, especially within evangelical circles (witness the popularity of such books as *Jesus CEO*). To clergy who have modeled their own professional role on the person of Jesus, such an association can suggest grotesque distortion for business purposes. But when was the claim to be modeling a worldly activity on Jesus never grounds for a turf battle in the church?

In general, the church's engagement in activist economics was the most contentious role in the eyes of the business interviewees. They criticized the church for protectionist or socialist tendencies in its alliance with unions, its defense of protectionist welfare policy, the liberal democratic social agenda, and market protection for developing nations. Ironically, clergy also criticized business for protectionist tendencies, citing an anonymous system of protectionism with the institutions controlling the movement of capital (banks, governments, and foundations). An example of these charges could be found, for example, in a *New York Times* article on new labor-clergy coalitions that have sprouted along the rust belt. Said Bishop Howard Hubbard of Albany, cochairman of the New York coalition: "We fear for the future of our society where a very wealthy elite benefits from government policies while the endangered middle class experience falling wages and increased economic uncertainty."[9]

Business executives who were as disturbed as Bishop Hubbard over proposed tax cuts were nonetheless furious over the alliance between labor and clergy. They expressed their thoughts in terms of role, thereby making the chief topic a question of proper role rather than critiquing their position on wages or health care. Taking sides formed the grounds for their discontent. They also argued that clergy do not understand how a union can hurt a corporation's—and the nation's—competitiveness, and that they often do not study the complexities of a dispute.[10]

"None of the clergy who signed on bothered to contact us," the president of a New Jersey dairy that was being boycotted said.

"Clearly they were manipulated. I lose a certain amount of respect for clergy who represent themselves as interested in justice but deny someone justice by not hearing both sides before making up their minds."[11] Once again, the larger principles on which one might hope for a common standard were fragmented into factional thinking and stereotypes. This stark equation of clergy's support *for* labor with a stand *against* management severely constricts the vision of role that clergy might play in their relationship with business as a whole. By contrast, there should be models for strong mediating figures who deeply influence both labor and management sectors, figures such as the eloquent John Ryan, who wrote passionately about labor during the Depression, or the great Bishop Henry Codman Potter, counselor to both Samuel Gompers and J. P. Morgan.

Get Off My Turf

Factions are a reflection of dispute over turf. In our study of attitudes toward the proper religious role of clergy and business laity, a number of turf problems contributed to the distancing and lack of ground for common dialogue. The businesspeople tended to rest these judgments on the perceived expertise—or inexpertise—of the clergy. The clergy tended to rest them on the perceived religious-oriented *motive*, or lack of it. Thus some businesspeople feared business would become the territory of the poor if the clergy were to be let loose on business issues. This was an interesting extension of the traditional positioning of the church to carry the responsibility to be "Christ's body, with the poor." Being with the poor meant not understanding how to create wealth, therefore disqualifying the clergy to speak out on economic or business factors in respect to the poor. Comfort, healing, soup kitchens—these were the areas of proper role.

Naturally, their conflicting views on the proper role of each group to hold authority over economic decision making led both business laity and church officials to seriously question the others' authority on practical religion. Clergy disabused businesspeople of having become allured by wealth to the point of religious insensitivity. They saw their own more modest lifestyles as evidence of a detached and fair perspective. Businesspeople saw it as one that carried many subjective blinders, envy and inexperience in the ways of power being the two most frequently cited.

What was a plus to the clergy ("Yes, I am different, I don't need big cars and large bank accounts!") became a liability in practice. When the church became involved in money questions, the clergy were depicted as vulnerable, even less well prepared to resist the temptations of greed, fear, and possessiveness. The many in-house fights over financial issues inside the church as well as highly publicized scams conducted in the name of religion only reinforced this view; the clergy demonstrated no special authority here. Others questioned the clergy's authority to give guidance on religion and business when they looked at the human relations practices of the church. As one person put it, "I think it is very important to ensure that my company dignifies every employee and recognizes the preciousness of every individual in the organization. I am frequently dismayed to see our church treating its employees worse than anyone."

The epigraph that opened this chapter was voiced by a vice president of public affairs who was actively addressing a number of difficult employment issues concerning the company's manufacturing facilities overseas. In exclaiming "Look at how they run their own shop!" she was citing the lack of women and minorities in positions of ecclesiastical authority as an example.

Many clergy agreed with these assessments, worrying aloud at their own failure to channel their faith into engagement with the institutional aspects of the church. They preferred to back off from uncomfortable incidents such as nonperforming employees, workplace abusiveness, and territoriality. They shrank from these roles. Clergy cited temperamental fear of conflict as a major reason for their disengagement, as well as belief that these things were simply not as important in the larger picture of their concerns. All of the employee problems are familiar to business managers, too, and there are many who would rather avoid them and look the other way. Yet role expectation prevented the clergy from turning these commonalities of the heart into discussion points about "faith on Monday."

More divisive assessments about overstepping turf were also in great evidence, pointing clearly to a mental and physical separation of the realms among both business and clergy. From a deacon at a Presbyterian church, who is a vice president at his firm:

> [The clergy] are so arrogant about business. They fix on a single issue and decide we [in business] are Satan in disguise. . . . They issue these economic directives as if they were commandments from God. "Get out of this business, stop doing that." They take no responsibility for the jobs that would be lost. . . . And yet they can't run their own parish budget. I really think some of the worst-treated employees in the world work for the churches. . . . Our pastor can't stand to be questioned, on anything. He thinks he's king. We have to tread very lightly here when we think he's making the wrong decision. Even when it's about the finances, which I think I and the other elders understand more than he does.

Reports a Presbyterian pastor from another church:

> [The leading businesspeople in my church] are always interfering. They want to treat everything the way they would in their business, and they don't understand that we are not about making a profit. That's all they care about, I'm afraid. Meanwhile, there are thousands of people who are really poor in this country. I really hate our discussions about the church budget. You get these people who are used to being kowtowed to all day. They always have to run everything. So they decide what they

think is right for the church and then just expect it to happen. They don't realize they are asking me to perform miracles. If they'd give away more of their money, *that* would be the best contribution they could make. But they don't seem to consider *that*.

The real surprise was how little each profession seemed to recognize of itself in its own portrayal of the other. Trusting their own abilities, they failed to trust the basic competence or motives of the other.

It would be reasonable to attribute part of this attitude to the relatively powerful professional authority of both groups of interviewees; top executives and clergy made up the majority of our interviewees. These people are habitually required to trust their own judgment, however much input they seek from other sources. A deep notion of needing to be an expert is ingrained in their self-understanding of responsibility. As a Kellogg Leadership Studies publication notes: "This [attitude] poses a profound conundrum for leadership today. The culture has trained us not to like ourselves or each other very much as beginners."[12]

The Professional Need for Authority

Both professional cultures reinforce this attitude in their power structures. Until recently, business has had a thoroughly hierarchical structure, only partially dismantled, as have most churches regarding the pastor's position. The clergy's sacredly endowed authority and self-reliance is heavily reinforced by a day-to-day culture in which the pastor or priest is often king of the institution. Staff may be selected more for their obedience and servantlike attitude toward the pastor than for their effectiveness at getting a job done.

The occasions on which this authority is questioned are likely to be emotionally charged, highly divisive, make-or-break situations, where the stakes are so high that people feel forced to question the pastor's position at the church—or so trivial and personalized (such as one man's absolute insistence on a lime-green banner for the pulpit) that they are easily overridden and mentally dismissed. Deaconate or other formal structures to which the clergy are ultimately answerable can in many cases only exacerbate the lone-ranger role of the pastor's authority. Some advisory or higher review processes rubber-stamp the pastor's decisions and kick in only when there is serious, job-threatening conflict. At that point, they are seen as being over and against the pastor.

The businessperson, whether CEO or middle manager, must also exert substantial authority if he or she is to gather resources, gain cooperation, and influence the choices of the firm. In many corporate cultures, the higher up the executive, the less his or her day-to-day decisions are openly questioned. The decisions that determine such events as layoffs or projected financial targets are still concentrated in a small, centralized group at the top. Gargantuan corporate work forces spread around the globe can further contribute to this isolation of top management. Many pastors find themselves working most closely with this type of authoritative senior executive, thus reinforcing the clergy's general view about the "arrogance" of businesspeople in general.

Several self-defining assumptions about authority are in fact shared. Both groups tend to see themselves as expert, benign, hardworking, concerned for the welfare of others, and somewhat at the mercy of outside forces over which they have little control. For the businessperson, these chaotic forces include the economy, change of ownership, competitive products, the vagaries of social dynamics in the workforce, and uncertain research and development outcomes. Expertise lies in anticipating these threats, making hard choices with decisiveness, providing economically viable solutions, sensing market needs, gaining cooperation, securing the admiration and rewards of other people, and getting things done.

For the clergy, chaotic forces are concentrated in the ongoing personal crises of church members (illness, death, divorce) to which they must attend; a largely volunteer workforce (at least some of whom have no incentives to do anything other than what they want to do and in their own time frame); and an expectation from the congregation to be all good things to all people, despite sometimes severe constraints of financial resources and time. Expertise is in being able to understand the disadvantaged person's point of view, provide comfort, gain recognition for public speaking, and harmonize the congregation. Getting things done may or may not be on this list.

The sources of the groups' authority obviously differ. The businessperson acquires authority largely from past success (in education and later on the job) and present affiliation with power. The pastor acquires authority from more diverse sources: on the one hand from the congregation; but also from the hierarchical, bureaucratic systems of the academy and their denominational authorities. Ultimately these institutions claim authority from God.

God and tangible success are two formidable endorsements in which one could rightly seat confidence. The problem comes with crossover. When religion and business are juxtaposed, they find each group's confidence in its own authority is not shared by the other. There usually ensues a battle for dominance. Barked one business executive: "I'd be crazy to go to my pastor if I had a business problem. He wouldn't understand it. I want him to support me and my faith so *I* can solve things."

This self-reliance and expertise is, after all, what is expected of him. Ironically, that expectation also seemed to apply to the businessperson's persona within the congregation, even if it drew envy or censure. A number of businesspeople mentioned that their congregation expected them to appear successful and well-adjusted at all times. When soul-wracking problems hit, they were unable to speak about them with anyone in their church. One person hid his own layoff from his church for more than six months, ashamed to appear to be a failure. Another shared his negative feelings about an unfair competitor with members of his adult Bible class, which then chastised him for not being sufficiently loving.

In these instances, one sees how the happiness principle of pastoral life (mentioned in Chapter Five) can actually cut off a situation where there would be great potential to explore the religious meaning of business life. Whereas the experience of failure can weaken some of the barriers by provoking new openness to self-reflection, other social expectations in the congregation construct a strong wave of resistance. By contrast, sociologist Nancy Ammerman has studied churches that squarely faced the financial difficulties of their congregants during a downturn of the local economy. Their sharing of the pain and their strategies for recovery led to the strengthening and revitalization of the whole church community. In these situations, however, the source of the problem was less personalized and the pain shared by more than one member of the congregation. Moreover, the church approached the subject of work from its traditional role as comforter of the suffering, only afterwards engaging in any celebration of for-profit employment as congregants reentered the workforce.[13]

Ammerman's congregation suggests that the entry point for the church's supportive engagement with business issues can make or reverse the distanced relationship. Some clergy we spoke to admitted that they felt very "shy" about discussing congregants' professional lives. They never asked how business was going for fear of embarrassing someone or revealing their own ignorance about issues that might be generally known. To the business congregant, however, this failure to ask only confirmed the impression that their identity as businesspeople counted for nothing with the church, as if it had no religious meaning or potential.

Expertise in the Trenches

The clergy's psychological failure to engage in the religious dimensions of the managerial role has real consequences in terms of managing the church itself. Remarked one Congregational minister: "How can we claim to be equipped to address business questions? If you look at the way churches are managed, it is not clear that we have any insights at all into how to integrate Christianity into organizational life. Take sexual harassment. It's an enormous problem in the church, and yet we are only beginning to address it, long after business created numerous programs. And we're only addressing it now because the insurance companies are forcing us."

A number of business interviewees cited poor ability to manage the church as an indication of a deeper turf issue: clergy have no business commenting on business. It's not their role. They have no business commenting on society or sex either, given their inability to clean house. The insistence on a perfect scorecard was directly contradictory to their own complaint that the church unfairly held business responsible for every problem in society.

Many other interviewees—clergy and managers alike—cited poor management of the church as the key arena for exploration of religion and business. Historic examples of institutional corruption in the church discourage businesspeople from accepting it as an authority on business in general. Incidents of religious financial wrongdoing are often well publicized and feed the general fear that when business and the Church meet, only bad things follow.

The media is quick to exploit and reinforce the public's emotional shock and disgust when the church is found to harm people *and* be making money; as with the church's stereotypes of business, the media has shaped the businessperson's stereotypes of the church. As one interviewee commented in connection with church corruption: "I don't think there's anything more sinful than someone stealing in the name of religion. And unfortunately, when churches get involved in business, they have the worst ethics on the block."

The contemplation of this juxtaposition is irresistible to the media. A profit motive makes things even sexier. It seems to help the public interpret incidents of exploitation or abuse in the name of religion, even when love of money is clearly not the most significant problem being reported. When, for example, the twenty-one women and men of the Heaven's Gate cult committed mass suicide, it was a key point that they had been engaged in running a for-profit Web site to fund their preparations to leave the world. The *Boston Globe* sidebar story to the suicide incident carried the headline, "Web Site Is a Mixture of Business and Religion."

It only takes a few well-publicized scandals, however grossly exaggerated, to confirm the general fear that the church can't handle money and power. The period from 1985 to 1995 saw a particularly salacious number of church scams: Jim and Tammy Bakker, Jerry Falwell, the New Era Fund, Jim Lyons. In each case, believers in a religious figure were bilked of millions while the culprits touted grandiose schemes for economic growth and redistribution. In several of these scandals, the key religious figures also engaged in sordid sexual affairs with close advisers or members of their congregation.

Nearly as significant as the fact of wrongdoing is the effect of failing to acknowledge it. Faint echoes of fifteenth-century exploitation in connection with the sale of indulgences seem to be fresh today. A particular concern today has been sponsorship of bingo games in churches. Such practices were thrown into sharp relief in several cities where casino gambling was being proposed by the government—but opposed by the church. Clergy who opposed the casinos were quickly forced to confront their own church's bingo games and raffles. Some of these efforts were paying prizes of up to $500 to participants, and at several Catholic schools revenues from bingo accounted for up to 40 percent of the tuition subsidy. When some church officials were quick to explain that gaming, like alcohol, was a complex issue, the conflict of interest questions were inescapable.

The laity form their attitude about the church's authority on religion and business from such incidents and expect the church to care about these failures. Any suspicion of cover-up can undercut the authority of important ecclesiastical discussions that would involve delivering judgments about management. Sexual abuse by clergy is perhaps the most sensitive topic and was seen as relevant to establishing in people's minds whether the church truly had the authority to offer guidance on the human dimensions of business. Gender and racial discrimination in the church, especially in its assignment of formal power, were also indicators of regressive behavior and a poor second to the admittedly imperfect track record of business in ending discrimination.[14]

Take, for example, a recent, highly sensitive treatment of the sacred potential of work by Stefan Cardinal Wyszynski. Echoing the rich Catholic tradition of writers who have sought to capture the dignifying aspects of work, Wyszynski writes of the permeation of work with religious meaning and obligation. He has many insights into the relevance of prayer, the meaning of little tasks, the possibility of a divine plan within the organization of work.[15] One group of Catholic interviewees who had read the book found it "interesting" but were essentially deaf to its wisdom because of another overriding concern: Why had the Cardinal not addressed the work of mothers? Weren't many of his views reflective of an antifeminist viewpoint that substantively shaped the institutional hierarchy of the Catholic Church around discriminatory ideals? In short, problematic values of discrimination and discriminatory hierarchies, accompanied by an age-old gender bias on roles of submission, seemed to have led the church to condone oppressive labor practices in the past. These same events led these parishioners to question Wyszynski's authority to be a religious interpreter of work today. Thus a potential resource for dialogue and inquiry was lost.

Who Shall Guard the Guardians?

Interestingly, there may be a dynamic new force for encouraging greater church financial accountability from the market itself. Several organizations are developing Web sites that track the performance of nonprofits, including where they spend their money, to meet the information needs of potential contributors. The creation of a formal White House position on faith-based initiatives has only increased public interest in how the churches handle power and money.

Ironically, when the church does exercise financial rigor, someone in the parish always worries that the institution has lost its values. A member of the board of a seminary day school worried about "selling out" when the chance came up for the school to rent out its gymnasium to a movie company. Adding to the difficulty is a propensity to get into businesses that are particularly vulnerable to economic failure or exploitation of consumers: financial investment, real estate connected to neighborhood revitalization, and gambling, to name three familiar church economic activities. When one parish held a raffle for tickets to a popular sporting event, it became clear that the bidding could be increased substantially with only a little effort. The priest enthusiastically endorsed an auction. When the tickets went for several thousands of dollars each, some parishioners wondered whether the whole thing was coming dangerously close to a celebration of big money.

Clearly, the church is as vulnerable to the problems of money as any other organization. Some of the most discordant events reported in our congregation interviews were over allocation of church funds. One interviewee told a sad story of how a proposed housing renovation had divided the congregation. People disagreed on everything from whether the idea was appropriate for the church to whether the design actually contributed to the historic identity of the particular community. Others thought the contractor had been chosen without full disclosure and wondered aloud at the resulting poor management of the project. In the end the building was completed, but it was a continuing drain on the church's finances. Concluded the interviewee: "We proved that the church had no business trying to develop housing. We proved that it didn't know what it was doing and couldn't hope to make good decisions. What's more, when people questioned this, they alienated the pastor. How in the world could I or any other congregant have any confidence in this person's views of business after that experience?"

This endeavor at positive social action through economic activity became a key source of conflict in the congregation. Ironically, most of the issues of conflict represented the type of problem business managers face daily, but for all that, there appeared to be no particular sense of shared problems.

Pastors in turn expressed great resentment at not being respected for their moral discernment of economic issues. Some who were aware of complaints about their attitude on labor practices resented the lack of deference their parishioners showed, attributing the criticism to selfishness. When clergy were asked if they felt strongly qualified to weigh in on the church's financial decisions, answers varied. Those who felt unqualified often mentioned a parishioner who served this function, but they rarely spoke of this person as potentially being a source of religious discernment. It was not that they did not value the laity's donation of personal service; rather, they did not visualize that person's *role* as offering a particularly significant opportunity to acquire religious insight.

Those pastors who did take on financial matters sometimes betrayed astounding naïveté about the rules of the marketplace. The New Era Fund, in which many faith-based institutions were persuaded by misguided advisers to invest in a Ponzi scheme, was a classic example, as was the more recent episode involving Jim Lyons's alleged misuse of church funds. The problems cannot be totally avoided. Business, too, has its dismaying share of scandals. Religious institutions are inevitably involved in business. They run real estate, hire people, contribute to pension funds. Some are even involved in marketing.

Relatively few of these practices result in illegal activities, but many churches have clergy who are so uneasy about having to be concerned with managerial or even fundraising tasks that they tend to go to extremes. Either they feel a self-righteous indifference to these roles—despite continuing to act in such a capacity—or they take a heavily authoritarian stand, refusing to share decision-making power. Both attitudes can unintentionally lead to severe financial and management mistakes.

Sometimes the financial issues got more personal, helping to explain how the clergy's negative attitude about money can be exacerbated by congregational life. Some pastors felt entitled to a level of financial prosperity that went far beyond a modest lifestyle. Justifications were often quite imaginative. A priest who cultivated strong ties with top businesspeople and was often treated to expensive vacations and dinners shrugged off these expenditures as inconsequential. He felt that they did not affect his priorities; besides, he did not personally own anything of worth. A member of his parish, however, felt that he was favoring the richest people in the church. So too, another congregant expressed dismay at her church's loan to a pastor for a new home. The price would put the pastor in a leveraged position no bank would have backed.

Several clergy reported great discomfort in discussing compensation. Others tried to put the question in perspective by comparing their salaries and perks to the average lifestyle of their congregants. As one head of an upper-middle-class parish reflected, "I have to be taken seriously if I am to do the Lord's work. Living at an unremarkable standard in this community is the only way I'm going to be respected." A number of parishioners agreed but were dismayed when the same pastor chastised wealthy lifestyles as evidence of not caring about the poor.

Some managers expressed hope that they could turn clergy and employees of faith-based nonprofits into good managers, and they have contributed substantially to this end through a number of programs. They see this as their mission work: to increase the capacity of the church to serve by using sound business practices. Clergy offered hope that they could exploit the management potential of their congregation more fully so as to free themselves from these issues (also to increase their capacity to serve), while retaining authority over distribution of church finances. No surprise then, that stories of disillusionment and conflict accompanied many of the examples of partnered decision making on financial issues and the mission work of the church.

As already noted, these conflicts were "explained" by examples of church corruption on occasions when the separation of the realms had broken down. On this view, the closer the church approached business, the more likely it was to cave in to corrupt values. One could argue that the problem lies in a curiously second-rate or paternalistic quality to many familiar types of church business, a tendency to go for cartels, unorthodox financing practices, and ineffective sales practices. When asked about this, a number of clergy objected to this assessment. They felt that many of these practices were not a significant problem or indicative of an ethical problem because the good religious cause, not the business principle, predominated. Who cared if the candy sold for the youth group trip was stale and the supplier was making a 300 percent profit in comparison to other competitors?

These examples suggested many a lost opportunity to engage in deeper understanding and education on religious ideas of good business practice. Would, for example, the youth group ever use the occasion of fundraising as a point of departure for exploring what makes a good business versus a bad one? Said one pastor, "Well that's very interesting. We've never thought about that. I'm not sure it's something we should take up. The candy sales are about a Christian Fellowship mission, not about business."

Although several clergy attributed active refusal of their colleagues to deal with moral questions of money to negative warnings in the New Testament, another was more self-critical: "We're afraid to be a voice in this area because we live off of these profits." Similar reluctance to engage in searching dialogue about church business practices accompanied use of pension funds, denominational decisions to downsize, and board decisions on faith-based operations such as hospitals.

In the end, however, it is fear of cooption rather than outright hypocrisy or corruption that seemed to drive much of the clergy's reluctance to extend their proper concern to business questions. Charges of clergy cooption are easily provoked, especially for a pastor in an upper-class congregation. Frustration over some richer congregations' self-imposed distance from problems of poverty can create another kind of cooption, the sell-out. Remarked one pastor who had been asked to leave an upscale suburban church: "They wanted your typical suburban pastor—the kind who will never make them uncomfortable. I'm afraid I haven't sold out yet."

As the stereotypes continue to be launched from each hilltop, the current search for integration of faith at work within the community of the church seems doomed to frustration; it is a battle between the self-righteous and the self-absorbed. The inward curve on thinking that Augustine attributed to denial of God can be found in many of these remarks, as each cuts off the possibility of a relational response to questions of faith and economic work. Simplistic caricatures abound, uncovering a mixture of contempt and desertion that is frequently at odds with how clergy and congregants relate on other occasions where business is not an issue.

The potential for money to coopt Christian religious experience is real, but it is also a stock charge launched by ecclesiastics seeking rhetorical cannon fodder. Ridicule of populist church practices associated with the money makers, as when pastors engage in Rotarian-type blessings of business prosperity, reinforce the association between intellectual elitism and religion (as opposed to the vulgar crowd). What might begin as a genuine effort of supportiveness and trust building evolves into a charge of being shallow or turning religion into a tool of business. Small wonder that a scrupulous pastor, turned off by business styles and concerned about cooption, might just conclude it is better to keep a distance.

Reflection

- Imagine your ideal person for the task of providing wisdom and judgment on business decisions. What characteristics does this person possess?

- Where have you seen these characteristics in people in business and the church?

- Where do you see them in yourself?

- What stereotypes about turf do you think you have? If you are a businessperson, what stereotypes do you think people you know in the religious community have about you or your business? If you are a pastor, reverse this question.

Action

- Ask for help from a church professional or a businessperson (whichever is *not* your professional group) to find or create a context in which you are asked to listen to people with different levels of authority discussing a common concern of business behavior.

- Gather this group. Together, pick a common concern. Then decide how each person will help prepare the group to discuss the concern from religious and business standpoints.

- After you meet and discuss your findings (it may take several gatherings), revisit the special talents and role each person brought to the group's understanding.

7

Different Voices

The Problem of
Language and Pluralism

*I ran a gas station for many years, and you know,
you see everything. You have to learn to deal with
people and with money. You hire some nice kid and
show him something about repair work and keeping a
job, and he gets a chance to make something of
himself. Suddenly he wants to go to vocational school.
So you help him.*

*When you're working on someone's car you get to
see a lot about people's lives, what's going on out
there. I always felt close to my customers, close to my
employees.*

*Now I'm going to become a pastor. I realize
I've always been ministering to people, but now I
want to change how the church looks at
businesspeople. I think I can do it. I know how to
speak their language.*

—Methodist divinity student, former garage owner

L anguage is both a means and a metaphor for communication. Knowing how to speak someone's language is an essential technique in, and symbol of, the effort to create mutual meaning. Religious authorities and businesspeople literally assign differing words to what business means from a faith standpoint, and they also fail to create meaning in relationship. Like two diners from different countries, even when ecclesiastic and businessperson sit at the same table they cannot critique the meal together. These dynamics pose communication problems across their institutions and create enormous problems *inside* each one—especially when businesspeople's spiritual interest threatens to spill over into religious language at work. Ultimately, these problems are expressed in the general difficulties of negotiating the expression of religion in American public life.

Language Gaps

From Old Testament times onward, religion has employed such economic terms as *debt, owing, stewardship, covenant,* and *trespass* to convey sacred relationships with God. Conversely, business adopted many types of religious symbols for economics, from the words and pictures on the dollar bill ("In God We Trust") to "redemption" of bonds.

Such language crossovers, however, have lost much of their original religious or economic syncretism. A new syntax, created by the sharper separation of institutional realms in modern society, has resulted in a double set of associations for these words. Church and business name things differently, but they also place differing meanings on names. *Redemption,* for example, carries either religious or legal meaning but rarely both at the same time.

Nothing characterizes an estranged relationship more clearly than when two people use the same word for different things. The betrayed sweetheart accuses the promiscuous date of "not knowing the meaning of the word *love*." No surprise then, that when clergy and businesspeople appropriate the same religious vocabulary for different understandings it exacerbates their distanced relationship. Chief among the examples we observed were *caring* and *soul*, or *spirit*. *Caring* is the common code word for justifying the additive or subtractive approaches of the yea-sayers and naysayers. Clergy and businesspeople expect *spirit* and *soul* to have quite different manifestations on earth. Nonetheless, business and church regard some forms of religious expression as more proprietary than others. The vocabulary of the liturgy, for example, is likely to be protected for use in a sacred domain to preserve its ability to represent human understandings of the transcendent. By restricting its use to certain "hieratic" or sacred social contexts, the church controls sacred language in a way that reinforces its authority over the sacred domain. It also preserves this language from contamination or trivialization. Such efforts have always been criticized by lay-oriented religions such as evangelicalism or the Quakers. They emphasize plain speaking as the voice of religious authenticity, minimizing the linguistic distinction between faith and everyday concerns and thus reducing one obstacle to integration.

Business also fears contamination from inappropriate uses of religious language, particularly from the capacity of religious language to evoke association with an espoused form of religion. It, too, tries to control these usages. As our coping strategies showed, when businesspeople stress that religion has no place at work, they are often referring to religious *affiliation* as a decision-making power at work, not a belief that personal religious faith has no rightful influence at all. Invoking the J word at work is easily misunderstood as proselytizing, which goes against the norm in nonsectarian corporate cultures even when they support the idea of spirituality.

Recognizing the power and associations attached to religious language helps makes space for the forms that are most likely to have some permissibility in a business discussion. Here the secular spirituality programs provide an example in their construction of generalized spiritual terms.

Miscommunication seems on the surface to be mostly about vocabulary. Clergy interprets the dense academese of theology as a sign of intellectual (analytic) superiority, while business calls it useless theo-babble. Their contrasting analytical styles, echoed in their language, assigns fundamentally different religious perspectives on the same events.

The Language of the Church

For the church, events tend to acquire a vocabulary that is otherworldly and sometimes nostalgic, full of biblical similes and arcane phrases such as "joy in the salvific" or "working out the plan for the coming of the Kingdom." Descriptive mental processes pass through the filter of liturgical and biblical words or an academic jargon of specialized terms. Thus problems of greed are problems with *mammon*, a term that signifies roughly a process of becoming overly preoccupied with wealth to the point of idolatry. Such compression of complex human experience into symbol is the strength of religious language and tradition. But it carries association with ecclesiastic institutions as well, and it may sound scolding or superstitious to a businessperson.

Theological notions take the vocabulary even further from the vernacular with which businesspeople describe experience. Religion academics speak of "indwelling," "Polanyian exploration," and a world of "moral normlessness." Steeped in complex abstractions, they tend to explore the effects of the religious worldview on history rather than on the individual.

Here, for example, is a word-for-word quote from a theologian's reflection on the social thought of Richard Niebuhr, with the author's own punctuation. The author, who published this in a prestigious journal, was asking how a human, who is fallen, can "know" values and develop an ethic that is truly reflective of God:

> Unlike the Thomists, however, who define values (*verum, bonum, pulchrum*) as among the "transcendental" or universal attributes of being *as such* (no matter where or when), for Niebuhr value is an attribute of being-in-relation-to-being. In the midst of plural, interacting, becoming existences, "value is present wherever being confronts being." It is "a function of being in relation to being." Values may always be defined as "the *good-forness* [sic] of being, for being in their reciprocity, their animosity, and their mutual aid," or as "what is fitting, useful, complementary to an existence." Apart from existences in interrelationship there are no values.

Tightly argued theories populate the normal linguistic domain of the ecclesiastical elite, but they are so embedded in the abstract that they have no point of context with concrete events or personalized expressive forms of religious experience—the stuff of the current spirituality interest. People who actually follow these arguments are themselves so embedded in this language they frequently have no desire to see it destroyed by practical translation and application.

The reward system of the academy and the ministry tends to reinforce this attitude. There is, after all, implied status to this language within the hierarchy of the church and its accrediting academic institutions. It is judged "superior" to plain preacher talk (in all but the evangelical denominations). Notwithstanding a few notable exceptions (such as Harvard's University chaplain, the Rev. Peter Gomes), sermons in congregational life are rarely regarded as holding intellectual authority today.[1] In contrast to the days when academics such as Henri Nouwen, Paul Tillich, or Reinhold Niebuhr were widely read and discussed by the public, the ability of those in the academy to acquire a popular audience has suffered a sharp decline. Up-and-comers are found, not surprisingly, in evangelical preaching on daily life, or in the chroniclers of religious practice such as Martin Marty and Harvey Cox, or those tracking religions outside the mainstream. Diana Eck's studies of Islam in the United States, for example, finds great response among lay audiences.

The culture of academic elitism may be one of the key barriers to the challenge of developing the church's ability to be a relevant force in the workplace. Theologians and future pastors who do not adapt to it are weeded out of the mainstream of the church's intellectual life.

No surprise then, that when clergy confront events and problems that are posed in language that is totally mundane, they have interpretive problems. This language does not evoke *their* language of faith and its application. They greet it with disdain. Fuller Seminary president Richard Mouw commented on this in his book *Consulting with the Faithful*. He persuasively argues that the church needs a new hermeneutics (interpretative language) that is a living reflection of the laity.

Certain linguistic patterns, generated by what we have called the critical idealism of the ecclesiastic worldview, reinforce the tone of disdain. Absolutes encourage a highly rhetorical, even polemical style. Economic dialectics assume grandiosity that is not accessible to interpretation on a human scale. An example is a commentary (to remain unidentified here) on a seminar specifically designed by one seminary to be of service to businesspeople. The group explored research development on two important questions: how the workplace shapes moral character and how people might bring their faith into alignment with their professional lives. We chose this passage, out of many similar examples, because it concluded that there was need for structured moral discourse to explore these questions: "[The seminar] taught us how far the language of economic materialism has eclipsed the language of the heart so that meaning, compassion, courage, and integrity are excluded from the common discussion and therefore from common view. Indeed, such matters are normally censored in the marketplace and are rarely included in the analysis of corporate policy, structure, and other strategic considerations."

The implication seems to be that religious language (should we agree on what it is) is the only language of the heart. This conclusion would be puzzling to businesspeople who spend millions on corporate communications specifically designed to capture and communicate the heart in their companies as well as its dedication to financial soundness.

Such patterns seemed to be learned early. Genuine need for moral critique is transformed into depiction of business as a relentlessly heartless and impersonal (read: unpeopled) place, while notions of justice or love are cast in dense abstraction or dramatic poeticism. Our review of seminary course material on business showed that when professors (rather than visiting businesspeople) taught business and religion courses, content and syllabus descriptions were heavily weighted toward economic theories on capitalism, pot shots at corporations, romanticized celebrations of church mission work, political activism, and organized labor. Business *experience*, presumably a fertile source for language of the heart, was far less in evidence.

The Language of Business

Businesspeople also have a language bias, tending toward the simple and pragmatic form of moral or religious expression.[2] They frequently speak in concrete terms, relating an action or personal sentiment to capture, rather than critique, a general principle. Good examples are investment dynamos John Marks Templeton (his *Worldwide Laws of Life*) and Max De Pree (whose leadership principles are summarized in material by the De Pree Leadership Center and in his books about his business experience as chairman and CEO of Herman Miller).

One business prayer group formed a general consensus that the people in the top tier of business are being paid an unholy amount of money. When one participant was asked if he drew on any biblical parallels for his assessment, he responded:

I'd say there's a lot of biblical supports of that kind of view. But I never looked at my religion for this question; that wasn't my process. My process was first to be both-ered by certain injustices and those two at the extreme bother me a lot. I don't see any good purposes served. I think it's just wrong to have people with the extremes of wealth [he cited the head of an investment bank who'd undergone a highly public divorce and subsequently scandalized his neighbors with his lavish expenses]. Whether this is an emotional reaction or an intellectual one, it comes out the same way. But I don't know where it comes from. Probably comes from my family.

This businessperson does not name the precise concepts from which his ethics originate, and it seems he doesn't care to know, so long as they seem to sustain his emotional moral resolve and that this resolve does not contradict his religious beliefs. He feels no need for a predetermined, carefully reasoned statement of norms to know the right rules for living. (This same attitude has colored many a man-ager's ho-hum reaction to a code of business ethics.) Businesspeople are skeptical that ethical choices are made by reasoning like a lawyer or a philosopher. In contrast to theological language, the vocabulary of business tends to encode religious meaning in nonexplicit moral vocabulary that emphasizes outcomes and enables relationships, rather than overt, dogmatic religious concepts. This comment is from the winner of a highly competitive business ethics award:

I was always meticulous in trying to save my customers money and in giving everyone a fair shake. So unlike others in my industry, I paid my vendors first and then my company, as the cash came in.

At one point a very good customer came to me and said, "You're not making enough money. I want to help you grow because you're good, and I don't want you to go out of business. Then I'd lose a good supplier. . . ." I wear a bracelet to remind me of these values. It says, "What Would Jesus Do?" That's all I need to keep me on the right path.

Academics talk of stakeholder responsibility. The businessperson describes being there for the customer, or being a good corporate citizen. As they talk past each other, they create negative assessments to explain their failure to be moved by the other's words. Thus communication that is an act of clarification for the religious community is deemed an act of fuzzy-mindedness to the businessperson. Placed in the crucible of pragmatism, it fails to offer ironclad guidance. Words per se symbolize the distance they feel— sermonizing in particular. Remarked one interviewee, "I can't stand all the hand-wringing that goes on in the church. Why don't they go out and generate what puts food on the table rather than crying over the plight of the poor?" Says another, "It is a wonder to me how people who claim to care so much [for the disadvantaged] actually do so little."

Behind these reactions is an extremely important debate over the relative strengths and weaknesses of deliberate moral reasoning in securing moral behavior. Seat-of-the-pants decision making based on good character and savvy about people may seem more reliable— or scarier, depending on your view. Rather than exploring these assumptions together, the communications bias of clergy and business prevents them from hearing what is valued in each approach to living up to and through one's religious views.

Preferred Religious Communication

Greenleaf's *Servant Leadership* (an extremely successful management book on servant attitudes and their application) has this to say about intellectual approaches in general:

Who is holding back more rapid movement to the better society that is reasonable and possible with available
resources? . . . The real enemy is fuzzy thinking on the
part of good, intelligent, vital people, and their failure to
lead and to follow servants as leaders. Too many settle
for being critics and experts. There is too much intellectual wheel spinning, too much retreating into "research," too little preparation for and an unwillingness
to undertake the hard and high risk task of building better institutions in an imperfect world, too little disposi-
tion to see "the problem" as residing *in here* and not "out
there" [italics in original].[3]

Businesspeople favor a personalized, experiential presentation
of religion over disciplined study of systemic cosmologies. They do
not look through the religious lens of ethical aspects of economic
theory; they are drawn by matters of the human psyche and the
spirit that defines greatness from the standpoint of faith.

Some theologians are keenly sensitized to the problems of religious language in the modern world. As Harvard Divinity School
theologian Gordon Kaufmann has pointed out, theological language
and even abstracted terms of religious morality do not capture the
sensory or linguistic richness of actual religious experience, which
heightens the worshiper's sense of being alive, of being alert to the
world's immediacy, even as one can rise to another perspective on
time and space. With theology's explicitness comes loss of the sen-
sual, the implicit, the layers underneath the surface. In other words,
it represents the loss of mystery, which seems to be a necessary
ingredient of authentic religious experience.[4]

As Michael Novak commented, quoting the *Imitation of Christ*,
"I'd rather feel compunction than know a good definition of it."
In *Business as a Calling: Work and the Examined Life*, he percep-
tively notes that there is a similar divide between theoreticians

and practitioners even within business. Economists and managers often haunt separate corridors of power. He suggests that it is the practical focus that gives access to the spirit of capitalism. Novak claims that this is also where the religious experience is most accessible.[5]

The problem of developing a richer religious language for the faithful businessperson's use is compounded in that ecclesiastics derive many of their economic attitudes from economic and political theories that reinforce the polemical vocabulary and use of absolutes. David Korten (author of *When Corporations Rule the World*), for example, repeatedly undermines his perceptive analysis of globalism with statements that pit one absolute against another in regard to business activity: the rights of people are replaced by the rights of money; free market ideologues engage in "a sanctification of greed."[6] These categorical aggregates stand in sharp contrast to his many nuanced descriptions of psychology, of how the quest for money and material consumption is a function of a lack of spirituality and love, and of the downward spiral of alienation that results.

The business perspective assumes that multiple and conflicting duties must be sustained in theory, if not always in practice. It does not create a fixed hierarchy of property rights over human need in every situation, nor do those rights reflect only greed and alienation; property rights were developed and endorsed by the church in part because fullness of life is difficult to attain if the rules of sharing are not completely clear, ordered, and enforced. The New Hampshire McDonald's owner who initiated a fundraiser for the local family whose barn burned down neither gave up the "rights of money" nor abandoned a spirit of community that is intimately tied in to his sense of doing business the right way.

Abandoning the abstractions can lower the polemics, but it also substantially reduces ecclesiastics' comfort level. It appears to lower intellectual content and does not allow idealism to maintain a comfortable distance from less-perfect contexts. The more that real events are held up only to an assumed ideal, the more coopted the clergy feel in acknowledging the ambiguity of everyday business pressures. If the polemics against business fail to match reality, the authority of the ecclesiastic is undermined, as is the source material on which it is based. As we saw, the businessperson concludes the church is perceptive in its own realm but unreliable on economics or economic institutions. If the conservative apologetics for capitalism are equally absolutist, they, too, fail to offer guidance or insight into the real problems of creating humane, responsive business decisions. What help are they for those whose religious heart says, "Make changes; leave the world and the system an even *better* place"?

Just as sermonizing and theory do not compute for the businessperson, ecclesiastics cannot hear the value of the businessperson's religious language. A number of interviewees strongly objected to the WWJD symbolism, feeling it had reduced Jesus to a corporate minion. When businesspeople explain faith explicitly, it frequently comes out sounding like a car advertisement, catchy and attractive with its contemporary flair. "My work is my worship," asserts the sincere executive. Instead of understanding, the phrase gives rise to ecclesiastic ridicule, politely disguised behind a façade of mild attention. Complained one businessperson, "We never seem to have a discussion with any teeth in it."

Behind the scenes, however, ecclesiastics were more open in their scorn of snake-oil self-help tracts and the new spirituality movement in general—forgetting, perhaps, that the great evangelist Dwight Moody began as a shoe salesman. So too, the marketing-savvy language of the megachurch invites extreme scorn from mainstream professionals, whether or not they have examined the actual congregational life of these new efforts. Given some of the language, their fears of cooption and marketing contamination are understandable. A blurb from the back cover of *The Corporate Mystic*, a best-selling new spirituality tract, is an example of this language, which not surprisingly, is taken from an advertisement: "In this spirited mandate for the future of business [the authors] have distilled the secrets of the hundred wisest businesspeople they know into nuggets of just-in-time wisdom you can put to work today."

Such presentations carry in the business community. A good example is the anecdote of the starfish, a tale that has been told by a number of business leaders and secular spirituality gurus, including Stephen Covey in his 1999 speech at Harvard Business School to a packed audience of MBAs: A man is walking down the beach and it is covered with starfish. They've been left behind by the tide. He sees a child ahead, picking up starfish, one by one, and throwing them back into the sea. He approaches the boy just as he throws another starfish. 'You know, there are thousands of starfish on this beach. What you're doing is not going to make a difference.' The boy looks up. 'It just made a difference to that starfish.'

The parable paints contrasting scales of justice: that of humans, and that of an order in which every living creature counts. It has obvious biblical parallels in Hebraic and Christian tradition, as with the Jewish maxim "You save one life, you save the world." Religious language, however, is implied; action vividly tells the simple, but profound message, and the listener fills in the rest. Some ecclesiastics described this type of story as feel-good religion, dismissing it as an inadequate response to the deep systemic injustices of a business system. In so doing, they failed to understand the businessperson's intense interest in creating a spiritual insight that changes how people inside companies actually treat each other or keep up their own sense of purpose when their energy to do the right thing flags.

The Hearing Gap

How does such a language gap create a hearing gap and provoke such hostility? Stereotyping, aggregate depiction, and conflict over turf and authority to control the critique are the obvious culprits, but an even deeper linguistic pattern drives these reactions. The two languages not only have their own vocabularies but also have differing conceptual syntax. Clergy and businesspeople each construct verbal connections as they assign religious meaning to the experiences of economic life.

These connections represent fundamental differences of direction and power that express their deeply divergent worldviews. Business-people tend to favor an additive approach, ecclesiastics a subtractive one. For example, when asked about solutions for economic injus-tice, the church frequently suggests giving away possessions and earn-ings, while businesspeople suggest creating more jobs. Both are contributions, but the directional emphasis differs. One is a path of redistribution (take away from one to give to another); the other is a path of creation. Both approaches are necessary conclusions about religiously motivated action, but each group tends to tilt heavily in one direction.

Their language and syntax support this approach. The ecclesi-astic tends to interpret along a path of self-denial (subtraction), the businessperson along a path of self-interest. Although both may be seeking the same ends—the common good, religiously under-stood, and personal spirituality—they base their speech on differ-ent models. The clergy's language is modeled on examples of sacrifice from Jesus and Mary. The businessperson's language is modeled on Enlightenment reasoning and utilitarian models going back to Adam Smith, who saw the vocabularies quite clearly: "It is not out of the benevolence of the butcher, brewer and baker that we expect our dinner, but from their regard to their own interest." Commented one business interviewee, "Look to the interests of all the parties, and you will find a solution. That is how to be a peacemaker."

Different Paths

The essential syntactical path each group takes in pursuit of height-ened integration of work and faith prevents communication and leads clergy and businessperson down different interpretive avenues. These examples of reflection on religious vocation are a good illus-tration of the directional approaches.

A Roman Catholic doctor trained in theological reflection writes, "Professional perplexity, like all perplexity, should be a call to come to him. . . . Devotion is giving up my right to myself, and the remainder of life will then be a manifestation of that surrender. Circumstances then lose their controlling influence, for Jesus is sufficient.[7] This reflection prefaced the doctor's decision to take action; he turned down a prestigious job offer, sacrificing a career boost.

Compare the words of this evangelical Protestant, the head of a major consumer foods firm, recalling a moment of reflection about his career during a long airplane flight: "I started to long for a vision of standing before God and having him say, 'Well done, thou good and faithful servant.' I realize my life doesn't deserve that vision, but I prayed a lot during that flight for the wisdom to know how to get to the vision and the discipline to do it. That's my vision; my objectives are to know and love God, honor and serve my wife, lead and encourage my kids, and use my specific talents to serve significantly." He concluded that most days he went home saying to himself, "I did none of the above; in fact I did just the opposite."[8] For all that, he has not given up the difficult commitment to take his religious and business responsibilities seriously.

The two groups' bias toward the additive or subtractive comes out most distinctly in interviewees' heated, almost gut resistance in encountering a religious interpretation that takes the opposite approach. As one theologian wrote: "Why is income generation so ambiguous? Why, if you tell me that you set up a sewing factory in Manila, can't I be wholeheartedly joyful and congratulatory? Because you may be defining work as a way to get money and get out of poverty rather than also as a way to serve others and express one's vocation."[9]

The emphasis on "wholeheartedly" is also telling, an example of the moral absolutism that colors the ecclesiastic framing of the issue and invites, as we argued earlier, a critical tone. Absolutist language, a common feature of utopian approaches, captures idealism but is less adapted to accommodating partial fulfillment of these ideals. The additive progress is threatening if one assumes it represents a devaluation of the ideal. Thus do the Cynics heatedly discount a businessperson's authentic sentiments of commonality in the face of business's flaws.[10]

Our use of terms drawn from human experience to approximate the meaning that is God limits our ability to express the ultimate. Thus every symbol and religious interpretation of God is also capable of being corrupted by its association with a human context. As Tillich commented, every myth is inevitably both transmitted and "attacked, criticized and transcended in each of the great religions of mankind."[11] Tillich was addressing the inevitability of change, but his comments could also be taken as a warning against supposing that our absolutist expressions should be above any accommodation of contaminating reappraisal of the mixed good and evil inherent in most human activities.

Businesspeople were similarly heated and ungenerous in their assessment of the subtractive language of the naysayers. Said one Episcopal executive, "There is always this assumption that business has to hurt. You're not truly acceptable to the church unless you can show yourself making sacrifices and suffering. It gets very perverted. And no one there seems to notice this." A Roman Catholic financial services executive told us: "If I help someone get on their feet and we both take pleasure in that, I think the church thinks I haven't really made a contribution. They won't even acknowledge that I might be a good person, because I made a profit somewhere. That's wrong. Everyone is better off in this situation than if I gave up all my money and joined the crowd of sufferers."

William James might have attributed these patterns to the respective optimistic and pessimistic psychological profiles he saw in some businesspeople and clergy. Though generalities are dangerous, there is clearly a rosy tone to one of the professional vocabularies and a gloomy tone to the other. Pursuing the psychological explanation further, we would suggest from our interviews that psychological discomfort indeed shapes these linguistic preferences.

Generally speaking, businesspeople are uncomfortable with a language that suggests weakness. If the church emphasizes suffering, poverty, and subtractive measures, it can trigger this discomfort. If hearing the religious message only summons up strategies for disempowering a business activity, the businessperson loses interest. Ecclesiastics, on the other hand, are uncomfortable with too close an alliance to worldly strength. Language emphasizing wealth creation, success, and partial solutions feels dangerously close to abandonment of their position "with" the poor and loss of spiritual sensitivity.

Language and Pluralism

A more obvious discomfort comes with introducing espoused language—pointedly religious speech—into business. Business today is composed of pluralism and diversity to a degree never before encountered. Religious language is a social minefield, posing a particular threat to values of inclusiveness and tolerance. It is naïve simply to say "Be open and tolerant." Religious language carries a strong power to establish distinctions; that is its point. Its otherness is more likely to interrupt ordinary experience and culture than to accommodate itself to the mundane. Use of religious language functions as a call to worship, formal or informal, or a call to membership.

If religious language carries an espoused message (such as commitment to Jesus or obedience to a specific religion's authority), businesspeople get nervous and claim their religion has no public relevance. Like John F. Kennedy, secular leaders go to great lengths to counter the assumption that their religion makes them vulnerable to intolerance, sectarianism, favoritism, or deference to the institution of the church on secular decisions.

Indeed, it is very difficult to separate the binding motive from religious language. When a coworker exclaims, "The Lord must be with us today!" it is not just a personal acknowledgment of thanks or spiritual awareness; it is a social act of invitation into the same belief system. Even a private statement ("This is what *I* believe, I just want you to know") requires heavy negotiating among people who respectfully disagree on their terms for the ultimate.

Caught between a problem of etiquette and a problem of personal authenticity, many businesspeople simply go silent. They privately vow never to combine religion and business, or they turn to personal spirituality as a way of putting social boundaries on their own espoused belief. Several studies in Canada and the United States have suggested that areas with greater religious pluralism have a lower rate of church membership and religious affiliation.[12] These correlations are tentative, but they suggest what we observed: that the more an individual personally identifies with membership in the pluralistic environment of the corporation, the more he or she is likely to prefer constraints on religious expression in the workplace.

As spirituality and religion in business gain momentum, new problems of religious etiquette and ethics in the workplace are arising. In his *New York Times* column "The Right Thing," Jeff Seglin reported on a court case in which a Buddhist worker who used epithets invoking God was chastised by his manager, who told him to conduct himself in accordance with the Ten Commandments. The ensuing religious battle was expensive, divisive, and distasteful.

Moderate believers, seeing such conflict, quickly decide privatization and disguise are the better part of wisdom. Such a reaction was most frequent among interviewees from mainline churches in the northeastern corridor, where pluralism is particularly evident. By contrast, a number of evangelicals from the south eastern corridor were adamant in their claims to be able to create strongly overt religious expression in their corporation without offending people. Assuming they were not all simply being insensitive, the big difference in the two experiences was the surrounding degree of pluralism in the setting.

When both lay and clergy seek to do something together on business, they need to be highly sensitive to how easily the espoused creeps into their language and its effects on a wider population.

As businesses based in the South and Midwest encounter a more pluralistic setting through national expansion and globalization, they will certainly encounter the same resistance and divisiveness over their religious expressions at work.[13] This warning is particularly relevant to evangelical language, with its strong emphasis on testimony. A language of exclusion arises as the community attempts to apply words to its own sense of fellowship. Asks one program that has successfully targeted top CEOs: "What exactly is corruption? Why is it wrong? Is there evidence of corruption mounting in our circles?" As the church employs its language of being chosen, of being righteous, such exclusionary terms become loaded with oppressive meaning. Gender-biased depiction of power, such as playful use of "brother" to indicate camaraderie with colleagues who share religious views in the male-dominated executive suite, only adds to the exclusionary tone. Personalizing religion into spirituality and other such coping strategies answers the need to keep business and religion (as institutions) separate, but it fails to confer the power that naming can do: the power to order chaotic impulses and assign weighted meanings of value. Religiously based naming is an important part of spiritual fullness. The problems of naming are inescapable in the new spirituality and business movement.

New Religious Language

How can we bridge these gaps of language and hearing? Businesspeople need new language for bringing the religious dimension into business, and they also need a religious articulation that they can respond to when they move out of their corporate setting into civic and church activity. Three strategies currently dominate this effort: boundary protection, open borders, and invention. We posit a fourth strategy, a new language for the future, which we term the evolutionist strategy.

The Boundary Protection Strategy

Boundary protection erects fences around using and practicing religious language in a business setting by establishing a mental or physical sanctuary. Some do this by taking time out for monastic practices at the end of the day. Others achieve it in church. Hieratic, archaic language, with its power to evoke mystery, is quite possible under these conditions, as evidenced in the popularity of Torah readings at lunchtime or Web broadcasts from monasteries. Vernacular rites in hieratic settings (the choice of the updated Episcopal and Catholic liturgies) are still in this category. Crossover, however, remains problematic. As one person put it, the hope here is that something will rub off on the businessperson's consciousness at work, but there is no way of expressing its effect.

Another form of boundary protection is the linguistic stealth strategy. Religious content is disguised in secularized form, thereby making the boundaries between sacred and secular disappear. Thus some programs "translate" biblical wisdom into a contemporary business presentation and disguise the source of their content. Said one successful publisher of religion books about its popular business book list: "They may be reading Isaiah and finding it common sense, but we leave out the references."

Humor is another common protective linguistic device. Religious language can be used humorously—as when evangelicals adopt a jokey patois and call each other brother or sister—thereby signaling that the conversants are not being seriously religious. Outsiders may find the humor merely corny. Some find it downright threatening. Missing the intention of fellowship, they may feel trapped by etiquette into being counted part of this espoused group.

This is a tricky strategy in terms of common understanding. Humor is crossover, dependent on a fixed context, which is then broken for the joke. The inappropriateness makes it funny, like a proper lady in a farce who belches at the table. To work, the joke has to preserve the boundaries it is going to break. A businessperson describes a killing on the market as "practically a religious experience." A pastor pronounces himself well aware of "the real bottom line." When Warren Buffett spoke to students at Harvard Business School, he peppered his speech with many crossovers from the past, including the Bible: "Aesop had the greatest investment advice of all time: a bird in hand is worth two in the bush. But he was a little sloppy. He should have said a bird in the hand is worth two in the bush over fifteen years at 3 percent interest. We have had a parallel of the Bible on Wall Street with a lean seventeen years followed by a fat seventeen years."[14]

Like all strategies containing a high level of ambiguity, this one is difficult to measure in terms of success. Whose boundaries are being preserved? What is the value of the crossover? Harvey Cox has suggested the pervasive crossover of religious metaphors in economic life has, if anything, turned the market into God. One could also argue that such secularization of religious language actually reinforces the separation of the realms by stealing away the platform for authentic religious sentiment when voiced in a business context.

The Open-Borders Strategy

To avoid problems of exclusiveness, other groups adopt an open-borders linguistic strategy. They emphasize religiously distinctive notions but invite all of them into the conversation, in a syncretistic orgy of multiple religious traditions and holistic scientific paradigms, centering on coping with modern life.

Trinity Wall Street's *Spirituality and Health* journal is one such example. A single issue may feature business guru Meg Wheatley, the Dalai Lama, an Episcopal monk, and a doctor of holistic medicine, each speaking from a specific religious standpoint. Such an approach achieves the contemporary, personalized slant that is driving the new spirituality interest, but with a sophisticated intellectualism in its descriptions of spirituality.

Whether these pluralistic presentations can capture the institutionalizing functions of religious community remains unclear, as does the degree of engagement of mainstream Christian clergy in this approach. In this, the open-border new spirituality faces the same dynamics of distancing from ecclesiastics as does the businessperson.

The Invention Strategy

Invention is another common linguistic strategy. Crossover to contemporary life invites contemporary symbols. Here is one example, from *Jesus CEO*: "Society is filled with turnaround specialists. Physicians reverse the progress of a disease. Artists take empty canvases and turn them into paint that takes your breath away. Entrepreneurs take an area of abandoned warehouses and adult bookstores and turn it into a thriving, bustling, revitalized downtown. A woman writes a book about slavery in the South, and *Uncle Tom's Cabin* fuels a war that changes America forever. In fact, if Jesus is our coach and Lord, it should be our specialty. He turned things around."[15]

Such crossovers work on vocabulary and syntax. They place an updated biblical vernacular in a business context. They tread a thin line, however, since they can evoke associations that give religious meaning to leadership roles but coopt religious meaning if too closely applied. The passage just quoted is sensitive to this problem: it does not intend for the reader to picture Jesus as Carl Ikahn. To avoid that much crossover, it takes care to emphasize the creative potential of business to change, just like art or the reforming power of abolitionist Harriet Beecher Stowe.

The ecumenical model suggests another kind of invention. There are attempts to create a language of universal religion that melds the common concerns of many religious traditions into a new hybrid language. From a linguistic standpoint, such efforts are naïve. A religious Esperanto is about as viable as the feeble inroads that Esperanto itself—now several decades old—has made on the culture. So too, secular spirituality's invented words capture a spirit of universalization, but most are so generalized that they are weak linguistic signals. *Inner power*, for example, is a concept so broad that it depends on a great deal of contextualizing and defining before its spiritual aspects become clear. Since these texts are not offered as catechism, few people have a language for sharing their usages. This increases the dynamic of self-discovery in discussion groups, but it is highly vulnerable to mutation. In moments of spiritual need, there is no power to evoke shared religious consciousness by calling up familiar religious terms.

The unfortunate effects of the current separation and incomplete crossovers can be seen in such obvious disconnection as the framing of racism, a problem of deep mutual concern. The church approaches race through the lens of poverty and macroeconomic injustice, while neglecting its own organizational reinforcement of segregation in practice. Business approaches race through demographics in the form of hiring and marketing practices, while neglecting the effects of income difference on the social structure of poverty. Each constructs a language reflecting these approaches, the former filled with polemical calls to note the injustice and the latter filled with concrete and optimistic indicators of progress. The problem needs both views, critiqued in concert and reflecting the actual power of those doing the critiquing to act on their convictions.

In this vein, Mark Chaves has suggested that the Church must propose clear distinctions in its own mind between the levels at which community problems are addressed, whether the congregational level or that of larger institutions such as social service agencies and government policies.[16] Our interviews confirmed this position. We found clergy totally unprepared in their training to cope, within a congregational setting, with the commitments formally posed by academic and denominational authorities concerning economic ideals.

Clearly, there must be movement within these separate languages rather than total collapse of the distinctive realms. As Martin Marty has observed, being religious does not mean that every minute of the day is spent in religious or spiritual contemplation. The same languages cannot be used to represent the different activities and states of mind without losing the original force of the vocabulary. Simplistic crossover or manufactured trendy terms run the risk of being hokey or artificial rather than offering authentic religious expression.

The Evolutionist Strategy

It is helpful to posit a fourth linguistic strategy for the terms in which business and church assess business in light of religious concerns. A common language is needed for such a critique, but it cannot be invented wholesale, manufactured out of general principles and vague terms. It must evolve. Hence the evolutionist strategy. Language evolves from social interaction. Expression of the role of religion in modern business life will only develop out of an ongoing interaction of the religious and business communities engaging in the same issues.

An evolutionist strategy recognizes this need for interaction and takes care to construct conditions of dialogue that avoid the predictable dead ends. For example, unremittingly additive or subtractive approaches are replaced by consideration of the key implications of both approaches through dialogue. This can only occur if the polemical, absolutist, or overly boosterized language is kept to a minimum. It is also important to recognize how deep differences of worldview may cause listeners to think they understand each other, when that is not the case. As we have seen, the businessperson's relation of a concrete, simple event represents a wealth of values. Many people, however, have no training in how to articulate these moral and spiritual processes, so they resort to platitudes or a highly instrumental depiction of spirituality as the best-case additive to business performance.[17]

A more responsive vocabulary must fulfill several conditions. It must represent both professions' key perspectives and provide critical and experiential syntax for religious expression at work. For both voices to be heard, they must be accurately represented, which suggests dialogue and mediation. Andy Smith, director of economic justice for the National Ministries of the American Baptist Churches USA, has come to a similar conclusion after many years as a board member of Interfaith Center for Corporate Responsibility (ICCR). He argues that many of the economic problems demanding a response from Christians better lend themselves to "dialogical" rather than polemical strategies.[18]

In his summary study of ICCR's twenty-five-year history, he discusses the institution's fear of corruption. ICCR faces a real conundrum: by investing and seeking profit, ICCR supports the very institutions whose policies it seeks to change. Since it places the churches' funds at risk, it must attempt to seek a good return. Some liberal churches with strong social action interests and some with conservative views on the social involvement of the churches have criticized ICCR for these reasons, feeling that participation within the accepted economic assumptions of society is seen as inherently tainted. But, argues Smith, this is a given tension of ICCR's mission, not a reason for giving up its activities.[19] There are many such situations where both business and the church share experience and wrestle with their sense of religious misgiving and opportunity. Groups such as ICCR can trump this debate by silencing it in a language of naysayer attack on capitalism, or fashion new opportunities to create a new business-church dialogue over their common concerns about the uncertainties attached to carrying out a prophetic vision in a large business organization.

Dialogue is one dimension, but conceptual crossover must also occur as a result of such dialogue. A good example is found in James Childs's book *Ethics in Business*,[20] which developed out of extensive seminars and lay work. Childs suggests that the Lutheran concept of "orders of creation" should be divided into two parts: orders of vocation, in which people carry out their call to service in the worldly arrangements of society; and orders of anticipation, in which striving toward the common good through business activity can be seen as an anticipation of God's promised future and a message of hope. This notion picks up both the critical idealism of the ecclesiastic view and the pragmatic optimism of the business view and gives them an ordering vocabulary. It is an example of how a mediating vocabulary for religious concerns about the economic aspect can replace the trigger words that silence dialogue. Concrete context is another essential element in the evolutionist strategy, and one of the best points of departure. The concrete and experiential mediate the divisiveness inherent in broadside opinions by refocusing attention to specifics and joint observation. Good case studies for such purposes, however, are hard to come by; we need much more development in this area, from experts who can listen attentively to both sides and assemble the facts. Many cases are far too simplistic and self-reported to serve as a substitute.

Time for probing, and safe space for questioning, as opposed to obedient deference to either the pastor or the top businessperson, are also essential. Here the new management techniques on participative decision making and team building would be very helpful.

There is much silencing to be overcome. Money and religion are *the* taboo topics of American social discourse; to make matters worse, church and business have developed startlingly different languages for considering these two realms and how they might relate. Both languages are only partially equipped for the task. Businesspeople's contentment with no ordered critical vocabulary for assessing business is a shaky scaffold on which to construct sustained commitment to moral leadership. Ecclesiastical idealism and negativity fail to acknowledge the need for constructive critique. Lack of common language means lack of sustaining community for completing these tasks.

The difficulties of the two languages will not be overcome automatically, but by being aware of the distancing paths on which these languages tend to take them, church and business laity can be prepared to resist these forces.

Reflection

- Review the observations on use of utopian abstraction, additive and subtractive languages, and trigger words such as *poverty.* Can it be that these patterns trigger some of your own assessments of the religious meaning and duties of work?

- How are your reactions to business and church colored by the language each uses?

- When do you think others use this language to assess your approach to business problems?

- What do you like and dislike about these conclusions?

Action

- Choose one article from a popular religious journal, and one from a popular business journal, preferably on a related topic.

- Note what does and does not resonate with you in each, and check the languages.

- Share your reactions with others in a study group.

PART III

Working Together

A New Integration Model

8

The New Terms of Religious Engagement

How Church and Business Can Work Together

*A religious community is where we practice our
"espoused" religion. In the workplace, we live out our
"sacred awareness."*

—*Protestant pastor*

As should now be abundantly clear, many businesspeople and clergy are caught in a circular trap. Businesspeople seek spirituality but feel queasy about religion as a spiritual resource for work. Religious professionals seek transformation of economics but shy away from anything that might endorse the market or turn attention away from the poor and suffering. The result: most contemplations of Christianity and business trigger a process of spiritual entropy. Those with strong religious beliefs cannot bring them to work. They are left feeling as if they live out a spiritual schizophrenia.

Some businesspeople seeking to bring Christianity into their work lives actually welcome the input of clergy, but they can't find it. Some lay groups, however, have begun to make inroads into the new territory of business-church integration. Two examples are

Manhattan's Trinity Church and a dedicated group of film professionals in Los Angeles.

Conversations at Trinity Church

The parish of Trinity Church in the City of New York sits at the intersection of two world-renowned streets: Broadway and Wall Street. Members of the financial community cannot walk down the most famous business street in the world without seeing the church's rose-colored sandstone walls and high gothic steeple;[1] in response the church offers morning and evening prayers every business day and a Holy Eucharist every noon. The church also sponsors several programs for the business community, including meditation and prayer groups. One program, a series of "conversations," was aimed at engaging business leaders in helping society rethink old problems in new ways.

The invitation-only Wall Street conversation that began in January 1997 was originally designed as four monthly meetings of three hours each. The participants, who were assigned background readings, included a dozen carefully chosen financial leaders and half a dozen Trinity Church staff. During the first two sessions, participants explained the major forces that had shaped their values, described how well their personal values fit in with today's society, and gave concrete examples of where they needed to make a major decision in the face of conflicting values.

The group went on to discuss such questions as how to be truly effective in diversifying workforces, how to deal with the values and business practices that are encountered globally, and how the Internet age is transforming business. Participants discovered that these issues challenged them to move beyond analytical and technical ways of knowing, but overall they were not finding this discussion very energizing. Over what became a six-month series, enthusiasm waned and several members left. As with many other lay discussions of faith and economics, this group felt the inquiry had not been contextualized well enough for them to walk away knowing how to use religious perspective concretely in their business roles.[2] At most, the shared concern of the group bolstered participants in their opinion that it was legitimate for Christian business leaders to take the imperfect moral outcomes of capitalism seriously.

The effort found new life when currency trader George Soros joined them to discuss his *Atlantic Monthly* cover story, "The Threat of Capitalism." Ironically, Soros's contention that religion had nothing to offer this debate breathed new life into the group's commitment. To the surprise of the organizers, the remaining participants chose to renew their commitment for five more months to examine the future of capitalism as their topic.

Soros modeled the group's task by demonstrating an entirely new way of looking at free markets. The future of free markets is utterly unpredictable, he explained, because a sensitive two-way communication process between the individual investor and the collective economic activity changes both the human actor and the marketplace. Soros calls this complicated interdependence between knower and known—between human actions and market responses— "reflexivity." If free markets are unpredictable, we humans are "fallible" in not being able to know our economic future. Economic thinking alone will not solve the terrible inequities and physical suffering in the world.

Soros's controversial point of view undercuts the classic theory of economic determinism, which has undergirded capitalist thinking for a long time. The Trinity group found that Soros's concrete challenge, couched in familiar economic paradigms, not only pushed them to critique the systemic problems of capitalism more rigorously but also motivated them to scrutinize possible moral and theological implications. Members established a new level of dialogue as they began to open up and share their ethical and spiritual values in a more vulnerable and concrete way.[3]

Perhaps the major lesson to be learned from the Trinity experience as it is unfolding today is that however strong the general interest, it is difficult to apply spirituality to contemporary business, both economically and theologically. The doorknob on religious-based insight into the current moral issues of capitalism was to understand that traditional analytical and technical tools have limitations that cannot be ignored. They leave out important human factors that influence market activity, as well as factors of inequality that are noted by secularists *and* spiritually driven people, from Soros to Robert Fogel (author of *The Fourth Great Awakening*). If free markets are more radically unpredictable than previously assumed, leaders of good conscience may be less in control of the human effects than they would like to assume.

With the help of social scientist Daniel Yankelovich, the Trinity group is still developing models that unite universalized, secular critiques of capitalism with theological concepts of human fallibility and the connectedness of all creation. But more difficult questions arise: How can business leaders apply these lessons in day-to-day decision making? How can church leaders incorporate these lessons into a Christian vision of a personally involved, relational, loving God? The task is still to bridge business and theological perspectives so that significant spiritual and ethical assistance can be offered to people in the workplace.

The most hopeful aspect of the Trinity Church efforts is their insistence on thoroughgoing dialogue and informed debate among peers with power to significantly influence the financial system. Notwithstanding the heritage of bifurcating human knowledge into subject versus object, heart versus mind, and qualitative understanding versus quantitative analysis, they are developing a new process for thinking, relating, and communicating. Empirical testing of the new ways of knowing will surely follow. The language and application of such a process are still evolving. It is encouraging that the collective input of business leaders and theologians seems to be staving off typical obstacles to substantive progress. Experiments like Trinity Church's seek to establish a new rabbinical model for shaping economic decisions in the global world of the twenty-first century.

The City of Angels Film Festival

The story of the De Pree Leadership Center (DLC) and the City of Angels Film Festival suggests that in seeking new formats for integration, it is important to consider strategic alliance and the possibility that a third-party organization may be necessary to create a bridge across the faith and professional realms. Though not technically under DLC auspices, the annual film festival was initially sponsored by Fuller Seminary and had from its start the ongoing participation of DLC's former executive director, Robert Banks.

As we have seen over and over, one of the key reasons for the distanced relationship between church and business is the modern tendency, as one interviewee expressed it, to "put our roles in separate boxes." Separation receives institutional reinforcement, especially from the institutions of church and business. One innovative answer to this problem is to create a totally new organization that carries none of the institutional contamination of the separate spheres.

Until recently, when he returned to his native Australia for personal reasons, Banks, a psychologist and theologian, was the chair of the Department of the Laity at Fuller Theological Seminary, the world's largest multidenominational seminary. The goal of his department is to provide strong theological training and preparation for students who see their mission in a lay profession. Mild mannered and a sensitive listener, Banks has an uncanny ability to organize people from a variety of settings to bring a new project to fruition. Banks commented on this with a simple observation: "My passion is to relate theology to life." In 1996, he helped found the DLC to give top professionals in business and academia the opportunity to reflect on spirituality, spiritual formation, and professional role, and to develop programs that cultivate the character of the leader and encourage integration of faith and public life. The De Pree Leadership Center continues to develop new programs on business and religiously based leadership principles under the direction of Walt Wright, who was president of Regent College in Vancouver for twenty-two years.

Several years before DLC's founding in 1997, Rob Banks was approached by an informal group of professionals in the film industry. They had been gathering to explore the role of religious faith in their own working lives and were seeking someone with theological training to be a resource person for the group. In their words, they wanted their own C. S. Lewis or Dorothy Sayers, someone they could converse with who would inspire faith, grasp the underlying concepts, and respond to lay issues. They had found other clergy unable to make a connection to their concerns. Banks said he would try.

They began to meet once a month on Saturdays. After about a year of increasingly probing discussions about their values and their work, the group felt it was time to create more contact with the larger community. They asked themselves, *What can we do to change things?* By *change*, they meant addressing both individuals and the Los Angeles community. They had formed the group out of deep awareness of the cynicism, exploitation, and personal disillusionment that surrounded the film industry. According to members of the group, no better example of the separation of faith and work could be found than in the Hollywood culture. As Cecilia Gonzalez, head of Family Theater Productions, put it, "It often comes down to the faith community (idealistic and artistic) versus the business community (ratings-oriented)."

Uneasy tension over religion inside the industry added to the difficulty. Historically, many industry insiders—from Louis B. Mayer to Steven Spielberg—have been Jewish. According to screenwriter and UCLA professor Ron Austin, this meant they were used to being marginalized personally or as a group. Thus any spiritual life in the industry had to address the deep sense of alienation its own professionals felt in the larger society. The same held true for Roman

Catholic immigrants. As both advanced in the industry, they tended to reflect a long-standing love-hate relationship between immigrant U.S. Catholics and Jews ever since the Depression. Frank Capra (who directed *It's a Wonderful Life*) was an example of the rapprochement that good film could effect.

The same, however, was not true of church-initiated discussion. In the experience of these producers, clergy were skeptical of the film industry. Not surprisingly, they tended to blame all bad things in "the culture" on this industry or failed to appreciate the message of such a popular medium. The animosity hit close to home. Said Austin, "Since the 1960s Hollywood has been opposed to authority, and religion is authority par excellence." Similarly, hard-nosed media professionals were skeptical that religious considerations could inspire any type of industry success. All that was changing, however, in the 1990s, when spirituality (though not organized religion) began to be seen as a legitimate interest. New productions featuring angels or religious sentiments began to trickle into the Hollywood culture.

After a year of reflecting privately with Banks, the group decided it was time to do something beyond supporting their personal interest in religion and work. Initially, Banks suggested a conference to address these issues. But the group replied, "No, that's what *you* do. We do film." He had the sensitivity to listen and even found funds from Fuller to underwrite the first festival. Together, they created a new group, the City of Angels Film Festival. They held their first event in 1994 and chose a theme of common concern: the city itself. They titled the event "Los Angeles in the Movies: Dreams/Conflicts/Lifestyles." Four days of films were aired at one of the best screens in town, the Directors Guild of America. The underlying notions were not disguised, as this program note indicates:

> The City of Angels Film Festival is a celebration of art and
> religion. The festival is both an event and a conversation.
> It grew out of a dialogue between some in the theological

community who are dedicated to thoughtful media and filmmakers who believe spiritual perspectives are an indispensable partner in the movie-making process. The festival is intentionally directed toward the screening of quality films that raise vital religious questions.

Banks had postulated that if they broke even it would be a great success; this would require about seventy-five attendees. They more than doubled the number on the first event, and by the third year they moved to a larger (and more expensive) theater. A success, the festival has now made it into the twenty-first century.

All agreed something special was happening. What started as an event for the audience became a resource encouraging the suppliers of film to integrate spirituality and humanism in their work. A screening of Capra's *It's a Wonderful Life* not only provided living proof of the possibility of creating religiously focused film, it occasioned a moving discussion of hope, miracles, and ethics in the City of Angels. Austin's observation that the conflict between art and business often comes out on the screen was being transformed. The films highlighted deep human conflict, but the festival was creating new attention to important religious notions—reconciliation, redemption—and a public acknowledgment of the relation between the spiritual and the industry. The committee had hoped that the festival would help people see that religion can be a good partner with the film industry rather than an antagonist (a deliberate antidote to the position of the Religious Right). Said Gonzalez, "This is redefining for the creative community that religion is not a bad word. It is not the last thing you want near you in the film industry. Instead, it's about finding meaning in life."

Several film professionals reported to us that it made a great difference to know that they were not alone in caring about content in an industry noted for its indifference to moral limits. Creating its own subculture, the film festival and private discussion group constitute a beacon for excellence in work and contribution to community. Exciting offshoots, such as a newly created award for young Hispanic filmmakers, suggest that an evolving approach to business action built on religious beliefs may accomplish more than a social action platform delivered from on high.

Dismantling the Monolith

As these examples show, it is possible to move from misconception or no conception of religious possibility in economic life to reconception of the Christian religious dimension of modern work—and it is time we did. Despite the hundreds of new popularizations of Christian tradition—from best-selling novels about the forces of good and evil to chart-topping CDs of Benedictine chant—there is still a basic need for religious programs capable of affording the possibility of integrating the rich traditions of the Christian church with the complex opportunities for living this faith in the modern workplace. There are many such programs out there, from the Woodstock Business Conference monthly business leader gatherings (now occurring in more than sixteen cities and fully supported with extensive program materials from the conference) to Ken Blanchard's ingenious Center for FaithWalk Leadership. Blanchard has created this nonprofit with a core group of business leaders to help draw on people of faith and build a network of leaders of faith. They offer a series of seminars on this topic, held in conjunction with Blanchard's highly visible public speaking engagements, and hosted by local CEOs.

One of the most exciting and ambitious new efforts is occurring in Fair Park, South Dallas. C. McDonald (Don) Williams, chairman of Tramell Crow, one of the nation's largest diversified commercial real estate service companies, is dividing his time equally between his business duties and the Foundation for Community Empowerment, which works on a number of projects with inner city neighborhood leaders and organizations. Don began this work out of a simple call of his faith to get involved in the human tragedy of the inner city—not just for personal religious reasons, but for the general welfare of society. He stresses that the goal is not to be a service provider, but a catalyst for internally generated change.

Don quickly learned that success would depend on a strong partnering relationship with the real community leaders. As he noted, mutual listening was essential. Any preconceived notions he had about solutions were quickly altered in light of the specific context of Fair Park. As a trusted and informed voice of the community, neighborhood church leaders have played a strong role here. At the same time, Don and other businesspeople have added their talents, including the ability to help mediate financing and acquisition of land for development.

It remains to be seen whether the churches can offer the same kind of moral mediation and willingness to partner with business leaders in the so-called advantaged communities in which many businesspeople live. We would argue the same brokenness and opportunity for religious-based change exists there. On the South Dallas analogy, however, progress requires cross-profession, cross-class dialogue and the willingness to share authority and develop a new economic perspective in an evolutionary, catalyzing way.

For such evolution to occur, we need a new way of approaching Christian concepts, a middle ground between the conservative apologetic for capitalism and the liberal ascetic rejection of the free market economy. This new way, however, cannot be created simply by moderating the intensity of the liberal church's anticapitalism and the evangelical right's apologetics. Nor will extreme syncretism of the world's religions answer the full needs of religious life any more than Esperanto has been able to create a living language. As we have seen from our interviews, the current understanding of religion's role in business is loaded with justifiable fears of inappropriate intrusion or favoritism and exclusiveness, or a ho-hum, unproductive discussion with people who "don't understand." *We must reconceive the language and understanding of Christian religion itself in terms of its scope and role in today's economic life.*

We call this reformulation "the new terms of religious engage-ment" because it requires a substantial rearrangement of conceptual models, along with a radically new relational process between busi-ness and church professionals as they approach questions of faith and work. It is important for church professionals and congregants to engage in deepening the religious connection in terms of both the rules by which business people guide their actions and, espe-cially, their state of spiritual consciousness. It is important to estab-lish a mental model that sets up a condition of creative, ongoing feedback for individuals as they navigate a fully meaningful life that embraces religious depth and economic productivity.

The first step is to loosen the categorical rigidity of the term *reli-gion* as it is commonly understood. As we have seen, one of the key mental blocks among businesspeople seems to be a continuing hang-up over this term, expressed in such statements as "I'm spiri-tual but not religious" or "I'm very religious, but you can't bring reli-gion into the workplace." Many people construct explanations of their behavior at work that totally exclude their religion, even when their actions are fully compatible with their religion. This is an absurd and spiritually limiting strategy. It is hardly plausible to claim, as top executives frequently do, that a religion deeply affect-ing their development has nothing to do with the most important conflicts of their career.[4]

To move forward, it is important to reconceive Christianity as a religion that takes many forms of expression, not all of which are equally appropriate to business and not all of which imply sectarian allegiance. Many of today's secular spirituality programs have restricted, even trivialized, spirituality so as to be almost exclusively about feelings and performance at work. Religion can and must be the important anchor for living a full life in all contexts: work, fam-ily, solitude, illness, and community. At the same time, reservations about juxtaposing business and the worldview of church authorities are well founded.

The history of Christianity itself is a history of the struggle to clarify the constant tension between worldly necessities and other-worldly saintliness, posed by the fact of being human with an immortal soul. Sometimes, the business setting can be one of the greatest trials a person encounters. Said one CEO, "My task is to constantly deal with questions that have no answer." At other times, the business setting has less religious meaning. The darkest hour of the soul is not spiritually equivalent to a bad day at the office or a church supper or a momentary lapse of creativity. The mundane tasks of getting a job done cannot be expected to evoke the mystery of a liturgy or a major life passage. The same holds true for a religious community. Membership in a faith community is not the same sort of relationship as membership on a marketing team. To expect the same spiritual payback from both is going to either trivialize faith or lionize workplace experiences.

Levels of Religious Engagement

If we see religion as a monolith, we lose these important distinctions. Religion becomes a slave to the worldly, or a place of retreat from it. We suggest dismantling the monolith of religion by seeing that it has three distinct levels of engagement: the espoused, the catalytic, and the foundational (see Figure 8.1). By understanding and recognizing these three levels, we can find a way out of ecclesiastical dominance over business without totally abandoning religious belief in daily life. As we perceive these distinctive levels, religion regains its complexity and begins to carry more relevance and meaning than "spirituality Lite." Paradoxically, it immediately becomes more compatible with public spaces.

Espoused Religion

Espoused religion refers to publicly proclaimed, mainly institutionalized forms of religion. Included are sectarian forms of allegiance, denominational creed, and proselytizing. Espoused religion is not

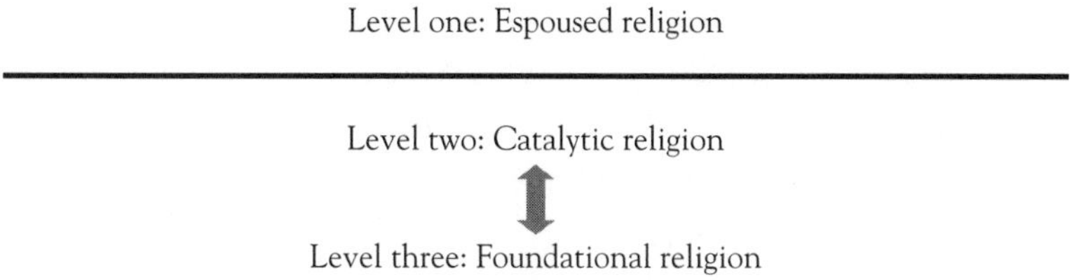

Level one: Espoused religion

Level two: Catalytic religion

⬆⬇

Level three: Foundational religion

Figure 8.1. The New Terms of Religious Engagement.

simply religious "talk" (as opposed to action); it is the intention to make a claim whose purpose is to bind claimant and receiver together in the same cause or understanding. The espoused level of religion is closest to the Latin root *religio,* to bind.

Espoused religion is religious expression that seeks to effect a promise, or elicit allegiance. In many cases, this allegiance takes the form of membership in a religious institution or deference to the claims derived from dogma, as when Christians observe the main holidays of the liturgical calendar, Jews rally around a denominational call to support antidefamation causes, or American Buddhists support the Dalai Lama's political agenda to free Tibet. An institution gives strength to the religious claim by guaranteeing a community that is committed to supporting the religion's goals and helping sustain its power over time. Sometimes the espoused act is personalized, as when someone bears witness to his or her belief. What makes it espoused is the strongly stated or implied connection of this statement to a larger religious culture, such as evangelical Christianity or Roman Catholicism. Put simply, "espoused" is any religious statement or act that carries and supports a label of membership and support of an institutionalized religious creed, even if the label does not fully correspond with an individual's actual beliefs.

Thus espoused is not the same as belief, which describes a worldview. For example, American Catholics who differ with the church on specific issues frequently try to separate themselves from the espoused forms of the church, but not its foundational beliefs (level three). Public creeds can be examples of espoused religion to the degree that their proclamation serves the purpose of reinforcing commitment to the religious community or specific claims of the belief system. This is the level of religious expression that is least likely to attract many businesspeople in the context of their economic life. Given widespread commitment to maintaining conditions in which all employees are free to worship as they please, the binding agenda of espoused religion cannot be tolerated in connection with life in the workplace. The individual believer may also be anxious to divorce himself or herself from the social history that an espoused label carries. The dynamics of espoused activities should not be underestimated, as we saw from the elaborate coping strategies business people developed (reported in Chapter Two). An action that would be considered laudable from a secular ethical standpoint becomes unacceptable in the workplace culture if it is couched in claims of institutional allegiance to a particular religious community.[5]

The hazards of espoused religion in business life are many, and frequently underestimated. Mere deference to a person in religious authority can be seen as an implication of one's allegiance to the church, as when a CEO closes the office to honor the Pope's visit to a city, or invites religious speakers from only one denomination to address the management team. To proselytize may be an exercise of one's religious belief (in that some beliefs require witnessing), but the attempt behind proselytizing is to bind others to one's claim of religious truth. This is an agenda deemed unacceptable for having been imposed on someone else's freedom of expression. Witnessing by someone with power over the recipient can all too easily invite abuse of power or a feeling of entrapment. Polite silence from the hearer may be mistaken for agreement, which only makes the problem more acute: there is often no way of knowing when the espoused expression has crossed the line of acceptability in the corporate culture.

The espoused level of religion is not easily defined by a set of core conditions. Depending on whether the recipient of the religious message perceives an invitation or pressure to make a vow of commitment, the definition of espoused is a product of culture and politics. For example, fervently proselytizing groups have claimed such strong ownership of Jesus that the J word is now widely perceived as unacceptably sectarian and conflictual. This makes any representation of the message of Jesus vulnerable to the perception of an espoused agenda, and hence dangerous territory from the businessperson's standpoint. (We noticed this effect even in reaction to our use of the word *Christian* in the subtitle of this book: "Are you trying to proselytize?") Religious writers who have popularized models of behavior based on Jesus' life are often surprised by the unwillingness of nonevangelicals even to read their books, unaware of the strong bias against espoused forms among the general business population.

Ideally, American insistence on tolerance and pluralism would have developed an etiquette for signaling that a person tolerates an espoused religion without feeling an allegiance to it. In reality, however, it is difficult to achieve such a balance. Tolerant silence in the face of proselytizing can be misunderstood to mean agreement with, and even partial complicity in, the religious claims of the proselytizer. When a particular economic policy is dictated by a denominational group, there is no way for the corporation to fully separate its consideration of the policy from the appearance of allegiance to the institutional church that made the claim.

This confusion is further heightened by the fact that espoused religious assertions are assumed to be an indication that a person agrees with many other claims of ecclesiastical dogma or politics. People who may be selectively and eclectically fashioning their beliefs—a large segment of the American population—have no way to signal a distinction between what they find acceptable or not in an institutional religion's beliefs. How to communicate that although one supports a particular church boycott, one disagrees with the same church's stand on reproductive rights? Or that one can see merit in Buddhist meditation and believe in Christian salvation? This is more clarification than most business settings facilitate, so the chances of being misunderstood are high. Why walk down that road?

Even sponsorship of ecumenical occasions, by failing to include all possible religions and gathering like-minded people to advance a political agenda associated with a specific denomination, places a company in the awkward position of appearing to choose and endorse one religious allegiance over another. Inviting Jesse Jackson, for example, to speak on racism may be misunderstood to be pressure to personally align oneself with liberal Protestant Christianity. Corporations walk this tightrope constantly in such areas as charitable contributions; they often take great pains to extinguish the binding power of their relation to a religious body when such contributions are made.

For these reasons, and because many institutional religious activities do have acquisition of power as one of their agendas, any form of contact or mutuality with espoused religion can seem inappropriate to the businessperson's professional setting. The espoused level of engagement generally raises real fear of generating sectarian strife, favoritism, or intolerance.

The exceptions prove the overall rule. Commonly accepted espoused practices in corporate culture are clearly wrapped in a protective context that signals personal, passive allegiance rather than an invitation to join in the vow. Most of these forms of the espoused occur in a radically personalized context, such as displaying a personal item of religious clothing (a cross on a necklace, or a yarmulke). Another privatized form of espoused religion in business is the industrial chaplain or religious-based employee assistance program. Sessions are completely confidential; they occur on the explicit condition that the corporation sponsors no public claim or invocation of a specific religious affiliation. According to the national code of industrial chaplains, proselytizing is forbidden. Similarly, companies that make available a space for religious practice during the day usually go to great lengths to make it ecumenical and use of the space optional.

Another tolerated public espousal is the generalized ecumenical gathering, such as the annual White House prayer breakfast, or religious representation at the funeral of a public figure. In these instances, people recognize that the religious authority has itself been transformed into a public figure, or that the public figure has a private religious belief that must be served in this specific public context. It is understood that creating or reinforcing a lasting attachment to a specific religious institution among all participants in the public event is not the primary purpose.

If the espoused level must be generally avoided in a business setting, then the role of the religious professional—living espousal of institutionalized religion—is difficult with regard to integrating economics and religion. Many clergy we interviewed were accustomed to adopting a strategy of engagement with the world that started with strongly signaling their espoused role and went on from there. Such a strategy can only work in a business-related setting if the person has no possibility of exercising abusive power over the corporation's employees and can be seen as embodying a way of doing things that makes sense for business. For most clergy, these conditions did not hold. These difficulties, and the ease with which they are overplayed by businesspeople and underplayed by clergy, suggest to us that a strong, solid line should be drawn between level one and the business setting (see Figure 8.1.).

Catalytic Religion

The catalytic level of religious engagement refers to personalized, experiential religion that is transformative of one's consciousness or actions. This form of religion does not demand a promise or vow of institutional allegiance from others. The many deeply privatized, appealing forms of catalytic spirituality today seem to have little in common with religion as many people know it from childhood, which is essentially that of the espoused level.

We call this level *catalytic* because this religious factor effects a direct change in the individual that sustains and empowers religiously consistent action or consciousness. The catalytic stimulates the process of personally (if only partially) knowing and experiencing God (or the nondeistic equivalent), of connecting to one's essential being as defined in religious terms, and being personally enhanced by this experience or knowledge.

The catalytic level refers both to accessing spiritual awareness and initiating specific actions as a result of this awareness. The catalytic religious experience takes many forms: maintenance of perspective, a sense of calm and confidence, a spark of creativity, a feeling of being anchored and fully operational. Catalytic religion links the interior life to action in terms of emotional, intellectual, or physical power. When, for example, an individual believes his or her religious faith holds every person sacred and unique, recovery of this belief as an active resource in understanding business problems is a catalytic religious act.

On this view, spirituality is that little extra bit of energizing that makes all the difference in one's creativity, emotional equipment, ethics, and sense of fulfillment. Spirituality in these circumstances is essentially an intensifying force; it heightens personal awareness and one's sense of connection with cosmic powers as defined in specifically religious or spiritual ways. It turns the four felt needs into avenues for worship, spiritual peace, balance, and ethics, directed toward the problems and opportunities presented in business.

Spirituality, as depicted in most of today's so-called secular spirituality programs, certainly falls into this category. Corporations tend to sponsor these programs because of their (sometimes exaggerated) claims of power enhancement and because they have effectively offered an outlet for religious belief in the workplace that is clearly disconnected from the espoused. A Buddhist-oriented program may draw on guided meditation or chanting and drumming without demanding any contribution to the Dalai Lama's political cause. A therapeutic program may include empathic listening exercises or T-group sessions that draw forth the ability to "love one another." A wilderness retreat, extreme adventure, hermitage, or even the simple lighting of a candle to smoke a room may all be seen as spiritual in that they evoke this ability to connect with the inner self and the larger, sacred forces of creation and love.

When Morgan Stanley partner Buzz McCoy took time out for such a sabbatical retreat, his experience in the Himalayas led him to write one of the most influential business ethics pieces ever published by the *Harvard Business Review*. McCoy's "The Parable of the Sadhu"[6] has been widely read and discussed by diverse groups of businesspeople and students. So, too, the fastest-growing element of Christianity in the United States, evangelicalism in its many forms, places strong emphasis on the catalytic. The ritual words of personalized prayer ("Lord, we *just* ask for . . .") evoke a personalized consciousness of relation to the divine. Were this form of religious expression not so heavily linked to proselytizing, it would undoubtedly vie more strongly with the popular secular spirituality programs in terms of capturing business interest. Instead, tipping point turns to tripping point for many businesspeople as an agenda to sign people up for Jesus appears to lie just beneath the surface.

Catalytic religious exercises appeal to today's interest in a self-discovered religion rather than instructional training from espoused sources. At heart, they are radically personalized, thus avoiding the pitfalls of espoused religious expression in the workplace. Many of the definitions of spirituality in Gallup's most recent survey pick up the catalytic elements of religious experience. When asked what the word *spirituality* meant to them, respondents answered:

Seeking to grow closer to God

Sense of awe and mystery in the universe

Inner peace or state of mind

Seeking to be a good person or lead a good life

Seeking the inner self, the being within the body or the essence of personal being, and evolving into a whole spirit or experiencing the spiritual side of the natural order

Reaching human potential and affirming a sense of personal worth

Last on the list in terms of frequency was "going to church and being a good person." Spirituality is therefore not about espoused religion in most people's minds, even among the Gallup interviewees, who tended to have a Christian orientation.[7]

Under these conditions, alternative worldviews among people with different faiths or no faith can be shared without sanitizing religion into secular humanism. Most world religions have a rich heritage of catalytic elements, from prayer to disciplined treatment of bodily requirements. But since the 1950s, mainstream churches have moved away from these forms of religious expression in favor of social action concern and denominational attachment that helped define neighborhoods, race, and status. Congregants reported losing their sense of personal discovery, and the feeling of awe and mystery in their church-based religious life. In reaction, they are drawn to other forms of Christianity, perhaps worshiping at their laptop along with others connecting to an online meditation from a monastery, or joining a megachurch whose emphasis on personal relation to Jesus and changed habits picks up the same need for individual experience of the religious. The current emphasis on the catalytic level of religion is both exciting and attractive, but the catalytic always runs the danger of degenerating into mere technique or self-referencing.

Religion, however, runs deeper than technique. It offers a worldview that goes beyond any individual's ability to answer the truly soul-racking questions: Why are we here? What higher purpose should our lives serve? What is the force that transcends biological fact? What is the nature of the good life? What is the meaning of death, or of misfortune? What connects me to others? The new spirituality programs reflect these larger perspectives without demanding acceptance of their dogma wholesale. People are free to pick and choose the parts they like. They share these books or parts of these books with friends, not to form religious community per se, but to signal friendship and support. Holistic in focus, underscoring the interdependency of life forms and describing systemic relationships, the new spirituality programs suggest a model for the social architecture of the corporation that "makes sense." They confirm classic Christian beliefs in a common humanity, the commandment to love God, and to love your neighbor as yourself.

Foundational Religion

When religious interests move beyond technique for developing an access to the sacred (the catalytic) to primary definition of the sacred, we enter the foundational level of religion, the level at which generalized (as opposed to personalized) statements of religious wisdom occur. These can be an explanation of cosmology or ethical precepts, a myth compressing the shared experiences of being human, or a commandment reflecting a divinely ordered way of living.

It is at the foundational level that individuals find words for the sacred force they seek to access in catalytic exercises: God, the Word, Tao, spirit, soul, heaven, cosmic order. Here, too, are the narratives that offer timeless representations of sacredly inspired activities. The Judeo-Christian foundational story of Abraham and Isaac, for example, is an example of a relationship between the devout leader and God that demands ultimate sacrifice and ultimate love. Attention to such narratives allows a deeper way of knowing the sacred, offers needed sustenance to the catalytic (which is largely internalized, experiential knowledge), and gives clues to the individual for replicating in business the foundational patterns of order that sustain life. A foundational cosmological narrative in the new spirituality literature may draw on fractals to illustrate the unseen ordering potential of even the most random and apparently atomized structural forces. If a simple fractal reiterated millions of times can create a beautiful image of a winged creature or the shape of a leaf on a tree, what similar forces can be generated in an organizational social architecture?

Because it draws on "wisdom texts," the foundational form of religious expression can seem synonymous with the espoused level, which often includes these texts to reinforce community attachment to their practices. The difference, however, is in how the foundational is presented and perceived. Foundational religious engagement does not necessarily require attachment to the community of faith that claims to have inherited the teachings. It separates the text from allegiance to a specific self-proclaimed guardian of these texts. This type of engagement implies more universal ownership of the religious message than would an espoused reference to the Bible. A wide variety of sects, for example, all make reference to the Old Testament figure of Abraham. The biblical text can be foundational or espoused, depending on the process by which it is presented and the relationship between the presenter and the receiver.

In our opinion, the connection between Christian forms of faith and business action is most likely to be strengthened through intensified attention to drawing new linkages between the foundational and the catalytic levels of Christianity (represented by the two-way arrow in Figure 8.1). For this to occur, the believer must create a new format and new relationship between church officials and businesspeople so as to avoid conjuring up espoused forms within the corporate context. Many attempts at these linkages are already in evidence, though most are still in the early stages.

A key example in the Jewish community is lunchtime Torah reading for businesspeople, open to people of any faith but with special religious meaning to Jews. Another example is ecumenical conversion of religious language into nonspecific, generalized principles for business guidance. These convictional statements tend to seek a common religious denominator among world religions, while avoiding the doctrinal messages that demand specific attachment to an institutional religious group.

The Universal Declaration of Human Rights, the Caux Principles of International Business Conduct, the Aga Khan Peace Statement, or Hans Kung's World Parliament of Religions also fall into this category but jump to the espoused at that point where they demand allegiance to the institutions that supported the development of the statements. Covey's *Seven Habits of Highly Effective People* would fall into the catalytic category with strong linkage to the foundational.

The "optional" factor that distinguishes the foundational from the espoused can be a tricky ingredient. Religious content without belief gets sanitized in great literature and loses its presentation as revealed truth. This in turn weakens the connection to the catalytic, experiential practices that help turn wisdom into inspiration leading to considered action. It is here that more work needs to be done inside the churches, and especially in lay groups that stress the personalized and seek to give guidance without much connection to deeper religious concepts. Turning foundational principles into simple axioms is one way of linking to the catalytic (which, ironically, tends to take both a personalized and a universalized form). John Templeton's analysis of "the laws of life" falls solidly in this category.[8] He notes, for example, the widespread use of the Golden Rule among people of all faiths. Invocation of this axiom within a faith context carries powerful normative force, yet because of its universal usage it defies espousing an institutional agenda. For this reason, it is easily adopted and authoritatively voiced in the workplace without apology. Many interviewees who claimed that religion had no place at work would invoke the Golden Rule as their guiding standard. As such, they were protecting themselves from an incursion of espoused religious engagement but were also publicly divorcing their own conscience from their religious identity.

To avoid this type of spiritual schizophrenia, we must develop ways of addressing and critiquing business through foundational and catalytic religious lenses devoid of espoused intention. Some of the most popular foundational texts in business programs are a resurrection of archaic or non-Western religious writing and rituals. The more ancient or non-Western, the less likely they are to be associated with modern espoused religious groups. For this reason, Buddhist teachings can be secularized by the Dalai Lama in spite of the heavily politicized and institutional forms of Buddhism, while recital of the parable of the Good Samaritan would carry much heavier espousing implications in a U.S. setting.

Because religious professionals by definition carry espoused associations, their participation in forming these linkages may require a less authoritative role. They may, for example, be more effective in simply providing spiritual support and intellectual resource for laypeople who would lead a discussion of religion and business. (Woodstock Business Conference has taken this approach by insisting that a business leader host the event and a priest attend as resource. The espoused element of the meetings is preserved in the association with Woodstock itself and when the cleric leads the prayer and bible reading.) Business gurus frequently help make foundational linkage. Ken Blanchard's parable formats for his books on values and business are one such example, and on several occasions he has partnered with such religious leaders as Norman Vincent Peale and Bill Hybels to create a business-church dialogue in these books. Tolstoy's novel *The Death of Ivan Ilyich* and other works of poetry and nonfiction dealing with spiritual and existential crises are extremely popular in executive workshops on spirituality and business. By selecting these relatively contemporary texts and offering interpretational authority, such programs help people learn foundational concepts and link them to a catalytic form of personal spirituality.

Metaphors of the search for a "corporate soul" have helped move the foundational to the catalytic in a specific business context. Take, for example, a popular catalytic exercise on team building and creativity in which participants stand in two parallel lines and are instructed to link hands. Most groups begin by holding hands with the person to either side. When they raise their arms in the air, it takes little effort to knock the "roof" down. But if they reach across and form four-way "arches," a grown person can easily hang from their "rafters." Thus the modern worker experientially discovers the cantilevered arches of the medieval cathedral. From here is it a short leap of analogy to team building and problem solving through an appeal not just to the structural pattern of the arch but to the spirituality that goes into its construction.

The technique of the exercise and participants' spiritual resonance can be further enhanced by making reference to the principles of religious expression that underlay the design of cathedrals. When a lay businessperson invokes these principles, participants do not fear being invited to participate in Roman Catholicism. Were the same exercise conducted among a religiously mixed group of executives by a priest, however, the resistance to learning would increase sharply in proportion to the increase in implication of an espoused agenda.

To ensure that such an agenda is not implied, most corporate-sponsored spirituality programs avoid foundational Western religious particularity in favor of developing "little traditions" of their own making. New cosmologies are particularly popular, drawing on the new science of chaos theory and mind-body connections to create a template for determining the right way to solve problems and live one's life. The widespread interest in these programs presents a strong argument for generating such new formats and languages for Christian religious engagement in the problems and context of business people's working lives.

The challenge, of course, is for a traditional religious foundation to maintain its core message as it is studied for business relevance. New adaptation of text to context is essential. For example, foundational notions of justice in the Christian religious community are based on an agricultural model that simply cannot bear up without complex adjustment to the intense diversity of social claims in modern economic life.

Considering the Three Levels

Consideration of the three levels and their appropriate settings can help in every aspect of the business-and-religion quest. To the degree that the contemporary religious message is linked to espoused forms of dogma, it requires isolation from settings where there is great diversity and strong institutional separation of church and state (or church and business). To the degree that foundational notions are developed without regard to their ability to link to the catalytic, they carry little religious insight into what must be done in one's business realm (the shaded circle). Many academic discussions of pluralism and Christianity seem to be suffering from this problem, constructing a theory whose only catalytic force appears to be generation of more theory, without practical effect.

All three levels are essential. The power of participating in tradition that has been repeated over the centuries in such a way as to feel immediately relevant and shared cannot be replicated in a totally privatized, personalized search referenced on the inner self. Rather than avoid particularity, the religious quest should seek it out for its ability to deepen spirituality. At the same time, particularity must be presented in a process that is able to transcend the particular claims of one espoused group. Otherwise the quester loses the spiritual strength that comes from freedom of choice,[9] and the message itself runs the danger of turning into a highly malleable human construction used for purely human political purposes.

New voices are helping in the process of fusing Christian faith and business responsibility. For example, women are playing a strong role in redefining the catalytic and experiential aspect of traditional practices in Christianity, with the result that they are redefining essential notions of women's power. The practical effects of such redefinition on the workplace practices of men and women can be profound if pursued such that understanding rather than triumphalism evolves. In the past, many of the foundational and es-poused religious precepts have advanced disempowering concep-tions of feminine spirituality and authority. After abandoning them wholesale for a time, women are now reconstructing their under-standing of the foundational texts by specifically reconceiving their connection to the catalytic. Cleansing rituals, for example, that once signified pollution are now being reinterpreted as an indica-tion of sacred rhythmic forces.

Such rituals are not for everyone. They inevitably spill over into the espoused arena because they are particular enough to pose a choice, a vow, an attachment. This is the price of religious power. It is naïve to think that practice and contact with the foundational can be supported for long without espoused spillover. A communion ritual can be sanitized into ecumenical sharing of a meal, thereby dramatizing a religious commandment to love one another, but it also loses religious meaning regarding the Last Supper.

The challenge, then, is to find the right setting for each level of religious engagement, and to strengthen all three types. By setting up some distinction between level one and the business setting, and forming stronger linkages between levels two and three, one can increase the ability to discern a religious perspective and personal spirituality in daily business life. Recognize that all three levels of religion are important, but that we are in a constant state of mutual searching for the precise form and contextual framework these lev-els should take.

Conditions for Reconnection

What can we do to help reconnect today's spirituality-and-business movement to religious roots? First of all, as individuals, business-people can begin to anchor their own actions in a religiously defined role for themselves that does not necessarily carry espoused associ-ations into the workplace but can find rich textual confirmation in the foundational literature of Christianity. Three of these would be:

1. *Personal calling:* the idea that creating goods, services, wealth, and corporate community can be an expression of God-given talents, and of an obligation to fulfill certain religious purposes in the world, such as honoring God, loving one another, feeding the hungry, and so on.

2. *Engine of justice:* accepting responsibility, religiously based, to correct the imbalances and harms of business activity. This includes promoting human rights processes inside the corporation and in its outside activities.

3. *Sacred awareness:* strengthening one's own experience of faith as a reality in the business arena, through spirituality, contemplation of decisions and accomplishments, or formation of relationships that extend the boundaries of the self into identity and connection with others.

In addition to the continued creation of such conceptual hooks, successful reconnection to religious tradition depends on three other characteristics: new voices, a return to basics (including the catalytic forms of religious engagement), and developed understanding of how business life should be an important expression of Christian social ethics.

New Voices

Participation of new voices and new sources for the religious narrative helps avoid the spiritual entropy that has accompanied the prospect of the espoused intruding on business culture. These new voices include lay businesspeople, women religious professionals, and futurists concerned with the interplay of new science and religion. Trinity Church at Wall Street has created a new journal, *Spirituality and Health,* with explicitly Christian sponsorship but drawing on multiple religious sources as well as biology, genetics, and psychology to explicate holistic approaches to spirituality. In so doing, the authorities of the church and of science have created new texts and learning, as well as essentially forming a new relationship.

Feminist scholarship of formerly suppressed ancient texts on women in church history has also opened up new forms of religious knowing and a new sense of the religious past. Their foundational-catalytic appeal to laypeople is in the aura of being a new discovery, yet somehow within the outer margins of the religious tradition. Sister Wendy Beckett's exposition of religious art is another example of this recovery of text, history, and biographical narrative, long disassociated from the espoused tradition, to stimulate new connections between foundational symbols and practices and catalytic spirituality. Universities are another new and potentially ecumenical voice, especially in those business schools that are combining spirituality and business ethics, among them Notre Dame, Loyola, Gonzaga, Harvard Business School, and Santa Clara.

Return to the Basics

Today's interest in the foundational is shaped by a bias toward the personal and experiential, most obviously in the connection between mind and body. Birth, sexuality, death, healing, knowing, and strength are topics of foundational narratives with strong potential for linkage to the catalytic, moving in a constructive feedback process from technique to cosmology to "new ways of knowing" that empower people's intellectual skills, so necessary in the context of the new economy.[10] By contrast, the espoused canons of the liberal mainstream have been primarily concerned with the political and the institutional, in some cases with almost no connection to biblical study. In our opinion, businesspeople find more resonance with the life passages material drawn from the Bible than with the texts that have suffered strong political filtering, such as passages on God and mammon.

Social Ethics

Although the personal and experiential continue to be strong elements, today's spiritual interest presents increasing opportunity for contemplation of social systems and their ethics. Of concern is that

the questions of Christian social ethics be framed and contextualized in such a way as to take advantage of this opportunity, not kill
it. The opportunity is already being exploited in new ways that promote self-discovery about social ethics among lay groups, such as
Don Williams's associates in the Dallas area, on the basis of the late
Jim Rouse's active conversion of his real estate acumen into developing low-income housing during his lifetime.

As people seek spiritual wholeness through consistency between
thought and action, they are forced to realize that social systems
must be engaged and changed in order to make such integrity possible. Individual behavior is not sufficient. At this point, religious
concepts of justice become paramount. This opportunity for contemplation of a just order is wasted, however, if cast into tri-
umphalist espousals of special privilege to impose a strategy for
achieving God's order on earth.

Another approach would be through modern texts that help
interpret religious notions of justice from a personalized standpoint,
such as psychology. In so doing, these texts avoid espoused associations and help link the foundational to the catalytic. One popular
example today is the fictional narrative *The Celestine Prophecy*, but
more interpretative examples include the modern classics of Henry
Nouwen, Herbert Marcuse, Norman O. Brown, or Erich Fromm.
H. Richard Niebuhr's *The Responsible Self*, or Martin Marty's *Being
Good and Doing Good*, also extract foundational and personalized
discussions of social justice from a heavily espoused context. Martin
Buber's *I and Thou* was instrumental in helping business leader Tom
Chappell create a corporation with "soul."[11] Biographical narratives
also explain religious notions of justice without specific denominational demands; Martin Luther King, Jr.'s writings, Erik Erikson's
Gandhi's Truth, and Toni Morrison's stories each offers linkage from
personal spirituality to normative social ideals. Similarly, catalytic
exercises on directed listening can inspire group discovery of underlying principles of inclusion and fairness that have many implications for creating a just marketplace.

Codiscovery

Should the church even try to be a force in the lives of business-people in their roles as managers and workers? Or should an es-poused religion confine its economic influence to underdeveloped economies and the underclass? Is the rightful place of the church to be a spokesperson only for the poor in their encounter with the rich corporations, while abandoning the so-called privileged? In our opinion, such a state of marginalization from the business powerful would be tragic for the church and tragic for business.

The new terms of religious engagement demand revision, not termination, of the church's relationship to businesspeople. Take existing ecclesiastical patterns of making an impersonal statement or demand about economic behavior. As we have seen, they have limited ability to penetrate the shaded circle where a businessper-son's religious views become active in relationships and decision making. They are so embedded in an espoused context, and so heavy on religious instruction rather than religious self-discovery, that they mark no point of convergence for the businessperson's own patterns of thinking and situational concerns. If this already threatening mes-sage is also condescending or even hostile to pragmatic basics such as economic effectiveness, the businessperson sees little point. Why join a game in which you are the predetermined loser?

On the other hand, churches that have tried to take a business-friendly approach run the risk of not knowing what they are talk-ing about, or of sounding no different from secular messages about business acumen or humanistic ethics. Their thin veneer of sacred-ness in attributing business success to God or Jesus adds little depth to spiritual understanding. Add in the fear that espoused religion tends to generate futile conflict, and there is little reason for the businessperson not to opt for the more challenging secular human-istic expression to determine work responsibilities.

Some church programs have attempted to innovate simply by bor-rowing wholesale from secular spirituality programs. Although this model has advantages in repositioning emphasis on the catalytic, all too often there is no developed linkage to foundational Christian notions to deepen this effort and bring out its distinctive spiritual perspectives. Meanwhile, there is intense pressure on the pastor to be a psychological cheerleader for each and every congregant—a circumstance hardly conducive to critical dialogue.

To move forward, church professionals have to adopt a revised understanding of their function and the content of their messages about economic life. As such, their power relation to the laity changes. They must abandon the role of instructional guru on the system to become a partner in a new quest for catalytic religious experience and foundational wisdom applicable to life in the new economy. The new operative goals are codiscovery of the catalytic aspects of religion in daily life and deepening consideration of business matters rooted in the foundational concepts of faith.

Shared Catalytic Techniques

A good place to start the process of codiscovery is in shared catalytic techniques drawn from many religious sources, and coexamination of shared functions in the professional lives of laity and clergy. Both the church and the laity have a great deal of unexplored common ground in terms of how religion should shape the management of an organization.

Communities of faith can also shift their orientation toward the catalytic and foundational in helping members recover a faith perspective rather than emphasizing the acquisition of members and political power. Most important, they can help individuals sustain their religious identity even in the role of businessperson. This is a longing that clearly drives the current spirituality hunger, with its insistence on getting back to the inner self and its connection with the divine.

To do this, however, the levels of religion must be recognized and accessed in varying ways and settings. The three levels of religion cannot simply be fused into one espoused form and foisted onto free enterprise in the hopes of integration, any more than a comprehensible language for two countries could be created simply by fusing the sounds of two native tongues. So, too, integration of faith and business will only develop out of referencing of both realms in their right syntax. The espoused level, which can offer the strongest support and recovery of religious ritual and commitment, must be clearly distinct from the more catalytic and applied business context, but distinct does not have to mean contrary.

Narrowing the Range

An important condition of the new way is to narrow the range of expression of religious power in business even when restricted to the catalytic or foundational level. On the surface, this condition sounds irreligious, but it is consistent with the idea of different realms. The religious view is, after all, a glimpse of ultimates; business is generally not. As we noted earlier, the threat to market share may be urgent, but it is not equivalent to the loss of a loved one. Many people find that spirituality helps them see this important distinction, and that this perspective gives them added strength not only in life but also at work. A CEO we interviewed, for example, was in the midst of an ugly lawsuit against his company. It felt like a threat against his life, until he remembered, through prayer and Bible study, where his real treasures were, and how Jesus had posed an example of unconditional love and sacrifice. This knowledge caused him to keep his head and his heart in the proceedings, and actually initiate a meeting that led to reconciliation.

Most religions, including Christianity, do not feel the perfection of the saints can be replicated on earth in any sustained way. The best we can hope for are punctuated moments of transcendence and sustained hope of acting in ways that lead us to know God and our role in the divine plan. Religion in the business realm must make room for these distinctions between everyday pragmatism and deeper levels of spirituality. It must also tolerate room for error and experiment.

All too frequently, spiritual integration in business is packaged in an expectation of absolute integration, a prospect so daunting as to be better left alone. This tendency to engage in utopian thinking encourages totalitarian assertion of religious power over economic life or perfect fit between capitalism and Christianity—precisely the questionable scenarios that cut short many businesspeople's spiritual quest.

Distinguishing among three levels of religious engagement can help avoid this trap. Integration of the religious dimension at work does not have to mean integration of all three levels to be legitimate or authentic. As one perspicacious pastor commented after considering our three levels of religion:

> A religious community is where we practice our "espoused" religion. In the workplace we live out our "sacred awareness." This is developed in religious community, but we don't share our espoused religion at work. Where our [the church's] model suffers is that it suggests a model of how things can happen. It's not reality. When I call my parishioners at work, they answer the phone differently than the voice I hear on Sunday. Do we say the model points to a way of creating a new reality for that kinder and gentler world, though church is not that world either?

This remark makes an important distinction: the church suggests a model, and exposure to the model can inspire changed attitude and behavior. But the model is not reality. Living the religion requires additional dialogue, insight, and experience.

The Four A's

What is missing is the linkage from the sacred awareness in a real setting back to foundational notions that shape at least four aspects of behavior, which we call the four A's: aim, attitude, actor, and accountability. These can be seen as benchmarks in the quest to apply one's spiritual journey to business life. The four A's are hooks on which individuals can hang their awareness of the religious dimension, a way of determining the effects of faith and measuring whether faith is truly having a transformative effect in the workplace.

To return to the pastor's example of the changed voice, the four A's could help determine what the changed voice indicated. How many of the four A's were radically "different" in a church setting, and why? Was the change superficial, an act of accountability to the etiquette of protestant pacifism and niceness, or are there deeper attitudes and purposes invoked by time at church that become lost or supplanted at work? Do these changes signify a significant change in the actor? How does one cope with such spiritual schizophrenia? Why are the sacred purpose and self lost in a business sitting?

Unless all of the four A's are affected by the claim of being spiritual at work, the practical faith journey is being truncated in some important way. This is not to say that behavior and goals should be exactly the same in the espoused and work settings. There must be movement between several types of religious expression to reach full transformation of the self.

A Network of Connections

One way to describe this movement is as a three-part referencing process that builds a network of connections between sacred and business realms:

- Stage 1: retreat

- Stage 2: renewal

- Stage 3: reconnection

In stage one, retreat, the individual slows down long enough to take a step back from business as usual and invoke a broad perspective that includes religious concerns or allows time for catalytic exercises. Stage two, renewal, brings deep sources of faith to the same context. These can be catalytic, foundational, or support from one's espoused community, provided the retreat setting is far enough removed from business. This is the stage similar to what Covey would call "sharpening the saw." As his metaphor implies, the process of retreat and renewal need not be triggered by crisis alone; it is a regular necessity or habit of those seeking a spiritually rich life.

Although stage one is usually provoked by a negative reaction to some situation—dissatisfaction with one's spiritual state, or ethical concern about the business environment—stage two is framed in positive terms, a time of renewal. Both the catalytic and the foundational can help this process, through prayer, meditation, ritual cleansing, notions of repentance, deeper ethical inquiry into the supportive perspectives of faith, and healing exercises. Given the sometimes overwhelmingly negative messages from the church about business life, it is important to develop a positive approach to this stage. One simple way to access this stage is with the question, "What is the spiritual opportunity in what I am doing?" The three conceptual points of engagement listed earlier—calling, engine of justice, and cultivation of sacred awareness are examples of this sort of opportunity.

Stage three, reconnection, moves from religious renewal to pragmatic transformations, summarized by the four A's. Here the catalytic form of religion is most evident, but certain foundational notions explored in a stage of renewal create particularly strong avenues to the catalytic. Again, calling or vocation is one such notion. Originally applied only to those "called" to the priesthood or nunnery, the concept has taken on catalytic import for living out religious commitment in a so-called secular profession. Studying the nature of this commitment can be an extremely important dimension of the religious person's understanding of business responsibility. As Robert Wuthnow noted in *Crisis of the Churches,* many people have simplistic notions of vocation as being happiness or self-fulfillment in one's career. The four A's can be applied to deepen the understanding of vocation, opening up a larger arena of sacred relevance in the activities of a firm. Robert Greenleaf's reflections on servant leadership are another example of the deeper kind of reconnection we are talking about.

The new way represents a state of heightened spirituality in which all three levels of religion are accessed in continuous feedback. The goal is to enable pursuit of one's calling, to create business practices that are functional, life-enhancing, and ultimately devout. The current state of integration of business and religion is so puzzling that there are not even standard terms for this kind of Christian religious integration in business. At one time, one might have called this process "trying to be a good Christian" in the marketplace, but today such terms trigger the espoused factor, with all of its coping challenges.

Exposure to the thoughts and support of the Christian community is all important here. Many spirituality programs today are so wary of espoused forms of religion that they have divorced themselves from any connection with Western particularity. Their nice and shiny principles are so thin as to be vapid when held up to the deeper problems of business responsibility. Already both Covey and the Dalai Lama have tried to deepen their programs with books that address religious particularities. The Dalai Lama has developed a program for "finding God without being religious," while Covey has written in depth about his own Mormon-based spirituality. Both books have proved to be personally inspiring but less adaptable to public sponsorship by a business program than the earlier books.

Two conclusions must be drawn here. First, spirituality is inevitably thin when studied among a general business audience inside a corporate context such as an executive workshop. To avoid entrapment, these exercises need to be confined essentially to the catalytic or carefully ecumenicized studies of foundational texts, or they will invoke charges of espoused religion. This does not make them useless, but certainly limited.

On the other hand, catalytic spirituality of any force almost inevitably provokes spillover into the other forms of religious expression. As spirituality is taken seriously, people seek ever deeper sources of truth and guidance, in which human experience in all its nuanced form is given full attention. To exclude the spillovers entirely is impossible; people are constantly seeking out new sources of spiritual development, including contemplation of foundational concepts. These interests must be nourished, not killed off. For this reason, it is essential to separate the espoused expression as much as possible from the workplace.

The central challenge today is to create new forms for moving from the generalized context of the executive workshop to the spillover religious search. The foundational and espoused forms of religion move beyond the corporate context and should do so. They need protection, however, in the form of safe spaces where private belief and communal religious affiliation can be expressed and nurtured. At the same time, they cannot escape responsibility for providing a way back into the mundane. Helping individuals nurture catalytic religious experience is an important part of the reconnection process.

The real challenge is to help businesspeople find conceptual linkages between the patriarchal agricultural societies of the foundation texts of Christianity and today's understanding of science, genetics, and economy. Certain principles are particularly adaptable to these purposes. Vocation is one, as we mentioned. Another is love and its various narratives of the opportunities and conflicts of compassion, filial love, stewardly love, romantic love, or aesthetic love. A third is life creation, and strict avoidance of its opposite, life destruction—of which there are plentiful examples in business.

Is it possible to echo the foundational notions without espousing them? Not entirely, but certainly searching for the foundational with a much lower level of the espoused can be encouraged, just as many non-Buddhists find great wisdom and relevance in studying Buddhist texts. Clearly, the sterile principle-based generalities of business ethics are not inspiring the leadership on ecological and economic issues that is needed in a global society. Neither are espoused religious languages providing the needed crossover to a modern, diversified population. The current intensity of interest in spirituality is a sign, we believe, of these failures, but also an indication of a widespread, even surprising, receptiveness to religion as an essential dimension of a sustainable future.

To move forward, however, we must recognize the general state of confusion about religion today, how rapidly our understanding of spirituality and science is changing the emphasis of religion toward the personalized and the experiential, and also its potential tendency to address the systemic. In our opinion, the distanced relationship between formal Christianity and business is not inevitable. It is urgent that the churches and businesspeople with Christian convictions find ways of drawing on each other's help, in relation. The point of the three levels of religion is to offer some coherent differentiation and ordering for this process at both conceptual and relational levels. The levels help refine an individual's sense of religion at work and religion in life without starting down the dead-end paths of today's typical coping strategies. Ideally, individuals move in and out of the three levels of religion in different settings, but with a chance to test religious belief in the context of modern economic life.

As we have seen, many factors work against the church's ability to help businesspeople in this process. Many ecclesiastic interpretations of foundational texts carry such hostile messages about capitalism or wealth that religious professionals find it unthinkable to support catalytic spirituality aimed at successful business activity. Yet more and more businesspeople are taking time out to attend adult Bible classes or divinity schools to become more acquainted with religious traditions and texts. Many of these people do not intend to abandon business, but rather hope to transform it into a more compassionate institution. Here, universities and lay groups carry a new and largely unanticipated responsibility for facilitating knowledge of practical religion in a nonministerial, religiously pluralistic context.

The three-level process outlined in Figure 8.1 is meant to encourage the religious quest of businesspeople in community, to effect the transformations of business on which a good life and a good society are to be based. Only if they are differentiated can the levels of religion be approached in such a way as to nourish each other rather than work in opposition, as they so often do today. Even under the best of circumstances, the confrontation between Christian religious principles and business ideals is inherently a source of intellectual conflict and personal stress. These tensions must be channeled into transformative, catalytic spirituality; otherwise the tensions become a reason to forget the whole thing.

Reflection

Using the framework for building a network of connections, ask yourself these questions about your business life.

Stage One: Retreat (Context Check)

- What is happening in my business life?
- What are the aims and attitudes here?
- Who am I becoming?
- Were I held accountable, how would I view that? Am I being accountable?
- What reality gaps exist between my intentions and the outcomes of my actions?

Stage Two: Renewal (Infusion of the Sacred)

- What is the spiritual opportunity in this context?
- Engage in prayer and meditation to evoke sacred awareness.

- Make reference to Christian ethics, biblical models, and principles.
- What is the Christian community saying on this issue?
- What are other communities of faith saying?

Stage Three: Reconnection (Creative Action)

- Complete a profile of the basics of religiously based, values-centered leadership.

- How have the virtues of your values-based leadership, such as courage, confidence, and insight, been changed by your spiritual quest?

- To be Christian is to be functional, life-enhancing, and devout. What actions of devotion, effectiveness, and life-enhancement have you completed in the past week? What more might you do?

Action

Here are specific examples of action in each level of religious engagement. Pick one action and practice it for a week, individually or with a group of like-minded seekers.

Action Arena One: Espoused

- Take a personal time-out from business for participation in religious community.

- Strengthen your religious community with a personal contribution.

- Ask for the support of the religious community for collective action on a worldly problem you feel you should be addressing.

- Find a concrete personal reminder of your religious identity, and place it where you can access it during your working day.

Action Arena Two: Catalytic

- Develop spiritual practices (meditation, discipline, prayer) that increase your personal effectiveness and ability to connect with God's patterns (diversity, ecology, and so on).

- Establish a clear set of moral guidelines for choice in the marketplace.

- Be a cultural catalyst in economic life (creating humane, dignifying workplaces and products; honest representations of financial dealings; and so on).

Action Arena Three: Foundational

- Familiarize yourself with biblical examples of leadership.

- Revisit sacred texts.

- Compare the messages you perceive in these texts with the assumed ends of espoused religion and business.

- Look at a visual depiction of the sacred or listen to sacred music. How does it refresh your perspective about the meaning and purpose of your life? of your business life?

- Convene a group of businesspeople and church professionals to contemplate these questions together. Determine one concrete problem you will continue to pursue together.

9

The Road Ahead

*We get them on Sunday, we used to get them in
school. Then we leave them to go back into business
alone. That's not what we claim the church is about.*
                                        —*Protestant pastor*

*This is an automatic relation, faith and work.
You can't put your finger on it.*
                                        —*Christian businessperson*

The alarming state of the church's ability to be a relevant force
influencing business can be summed up in a simple observation:
we already see many signs of Christian businesspeople from every
denomination rejecting their religion, and religion overwhelmingly
rejecting businesspeople. The standoff is so embedded in our current
culture that both groups assume Christianity and humane capitalism are at best compatible but separate. To deal with this assumption, both groups have developed severely limiting coping strategies

for thinking about faith and business career that are so pervasive they are considered accepted truth.

Not one of these strategies posits an active, developing synergy between faith and business, yet the role of faith is extremely important to business. As a source of strength and perspective, it is the baseline of conviction by which businesspeople may risk disappointment or failure in the search to make the world better. It reasserts a larger framework in which to measure progress toward the good life and purposes of God. These perspectives are vulnerable to corrosion by both extreme business success and extreme business ruthlessness. Formal religion allows time-honored articulation of belief, to be shared, celebrated, and held up as a standard to which communities of faith help keep each other accountable. These beliefs are messages of personal salvation and profound social obligation. Few people want only to work for a paycheck. This does not mean, however, that they believe it best to throw out the entire economic arrangement of capitalism.

In seeking a road map to live out these felt needs, people feel misunderstood by the clergy, who negatively stereotype their sentiments and diminish their contributions to daily life. What is particularly disturbing is the seeming inability of the Church to come to terms with this problem. Unless churches face up to their continued tendency to romanticize business on the conservative right or adopt thinly disguised leftist hostilities to capitalism in the mainstream churches, there will continue to be a steady race to alternative forms of religious guidance concerning the many challenges facing the businessperson of faith today.

Given the current lack of attention to the businessperson's highly privatized spiritual questing, it is difficult to give credence to the church's desire to be a force within the mainstream of economic life. One cannot address truly difficult questions without a basis of trust. In our interviews, both business and the church show a great deal of mistrust toward each other's motives, understanding, and morality.

The churches and businesspeople inside and outside the congregation must take the overall lessons of today's spiritual quest seriously. Given the individualistic, self-reliant focus of Protestant pragmatism, the fears of espoused religion in a pluralistic environment, and recent inability of the Christian religious voice to adapt to the economic problems business faces today, it's not surprising that businesspeople underestimate the importance of religious community to the development of an active and robust spiritual life. Many people assume that a severely isolated, personal responsibility for keeping true to their convictions is the only appropriate pilgrimage for ensuring that business life has a soul. We believe there is an urgent need to develop stronger community support within religious institutions for congregants who seek to live their faith in worldly occupations.

In *Crisis in the Churches*, Robert Wuthnow has underscored the church's failure to effectively engage in the personal economic lives of its congregants.[1] He posits alarming consequences for the values of the culture as well as the ability of the church to sustain itself fiscally. Our study of faith in a corporate setting reinforces many of Wuthnow's conclusions. The connections between Sunday and Monday are quite slim for many nominal Christians. There are very few successful models inside the churches to help people make these connections and still stay in business.

Today's spiritual quest in business is transforming how people think about corporations, success, career, and their own relation to the sacred. Seekers can be found in every congregation and corporation, determined to embark on their spiritual journey toward vocational awareness with or without the church. The church is challenged to respond.

A Wakeup Call

Our purpose in writing this book has been to offer a wakeup call: the task of creating bridges between faith and business has been neglected for too long. As it currently stands, the religious identity of businesspeople has been reduced to a set of caricatures; they can only act like moral menials or moral genials, doing the necessary evils or taking on the role of Santa Claus. The inability of most clergy to understand businesspeople in a nuanced light threatens the church's relationship as a living presence in the lives of the laity.

Currently, there are few resources for personalized, catalytic Christian spiritual experience directly accessible in the cognitive arsenal of business problem solving. Businesspeople who do have spiritual interest have lowered expectations about religious relevance in their working lives. As one religiously devout business school professor said to us, "It's not really clear that the church has anything to say in this area that's of any use."

This nonengagement between church and business is both ironic and alarming from moral and practical standpoints. It is neither fully perceived nor remotely satisfactory. The old term "comfortable Protestantism" is not just about failure to engage in social action of a radical sort, but rather failure to address the challenge of helping congregants negotiate the multiple responsibilities and pressures of modern economic life.

The simple mapping we explored in Chapter Four brings home with startling vividness the lack of church-associated religious penetration into the private sector in any form—values, sacred consciousness, or character-based behavior. One Presbyterian pastor reacted with shock as he studied the framework during a focus group session: "We do almost nothing to minister to businesspeople where they *live*."

Although many of the clergy and theologians we interviewed felt that the church was actively addressing economics in a way that offered effective guidance to business congregants, the reported reality from the businesspeople is different: the efforts of the church in this area are often dismissive and therefore often dismissed by the very people it seeks to influence.

The vacuum of faith-based reference within the shaded circle of our framework is so embedded in the culture of the corporation and the church that it is taken for granted. Coping strategies and common acceptance of vaguely understood distinctions such as "spiritual but not religious" rationalize away the separation when it cries out for new thinking. As a result, the complexities and paradoxes of Christian faith and of business are reduced to diatribes, platitudes, or vague—even weak—notions of generalization, nihilism, or justification.

The rationalizations of this status quo, the failure to address conflict and dissent constructively are serious problems. The mutual sense of distance, and sometimes abandonment, in the two professional groups is like a case of internal bleeding within the church community. The consequences of this distance are weakening the practical force of people's religion and the church's role in society.

Unless addressed constructively, the distanced relationship is likely to lead to further marginalization of the church. Mainstream businesspeople are leaving the mainstream churches; they are participating in many other programs that offer help in shaping the attitudes and behaviors that negotiate spirituality and economics. This trend flies in the face of the transformative aspirations of the church. It fails to serve the Christian religious community, and it fails to stimulate the personal and systemic insights that lead to the radical changes of culture and priorities that the church's social vision suggests. Said one interviewee with long experience in business and in doing volunteer financial work for the church: "Lay ministry used to mean telling people to stay out of the bars, be home, and cook dinner. Now we need a more nuanced view that takes men and women's professional lives into account. The old authoritarianism—'Pray, pay, and obey'—no longer works."[2]

Today's dropouts from church traditions—Wade Clark Roof's "Seekers"—have an even stronger negative view of the church's potential to be of help in addressing the deeper questions of faith or spirituality and daily life.

Moreover, marginalization has spillover in terms of the economic and social health of the church itself. As Wuthnow has reported, mainstream churches are experiencing weakened commitment from congregations on economic issues, from maintenance of the facilities to funding of mission projects. Withdrawing from economic issues only exacerbates these conditions.

Comments inside and outside the church suggest a certain blindness in the ecclesiastical self-assessment process, which has practical implications for the seminaries. Ecclesiastic training and accrediting structures continue to reward the specialized conversation of ecclesiastics speaking to each other but excluding the pragmatic optimists who conduct business and sit in the pews. This raises serious questions about whether the seminaries are really preparing the ministry to go out into the world. Our survey of seminaries indicated that a number of students were disappointed with their lack of training on contemporary economic institutions. Some commented on the misplaced self-satisfaction they saw around them as faculty and students develop strong theological positions over and against business and use them to justify substantial curriculum gaps in this area.

The most disturbing finding in our study was the degree to which the ecclesiastic community appears unconscious of the distancing and its role in contributing to the underlying causes. If the pace of disconnection is not to accelerate, the church must engage in a serious critique of its own triggering patterns so as to develop new approaches to being a critical force in businesspeople's lives. As we saw, this failure has many complex sources, including deep-seated differences of worldview, ignorance of business and economics, problem definition, language, and unresolved conflict over proper authority.

Deep ideological confusion, a hidden political agenda, poor track record in dealing with fiscal responsibility, and foundational traditions that have been used to support sexist and racist views must be considered in reviewing the church's stand on economic life. No doubt it would be quickly discovered that ecclesiastics and businesspeople have many professional problems in common, and that neither has exhausted the possibilities for deepening the religious dimension of addressing these concerns.

Still, although the dynamics of distance have many sources, it is clear that churches must come to terms with the intellectual bankruptcy of their existing economic ideologies. This is not necessarily a call for another round of theory, but for more perceptive and inclusive discussion of the gap between theory and practice. The conservative right's apologies and romanticization of capitalism may be more effective in promoting wealth creation and freedom than the liberal left agenda, but these approaches have failed to give guidance to the many obstacles to "caring capitalism" on the ground.

The tendency to seek resacralization of the workplace at the level of espoused religion continues to be more divisive than helpful. The right cannot paper over the systemic pressures businesspeople face to opt for ruthlessness. Moreover, continued association of the religious right's economic program with religious and social intolerance severely undermines the extremely useful relational approach of evangelicalism in general. Religious perspectives that make sense from the standpoint of personal responsibility and spirituality at work are nonetheless suspect if they gloss over deeply troubling failures to expand economic opportunity for those at the bottom rung of the ladder.

The economic messages of the liberal left church are equally problematic. Ecclesiastic elites are still promulgating autocratic, statist solutions to poverty and a profound anticorporation bias. If the church regards some form of capitalism as a legitimate economic structure, it must recognize the need to abandon an absolutist antibusiness stand. Ecclesiastics must come to terms with the fact that their widespread theoretical bias for communalism continues to favor economic solutions that have not brought human rights or economic development to the disadvantaged. They must reexamine their failure to acknowledge the essential social assets to be found in the basics that support free-market business: financial accountability, risk taking, open competition, value creation, legal infrastructure. Backing representatives of the poor who have frequently committed outrageous acts of theft, monopoly, or ethnic and racial intolerance, these blueprints for a responsible economic approach sit poorly with those who toil to be responsible stewards of other people's money. Macro plans for principled global capitalism are as naïve as the generalized secular spirituality vocabulary, and personally of little relevance in the business actor's decision-making arena. Meanwhile, the seminaries celebrate continued promulgation of elitist polemic.

There are signs of change within the ecclesiastic and lay institutions. Progress, however, has been slow, in large part because of the continued failure to achieve intellectual crossover between the two professional worlds at the foundational stages of these programs. Once again, it is unclear that either fully appreciates the impact these failures have on the life of the church, or the businessperson's ability to understand Christianity as a respected source of strength and guidance.

What You Can Do

Clearly, the dynamics of spiritual influence in practical life are not as well understood as we might hope. Moreover, the context of business is surely one of the most extreme challenges to applied Christianity faced by believers. More effort is needed. Any businessperson serving on a visiting board of advisers or deaconate should be holding their church institution (which includes faith-based nonprofits and seminaries) accountable for the job of bridging the two realms—and helping it find the means to do so. This should be occurring not only in terms of contact and information sharing but also in developing an exchange of deeper levels of consciousness that mark the two professions.

More research and discussion on the dynamics of the causes of distance is especially needed, but we cannot do it here. As one simple example, take the use of slogans by businesspeople. Frequently ridiculed as shallow, it is not evident that we really understand the moral function of such linguistic patterns. Nor is it clear what other form of articulation would deepen application of religious perspective to daily life.

Guidelines for Connecting Church and Work

We encourage you to use this book primarily as a diagnostic tool for testing the attitudes and accomplishments within your own experience, and as a common resource for discussing these factors together with other concerned individuals inside and outside the church. In Chapter Eight, we suggested a process and framework for a personal religious engagement in questions of business, and for encouraging a dialogue with peers. Below are additional general recommendations for moving forward to create a better business-church dialogue. These are guidelines for both business and church professionals. They can be seen as a cautionary warning so as to avoid the predictable pitfalls in taking up the question of business and religion—or in understanding when they do occur why they occur and how to hear beyond them:

Entry Points

Be aware of and rework the conceptual entry points:

- Start from the personalized, experiential, and contextual, and avoid generalized lionizing or attacks on the system.

- Rethink the first questions carefully from the standpoint of unstated stereotypes or radical naysayer–yea-sayer agendas.

- Avoid material that begins with an assertion of institutional territoriality over the right to dictate a solution.

- Work from religious concepts expressing the personal opportunity to fuse faith and work: calling, engine of justice, sacred awareness.

Avoiding Triggers

Avoid starting from the trigger-point words that cut dialogue and mutual inquiry short:

- For clergy: "the four P's": profit, poverty, polemics, and proselytizing

- For businesspeople: the platitudes on doing good to do well, Jack Welch's sainthood, and equating business activity with Jesus.

Differing Worldviews

Check for inherent differences accountable to worldview:

- Critical idealism versus practical optimism

- Subtractive versus additive approaches to securing a moral marketplace

- Personal resonance toward images of strength or weakness

- Overuse of romanticized religious metaphors to describe contemporary situations or villainous depiction of corporations

Knowing Thyself and the Other

Know thyself and know each other; don't assume you understand:

- Pay attention, listen for the hidden texts as described in Chapters Five through Seven. Test how they may be limiting your desire to understand and listen.

- Help inform the clergy of how key changes in the business environment are affecting the problems you see businesspeople having to handle.

Build Bridges

Build bridges between the professionals:

- Form new connections between the professional realms structurally, cognitively, and relationally.

- Build bridges from catalytic to foundational to espoused religious levels.

- Identify overlapping realms of religious opportunity and obstacles to religious action or consciousness in professional work.

- Bridge secular spirituality efforts (in which congregants find value) to foundational Christian concepts.

- Offer career counseling for seminary students to enter business and nonprofits when the ministry is not their calling.

Context

Develop particularized contexts:

- Share concrete experience as a point of departure for religious interpretation.

- Help convene occasions for reflection on contemporary problems.

- Fund and participate in case studies, fully developed and led by experienced discussion leaders.

Improve Professional Preparation

Weigh in and advise on how to retool formal educational preparation of ecclesiastics and businesspeople so as to address:

- Acute curriculum gaps on business and religion

- Lack of education on basic moral thinking in universities

- Case development and research development

- Funding problems

- Replication of distancing effect in the dynamics of academic advisory committees on which business people sit

- Deeper preparation for dealing with moral complexity in practice

- Clarification of the distinctiveness of the religious tradition

- Development of support for business schools to generate new participation in faith and work education separate from espoused agendas

- Encouragement of religious attention to the question, Why be ethical in business?

New Format for Inquiry

Develop new delivery formats for religious inquiry:

- Explore less-familiar theological concepts that avoid espoused associations already in place.

- Resurrect Christian exercises in catalytic spirituality.

- Create tangible symbolic expressions of respect for work and personal religious reminders that carry into pluralistic environments.

Share Authority

Rethink how authority is developed and communicated:

- Develop new neutral settings and zones free of fundraising.

- Create joint leadership for mutual journeying.

- Build new ongoing associations through lay groups.

- Invest in building new expertise on business and religion. Don't cherry pick partial expertise for your own conference program without giving something back to developing further learning.

- Include third parties for mediating turf, expertise, and interpretation of religious and business perspectives.

Participation

Show up and be interested:

- Clergy: attend the business seminars.

- Businesspeople: spend a day walking in your clergy's shoes.

- Ask what people do and think.

- Create opportunities for your personal participation in social service, in roles that do not match your business life or status.

- Develop in-residence programs for businesspeople at seminaries, and take your own sabbatical for study, dialogue, and reflection.

Create Language

Frame language for practical, business contexts:

- Use evocative and poetic vocabulary and syntax.

- Avoid scolding and dense abstractions.

Clean House

Clean house within the church itself:

- Model successful, religiously coherent administration.

- Educate clergy about management, including underlying attitudes about financial accountability and effectiveness.

- Subject fiscal and organizational problems to full ethical inquiry. Do not cover up or ignore personnel misconduct or discriminatory hiring and promotion practices.

The Journey Has Begun

Each of these recommendations has examples under way at the moment. There are signs of progress. Substantive shifts have occurred in the recent past, primarily in lay partnerships. The evangelical lay groups, such as Fellowship for Companies for Christ International, FaithWalk, Leadership Forum, Marketplace Network, and a host of others are reporting steady increases in membership.

New alliances between business guru and pastor, such as that of *One-Minute Manager* consultant Ken Blanchard and Willow Creek pastor Bill Hybels, offer exciting examples of dialogue in place of diatribe. Hybels and Blanchard have published a conversation on faith and work that has created an overall design for a new nonprofit seminar on faith and leadership, called FaithWalk. Like the

Fair Park/South Dallas efforts, this group is creating new alliances between business and religion in practice, reaching out to the San Diego community with new civic programs involving business leaders and church groups.

The power of such efforts seems to lie in their ability to create new, working partnerships between ecclesiastic and business gurus or leaders who are used to management training and public speaking on social issues. James Gustafson and former General Motors outside counsel Elmer Johnson (now president of the Aspen Institute) formed one such partnership, which was captured in an extremely challenging essay on the virtues of leadership.[3] George Soros managed to jump start the Trinity Church at Wall Street seminar back to life with a frank confession of his reservations about religion and capitalism before a group of CEOs. Fuller Seminary's alliance with the De Pree Leadership Center has recently formed a partnership with real estate executive Robert Anderson, an elder in his church, to hold a series of discussions for local business executives; attendance has doubled after each event.

What Does a Life of Faith Mean in the Context of Business?

The interest in foundational religious forms seems to be increasing, but there is still widespread belief that religion and business should not mix. What, then, does a life of faith mean in the context of business? If not based on incorporating explicit religious symbols, language, and authority into the workplace, then how do you know it when you see it? A starting point for this conversation is to clarify the three levels of religion as discussed in Chapter Eight, and to elicit people's reservations about business and religion together.

In the absence of more examples of applicable forms of religious insight, society has found many other mechanisms with which to guide and constrain marketplace activity. The overwhelming increase in legislative control of corporate activity forms a large litigious fan moving out from the upper right-hand corner of the integration framework of Figure 4.5 (social action), reaching out over just about every aspect of corporate life except the question of individual consciousness. This framework has penetrated business consciousness nonetheless, to the degree that businesspeople feel they cannot consider nonlitigious, personally relational strategies for resolving conflict without jeopardizing their business. Businesspeople lose the capacity to empathize and tolerate the risk of pursuing a solution that defies the adversarial framework. Secular spirituality programs, starting at just the opposite point, delve deeply into individual consciousness and cognition, reawakening the sentiments left dulled by the legalistic takeover of business decisions, but they fail to stimulate new civic solutions (supported by legislation) to problems created or solvable by business forces.

Together these two secular perspectives cover the map, but they do not give full play to Christian religious concepts. Nor do they really work in tandem with each other. There is little indication that Coveyites go out and reform labor laws, or that labor lawyers are transforming their inner selves to adopt practices that are more respectful and empowering of those outside the labor group.

These programs are competition for the spiritual and ethical consciousness of the businessperson, but they need not be so. Neither advocates a totally Secularist world. Most of the secular spirituality programs suggest the need to draw on personal faith traditions without taking the responsibility for helping people do so. Many of the quasi-legal business ethics programs are populated by people professing belief in God, if not Christianity. Churches should tap, rather than ignore, the dynamism of these movements. The Church should be actively exploring ways to bridge the void in its efforts to achieve a just, free, and humane society. To adopt such an additive approach, however, the church first has to understand the nature of the subtractive bias in its own patterns of economic engagement.

As we saw from our case profiles, it has become clear that lay programs need to be supplemented with substantial educational development of research and course material. Given the strong culture of specialization in academia, crossover education efforts need strong and extended funding, solid support from deans and presidents, and access to business leadership for help.

Currently, many programs at divinity and business schools are understaffed, created as a concession to major funders who will hopefully be diverted to other university funding needs. The donors themselves need to be much clearer from the start on how the university supports and develops new programs. Business and alumni must offer substantial support and a buffer of security around these programs, even though they meet enormous academic resistance from entrenched faculties. For these very reasons, there may be more slack in private foundations, and research and programs may thrive better under their auspices.

There also seems to be a recurrent problem in moving from the big-patron model of funding to multiple sources in the business community. (By contrast, look at the vast and diverse corporate resources invested in programs and books like Covey's). Typically, a single businessperson seeds an effort to sponsor activity on faith and work in a faith-based setting, and attendees from the business community regard these as free services. They seem surprised at the idea of actually contributing money to institutions that are not their alma mater or local church.

Although critical funding is needed from the business community to spur changes in the training and programs of the seminaries (and to a lesser degree the business schools), it is also important not to let programs fall back into narrowly defining the businessperson as a potential donor to the church. Fundraising has cynical associations and can undermine the ability to deliver any message about faith.

On the other hand, the current funding for development of programs and educational material on faith and work is weak. There needs to be much greater clarification up front on funding needs, so that donors can be found. An example of the careful planning and support that needs to occur is a Jewish business group in Los Angeles. Seeking to reconnect to its religious roots, the group privately formed a club in which each member is required to donate $30,000 a year for maintaining a rabbi and research staff to conduct various scholarship efforts on Judaism, society, and business. They meet monthly to explore these issues and have also created a strong philanthropic program within the overall club. The group is quite private in its meetings and does not publicize them in the workplace in any form. This has allowed a level of seriousness not replicated in many of the programs we saw. What it does not do, however, is share this learning with a wider academic community for discussion and critique. The need for institutional crossovers is obvious.

As we review these recommendations, there is a temptation to become too prescriptive at this early stage in the general repair of the business-church relationship. In the end, our strongest recommendation is to concentrate on the original focus presented here: the interest and the relationship. What we see most lacking is a mutual reaching out—from church and business alike—to offer support and guidance instead of dismissiveness or wholesale condemnation.

Our vision of a new approach to the business-church relationship does not mean that the church must abandon its priority to represent the needs of the disadvantaged. Nor that religion should cease being a voice attempting to influence public policy on economic decisions. Rather, we suggest that the church not confuse ultimate priorities with where one should first start a religious dialogue. An informed religious community must make careful distinctions among what a public policy concern is, what is tractable within the corporate sector, and what carries the religious dimension into the daily lives of congregants high and low on the business ladder.

Tocqueville's observation of the extreme religiosity and pragmatism of the American culture has not become obsolete. We still see Americans channeling much of their energy into exciting new forms of trade, only to sail off into novel forms of spiritual inquiry at the drop of a hat. As the Puritan merchant Robert Keayne demonstrated, crossover has never been smooth. Today's environment has only intensified the juxtaposition of spiritual and business impulses in the United States. These impulses can be trivialized into fleeting expressions of sentimental idealism or captured and developed into a full understanding of the good person.

Our findings suggest that the religious development of congregants who are in business is a two-way process, not an instructional statement from on high. It comes from participation and relationship. The best focus for moving forward with the businessperson's current spiritual quest is for both ecclesiastic and business professionals to attend to their mutual relationship.

A Hopeful Challenge

We invite you to consider the new search for integration as a hopeful challenge: one not simply to strengthen the connection between the concerns of Christian faith and the believers in the world of business but also to strengthen the church itself.

The opportunity for deeper religious meaning in work must be posed and developed inside and outside the church. In the foundational notions of the church's older social arrangements, there are themes that resonate with the most progressive spiritual concerns of the day: economics structured in harmony with nature's rhythms, a notion of work that is spiritually equal to a life of contemplation, a sense of religious mission for the community as a whole to advance just purposes. The conditions of the righteous community, described in Exodus, are a rich starting point: deliverance from unjust, oppressive systems into a state characterized by righteousness, religious joy, and abundant provisions for life on earth—a land of milk and honey.

At the same time, we must not forget the new commandment: to love one another. Finding a richly developed notion of love and devotion in the marketplace is at times a puzzle, though at other times as apparent as a simple act of service to another in need. Our hope is that these moments can be strengthened and sustained through the business community's investment in its own search for religious meaning—and in a church that supports that search.

A Note on Methodology

As we conducted our interviews for this book, two responses surprised us over and over again. Some people were totally turned off and had no interest in addressing this problem. Others held to initial insistence that they had a good relationship—businessperson with pastor, and pastor with businessperson—until we probed a little deeper. In both cases they had come to accept the status quo and wondered why we would even want to address the issue.

Given extreme sensitivity and reluctance to participate meaningfully in the questions about the role of the church vis-à-vis business, we have had to rely on a rather messy sample, finding evidence of worldview, attitudes, and experience where we could. Our research consisted of in-depth interviews of businesspeople and clergy from primarily Caucasian mainstream and nonaffiliated Christian denominations and lay groups (approximately ninety-five individuals, with a larger number attending but not always commenting); case studies of programs that appeared to be offering particularly noteworthy programs for businesspeople at ten sites, reviewed for accuracy by the institutions profiled; a written survey of seminaries; and an extensive review of more than a hundred books, articles, and programs (secular and religious) appealing to executive spiritual development. It also builds on material gathered from *Believers in Business*, a previous book on eighty-five Christian CEOs published by Laura Nash.

Our chief focus was on businesspeople in positions of management authority and the Christian clergy and lay groups serving this community.

Our sample congregations were chosen to highlight middle and upper management. We conducted the majority of interviews in the greater Boston area, with significant input from several congregations along the eastern seaboard, Chicago, and the Los Angeles area. We have been warned that our sample may be overly skewed toward the most liberal, secular-humanistic population in America. It is a point well taken. For this reason, we have tried to present this data as *representative of key issues* in the faith-and-work movement without making claims to depicting the definitive state of church-congregant relations in America today.

Many people expressed an intense sense of privacy about the topic and their participation, so we have chosen to keep all remarks anonymous unless previously published elsewhere. For this same reason, we have not acknowledged the names of the pastors and businesspeople who helped us on this project. Our gratitude to their contribution is enormous and can best be expressed by preserving their privacy.

The difficulty of gaining access to executives concerning the state of their relation to the church on business-related topics cannot be overestimated. For many businesspeople, especially those outside an evangelical confessional tradition, personal religious affiliation is a private thing, inappropriate to discuss as it relates to one's official executive role. They often seek to disguise, not advertise, their relationship to their church. Businesspeople were reluctant to offer names of colleagues for participation in interviews, for fear of appearing to use their power to coerce people to discuss private matters. Many clergy, unwilling to approach members of their congregation who were in a position of significant business responsibility, refused our request to participate. In one example, a large suburban Catholic church with an upscale executive congregation published such an invitation in its bulletin for three weeks. Only one businessperson expressed interest in participating. The church leader who gave permission to run the ad did not feel it would be appropriate to contact anyone personally for fear of appearing to coerce them. Even lay groups that knew our work and trusted us personally did not necessarily feel it appropriate to let us have any kind of access to their membership, not even a flier indicating the existence of our study and an invitation to contact us.

In general, we gained access through clergy who graciously were willing to take the risk and assemble a focus group, by personal recommendation of another businessperson (the snowball method), or from serendipity. Some of the best interviews were achieved through the back door—in connection with a gathering for some other expressed purpose concerning business or religion. Clearly, more methodical work is to be done, and we hope this study is the impetus for further inquiry by the churches themselves.

Most unchurched interviewees had been members of a church in the past. The ratio of clergy (including theologians) to businessperson was approximately one to four (in about ten cases, people held both professional positions). An interview normally took place over a private meal or in a convened discussion group at a church or university. In a few cases, clergy participated in a group gathering hosted at a church. The majority of discussions, however, were conducted with businesspeople and clergy separated from each other.

We shared our conclusions and integration framework with several large groups of clergy and businesspeople outside Boston. Even where local experience differed from the findings, the findings themselves gave clergy and businesspeople insight into the general dynamics and problems of church-based interest in spirituality and work today. If this is so, our goals have been fulfilled.

Our study did not include non-Christian religions, African American churches and congregations, and churches whose congregations are primarily blue-collar workers. Blue-collar workers were not included on the assumption that most of the "secular spirituality" programs sponsored by corporations have been geared toward middle and upper management. We also felt that the business problems of managers were often of a different nature than those of blue-collar workers, and that managers had been less studied by the church than the labor movement. Our focus does not in any way reflect an opinion that blue-collar jobs have less spiritual potential than white-collar ones.

Originally, we planned to include churches that have predominantly African American congregations, but we abandoned this idea after some interviewing and case study work. We soon found that in many areas both the economic and social profiles of these congregations and the historic role of the black church as mediator to congregants' economic life were radically different from those of white churches. To tackle both was beyond our capability.

It is an unfortunate fact of American life that churches are among the most segregated institutions in the country. It is dangerous to extrapolate the religious experiences of one denomination or social class onto another. Indeed, our preliminary screening showed many differences. On the surface, black churches appear to cross the realms much more frequently than white clergy. They have been the predominant institution in many of their congregants' lives, in part because the community's economic or educational prospects have been so constrained. The church remains an important gatekeeper—spiritual and economic—for a population without easy access to other institutional supports from the private and public sector.

African American churches perform many functions. They are the site of local political action. They help people network for jobs or loans. They are a platform for information sharing about the financial activities of their members. They secure assistance for the needy in their own congregation and community. They open their pulpit to political figures who might bring economic improvement to the community. They help members develop job skills (including acquiring education). They also sponsor startup businesses.

By contrast, for many whites it is corporations and secular humanistic educational institutions that have been the predominant gatekeepers to their financial and career performance. These same institutions compete with and share moral concern with the white churches about many important activities associated with Christian doctrine.

The gatekeeper role of the black church, and the economic marginalization of many of its congregants in respect to traditional business, are just two factors that predict a differing profile for the church on the question of integrating faith and work. A detailed and comparative study of black churches would be most useful, but it was beyond the scope of our expertise and this project.

Similarly, we did not try to study Jewish or Islamic congregations because of fundamental differences of economic theology and congregational practice that would have made our findings overly complex. Again, comparative research is surely useful but beyond our intended scope.

A word about the survey. We attempted to contact twenty-five leading seminaries and divinity schools in the United States by phone. Each was asked to distribute a written questionnaire to twenty students and five faculty members. The purpose was not to single out specific schools for particularly good or bad preparation, and for this reason we have not attributed the source of any remarks drawn from the surveys. Our sample was much too limited to draw any such conclusions. Fourteen of the fifteen institutions that agreed to participate responded (154 responses in all): Andover Newton Theological Seminary, Boston University School of Theology, Catholic Theological Union, Episcopal Divinity School, Fuller Theological Seminary, Gordon-Conwell Theological Seminary, Harvard University Divinity School, Holy Cross Greek Orthodox School of Theology, Institute for Buddhist Studies (Graduate Theological

Union), Nazarene Theological Seminary, Princeton Theological Seminary, Southern Baptist Theological Seminary, St. Vladimir's Orthodox Theological Seminary, and Weston Jesuit School of Theology.

We asked schools to choose a mixed sample that included, but did not exclusively comprise, people they felt were teaching or doing course work that would relate to business and religion in any way. We also asked that they try to reach students who were nearing the end of their graduate work, so as to better reflect the experience of their training. Given the wide differences of curriculum, it was impossible to set up any further parameters on the choice of students. (A survey of catalogues was only minimally helpful.) We did ask respondents to indicate any courses they had taken or taught relating to business, but without extensive interviewing it was impossible to determine the depth and nature of the coverage in these courses. There did not appear to be any correlation with such exposure and the responses on other questions. All answers were cross-tabulated by school, question, status (student or faculty), and gender. A sample Biographical Profile of Respondent and Questionnaire are included at the end of this section.

The data from these responses are fascinating but should not be overstated, given the sampling method. For this reason we have reported general patterns in the responses rather than actual percentages, for fear that once put on paper the percentages will be overblown in subsequent discussion. In our opinion, the role of academic institutions in the church's ability to give guidance to businesspeople deserves continued study and reflection. We hope the information here is of help to others undertaking such an effort.

Biographical Profile of Respondent and Questionnaire

Object of questionnaire: To explore how seminaries prepare students to minister to members of the business community. This survey is part of a larger study that includes interviews with clergy, rabbis, and business leaders, with a focus on executives who hold senior positions and have significant stewardship functions.

Confidentiality: All information will be reported in generalized form, e.g., "A first-year Jesuit seminarian who had once owned a business commented as follows. . . ." Participants' identities will not be disclosed, unless agreed upon in writing by the author and the participant.

A. Personal Information

Name: Parents' profession(s):

Address: Past profession (if any):

Telephone: Current seminary or school:

                                              Academic field of concentration:

Gender: F   M   States and countries where you have
                                              lived:

Education:
Religious affiliation: Past religious affiliation (if different):

B. Curriculum

(Please circle Yes or No where appropriate.)

1. Are there any business-related courses included in your curriculum?
   No   Yes (Please specify title of course or courses.)

2. Are any business or economics books, journals, or TV programs assigned as required reading or viewing?
   No   Yes (Please specify.)

3. How important do you feel it is for your curriculum to include ministry issues regarding businesses and businesspeople?

C. Scripture

(Please circle Yes or No where appropriate.)

4a. Do you include any scripture passages in your courses with the explicit purpose of discussing their implications for businesses or businesspeople?

        No   Yes (Please describe.)

4b. Have you ever tried to apply any scripture passages to what you see is going on in the world of business?

        No   Yes (Please specify the passages.)

5. Have you given or heard any sermons on how businesspeople form part of the religious community and how they fit into the fabric of society?

        No   Yes (Please specify the key messages conveyed.)

D. Religious Tradition

(Please circle Yes or No where appropriate.)

6. What were the main images or themes, or what do you perceive as the main issues, regarding the relationship between the church/temple and businesspeople?

7a. Do you feel that your religious tradition has any particular view about businesspeople or business?

        No   Yes (Please explain if this view is positive or negative.)

7b. Is there any attention to this in courses?

        No   Yes (Please specify.)

7c. What is your own view with regard to the above?

8. Do you think that in general the church/temple's relationship has changed with respect to business?

        No   Yes (Please specify.)

E. Personal Experience and Development of a Worldview

(Please circle Yes or No where appropriate.)

9a. Does your program include some kind of contact with businesspeople who hold positions of responsibility, e.g., talks, informal gatherings, etc.?

        No   Yes (Please specify.)

9b. Do you participate in any activities that bring you into contact with businesspeople?

  No Yes (Please specify.)

10. Do you have any family members or friends who may be considered senior business executives?

  No Yes (Please specify.)

11. Do you feel that you understand the role that business plays in our society today?

  No Yes (Please comment.)

12. Do you have opportunities to discuss your views with other colleagues in this regard?

  No Yes (Please specify with whom and how frequently.)

13. Have you ever prepared a sermon or given a talk that is addressed to the business community?

  No Yes (Please specify the title or main theme, and include a copy, if you desire.)

14. How do you understand the ministry needs of businesspeople?

15. If you could, how would you like to influence the church/temple's role or attitude toward large businesses?

16. If you could, how would you change business?

17. If you could, how would you like to minister to the businesspeople in your religious community?

Thank you for your participation.

Notes

Preface

1. *The Apologia of Robert Keayne; the last will and testament of me, Robert Keayne, all of it written with my own hands and began by me, mo: 6: 1: 1653, commonly called August; the Self-Portrait of a Puritan Merchant.* (B. Bailyn, ed.). New York: Harper Torchbooks, 1965.

Introduction

1. See James, W. *The Varieties of Religious Experience: A Study in Human Nature.* New York: Macmillan, 1961, p. 90. (Originally published 1902)

2. Fogel, R. *The Fourth Great Awakening and the Future of Egalitarianism.* Chicago: University of Chicago Press, 2000.

3. The term is Wade Clark Roof's, used in his excellent surveys of the new religious profiles of baby boomers. See *A Generation of Seekers: The Spiritual Journeys of the Baby Boom Generation,* with Bruce Greer (San Francisco: HarperSanFrancisco, 1993); and *Spiritual Marketplace: Baby Boomers and the Remaking of American Religion.* Princeton: Princeton University Press, 1999.

4. See Cimino, R. P., and Lattin, D. *Shopping for Faith: American Religion in the New Millennium*. San Francisco: Jossey-Bass, 1998; Gallup, G., Jr., and Castelli, J. *The People's Religion: American Faith in the '90s*. New York: Macmillan, 1989; Jones, T., and Gallup, G., Jr. *The Next American Spirituality: Finding God in the Twenty-First Century*. Colorado Springs, Colo.: Cook Communications, 2000; Marty, M. E. *The One and the Many: America's Struggle for the Common Good*. Cambridge: Harvard University Press, 1997; Roof, W. C. *A Generation of Seekers*. San Francisco: HarperSanFrancisco, 1993, and *Spiritual Marketplace*. Princeton: Princeton University Press, 1999; and Wuthnow, R. *The Crisis in the Churches: Spiritual Malaise, Fiscal Woe*. New York: Oxford University Press, 1997. George Barna of the Barna Research Group calls the new mainstream generation of believers "the Mosaic." See also Mitroff, I. I., and Denton, E. A. "A Study of Spirituality in the Workplace." *Sloan Management Review*, Summer 1999, 83–92; and McLennan, S. *Finding Your Religion*. San Francisco: HarperSanFrancisco, 1999.

5. For example, the United Methodist Church declined from 11 million members in 1965 to 9 million today; the Episcopal Church went from 3.6 million to 2.5 million.

6. For further discussion of our methodology, see "A Note on Methodology."

7. Jones and Gallup (2000), pp. 184–185.

8. Mitroff, I. I., and Denton, E. A. *A Spiritual Audit of Corporate America: A Hard Look at Spirituality, Religion, and Values in the Workplace*. San Francisco: Jossey-Bass, 2000. They report that 60 percent of their sample felt positively toward the idea of spirituality and negatively toward religion. Another 30 percent felt positively to both. See also, Grossman, C. L. "In Search of Faith: For Many, Self-Defined 'Spirituality' Is Replacing a Church-Based Faith." *USA Today*, Dec. 23–26, 1999, pp. 1A, 2A. In a CNN Gallup Poll survey reported in this article, people see themselves as "spiritual but not religious." For the trend toward grassroots, self-defined religion, see Roof (1993, 1999); see also Creedon, J. "God with a Million Faces." *Utne Reader*, July–Aug. 1998, 22–28; and McDonald, M. "Shush.

The Guy in the Cubicle Is Meditating. Spirituality Is the Latest Corporate Buzzword." *U.S. News & World Report*, May 3, 1999.

Chapter One

1. Many others repeated this interviewee's comments. For confirming and contrasting views, see Wuthnow, R. *God and Mammon in America*. New York: Free Press, 1994, 55–56. He cites contradictory survey results regarding participation in and understanding of the church concerning religion and work. In one survey, 90 percent of church members claimed never to have heard a sermon relating faith and their work; Wuthnow's Economic Values Study revealed that 40 percent had heard a sermon that inspired them to work harder; and only 24 percent of the labor force agree with the statement, "Members of the clergy have very little understanding of what it is like in the real workaday world." He also noted, however, that only 20 percent of church members say they have talked about their work with a member of the clergy in the preceding year. See also Wuthnow (1997), p. 66, citing the attitude that a worker would not turn to her pastor for advice on a serious ethical decision at work.

2. See, for example, Wuthnow (1997), p. 6. He reports a strong tendency for the clergy to preach on topics presented by the media reflecting large political issues and the culture wars rather than the reality of everyday life.

3. Kelly, K. *New Rules for the New Economy: Radical Strategies for a Connected World*. New York: Viking, 1998.

4. From a study by business professors Albert Vicere, Pennsylvania State University, and Robert Fulmer, College of William and Mary, reported by Farnham, A. "In Search of Suckers: A Growing Army of Tom Peters Wannabes Are Making Millions Peddling Advice to Managers." *Fortune*, Oct. 14, 1996, p. 119.

5. In this same vein, some Christian conservatives use *secular* to indicate any ultimate claim not centered on Christ, including Buddhist practices.

6. William James noted the frequency of what he called the language of "respiratory oppression" in the Bible, and the even stronger use of expiration and inspiration of breath in Eastern religious practices. James (1961), p. 278.

7. Covey, S. R. *The Seven Habits of Highly Effective People*. New York: Simon and Schuster, 1989, p. 292.

8. Block, P. *Stewardship: Choosing Service over Self-Interest*. San Francisco: Berrett-Koehler, 1993, pp. 48–49.

9. Though the four needs were drawn from a variety of spirituality programs and our interviews, note that authors John B. Izzo and Eric Klein suggest four paths to corporate soul that roughly reflect a more functional description of our four felt needs. Their categories are doing work that has the potential to become a direct expression of one's values; work that enables people to feel they are making a worthy contribution; work that allows people to find and discover new areas of mastery and artistry; and work that fosters community and teamwork in an organization. Izzo, J. B., and Klein, E. *Awakening Corporate Soul: Four Paths to Unleash the Power of People at Work*. Edmonton: Fair Winds Press, 1998.

10. See especially Shor, J. *The Overworked American: The Unexpected Decline of Leisure*. New York: Basic Books, 1993; and *The Overspent American: Why We Want What We Don't Need*. New York: HarperCollins, 1999.

11. Greenleaf, R. K. *Servant Leadership: A Journey into the Nature of Legitimate Power and Greatness*. New York: Paulist Press, 1977, pp. 28, 186.

12. Rogers, F. *You Are Special: Words of Wisdom from America's Most Beloved Neighbor*. New York: Penguin, 1994.

13. For a comparative discussion of religions and social justice, see Green, R. M. *Religion and Moral Reason: A New Method for Comparative Study*. New York: Oxford University Press, 1988, pp. 162–194.

14. For further discussion, see Nash, L. *Believers in Business*. Nashville: Thomas Nelson, 1994, pp. 6–8, 124–162.

15. Coué, E., and Orton, J. L. *Conscious Auto-Suggestion*. London: T. F. Unwin, limited, 1924.

16. Kaminer, W. "The Latest Fashion in Irrationality." *Atlantic Monthly*, July 1996. Also, Kaminer, W. *Sleeping with Extra-Terrestrials: The Rise of Irrationalism and Perils of Piety*. New York: Pantheon Books 1999.

17. Dykstra, C. "Religion and Spirituality." *Responsive Community*, Winter 1996, p. 6.

Chapter Two

1. According to Ian Mitroff, about 60 percent of businesspeople claiming some sort of belief adopt this stand. See Mitroff, I. I., and Denton, E. A. *A Spiritual Audit of Corporate America: A Hard Look at Spirituality, Religion, and Values in the Workplace*. San Francisco: Jossey-Bass, 2000.

Chapter Three

1. Wuthnow (1997), p. 11. See also Ammerman, N. T., with Farnsley II, A. E., and Adams, T. *Congregation and Community*. New Brunswick, N.J.: Rutgers University Press, 1997.

2. Marty, M. "Number of Centers Studying Public Religion Grows." *Sightings*, June 19, 1999.

3. See, for example, Bellah, R. N. *Beyond Belief: Essays on Religion in a Post-Traditional World*. Berkeley: University of California Press, 1991; Bellah, R. N., and others. *Habits of the Heart: Individualism and Commitment in American Life*. Berkeley: University of California Press, 1996; and Madsen, R., Sullivan, W. N., Bellah, R. N., and Swidler, A. *The Good Society*. New York: Vintage, 1992.

4. As reported by Greenhouse, S. "Clergy and Unions Teaming Up Again. Roots of Labor Day Recalled in Services." *New York Times*, Sep. 6, 1999, p. A9.

5. In all, we reviewed more than 125 books in the areas of new spirituality, science, and religion, or management and religion. The top 25 from which we drew our main conclusions about the content,

underlying assumptions, and techniques of the new spirituality and business movement were Allman, W. F. *The Stone Age Present*. New York: Touchstone, 1995; Autry, J. A. *Love and Profit: The Art of Caring Leadership*. New York: Avon, 1992; Blanchard, K., Hybels, B., and Hodges, P. *Leadership by the Book: Tools to Transform Your Workplace*. New York: William Morrow, 1999; Blanchard, K., and Peale, N. V. *The Power of Ethical Management*. New York: William Morrow, 1988; Block, P. *Stewardship: Choosing Service over Self-Interest*. San Francisco: Berrett-Koehler, 1993; Briner, B. *The Management Methods of Jesus: Ancient Wisdom for Modern Business*. Nashville: Thomas Nelson, 1996; Canfield, J., and others. *Chicken Soup for the Soul at Work*. Deerfield Beach, Fla.: Health Communications, 1996; Carlson, R. *Don't Sweat the Small Stuff . . . and It's All Small Stuff*. New York: Hyperion, 1997; Chappell, T. *The Soul of a Business: Managing for Profit and the Common Good*. New York: Bantam, 1993; Chopra, D. *The Seven Spiritual Laws of Success: A Practical Guide to the Fulfillment of Your Dreams*. San Rafael, Calif.: Amber-Allen, 1994; Chopra, D. *How to Know God: The Soul's Journey into the Mystery of Mysteries*. New York: Crown, 2000; Covey, S. R. *Principle-Centered Leadership*. New York: Fireside, 1992; Covey, S. R., Merrill, A. R., and Merrill, R. R. *First Things First: To Live, to Love, to Learn, to Leave a Legacy*. New York: Simon & Schuster, 1994; Covey, S. R. *The Seven Habits of Highly Effective People*. New York: Simon and Schuster, 1989; Lama Surya Das. *Awakening the Buddha Within*. New York: Broadway Books, 1997; De Pree, M. *Leadership Is an Art*. New York: Doubleday, 1989; Edelman, J., and Crain, M. B. *The Tao of Negotiation*. New York: HarperCollins, 1993; Garfield, C. *Peak Performers: The New Heroes of American Business*. New York: Avon, 1986; Greenleaf, R. K. *Servant Leadership: A Journey into the Nature of Legitimate Power and Greatness*. New York: Paulist Press, 1997; Guinness, O. *The Call: Finding and Fulfilling the Central Purpose of Your Life*. Nashville: Word, 1998; Handy, C. *The Hungry Spirit*. New York: Broadway Books, 1998; Harner, M. *The Way of the Shaman*. (3rd ed.) San Francisco: HarperSanFrancisco, 1990; Hendricks, G., and Ludeman, K. *The Corporate Mystic: A Guidebook for Visionaries with Their Feet on the Ground*. New York: Bantam, 1997; Hillman, J. *The Soul's Code: In Search of*

Character and Calling. New York: Warner Books, 1996; Hutchens, D. *Outlearning the Wolves: Surviving and Thriving in a Learning Organization*. Waltham, Mass.: Pegasus Communications, 1998; Inamori, K. *A Passion for Success: Practical, Inspirational, and Spiritual Insight from Japan's Leading Entrepreneur*. New York: McGraw-Hill, 1995; Jaworski, J. *Synchronicity: The Inner Path of Leadership*. San Francisco: Berrett-Koehler, 1996; Jones, L. B. *Jesus CEO: Using Ancient Wisdom for Visionary Leadership*. New York: Hyperion, 1995; Kauffman, S. *At Home in the Universe: The Search for the Laws of Self-Organization and Complexity*. New York: Oxford University Press, 1995; Komisar, R., with Lineback, K. *The Monk and the Riddle: The Education of a Silicon Valley Entrepreneur*. Boston: Harvard Business School Press, 2000; Noble, D. F. *The Religion of Technology: The Divinity of Man and the Spirit of Invention*. New York: Alfred A. Knopf, 1998; Oakley, E., and Krug, D. *Enlightened Leadership: Getting to the Heart of Change*. New York: Fireside, 1994; Peck, M. S. *The Road Less Traveled: A New Psychology of Love, Traditional Values, and Spiritual Growth*. New York: Touchstone, 1978; Pollard, C. W. *The Soul of the Firm*. New York: HarperBusiness/Zondervan, 1996; Redfield, J., and Adrienne, C. *The Celestine Prophecy: An Experiential Guide*. New York: Warner, 1995; Robbins, A. *Awaken the Giant Within: How to Take Immediate Control of Your Mental, Emotional, Physical and Financial Destiny!* New York: Fireside, 1991; Wheatley, M. J. *Leadership and the New Science: Learning About Organization from an Orderly Universe*. San Francisco: Berrett-Koehler, 1992; Whyte, D. *The Heart Aroused: Poetry and the Preservation of the Soul*. New York: Currency/Doubleday, 1994; Wilber, K. *Spirituality: A Brief History of Everything*. Boston: Shambala, 1996; and Wilber, K. *The Marriage of Sense and Soul: Integrating Science and Religion*. New York: Random House, 1998.

6. Bellah (1991).

7. Hendricks and Ludeman (1997), p. xviii.

8. Conservative or fundamentalist believers in the Muslim, Jewish, and Christian (including Mormon) communities have disagreed with this assessment and have on occasion sued corporations for imposing "new age" religion on them. This has led to reassertion of

Title VII as having implied no discrimination on the basis of religion and right to freedom of expression (but not oppression) in the workplace. Although these complaints are important, they do not appear to represent the general business population. In our interviews and work with executives, a number were somewhat concerned about the corporation acting as Big Spiritual Brother, but they also felt fully capable of maintaining their personal religious commitments. In their view, participation in these exercises did not present a threat of imposing on their freedom of religion, partly because they did not see them as religion in the traditional sense of the word.

Chapter Four

1. For a discussion of this trend, see Nash, L. "The Nanny Corporation." *Across the Board*, May/June 1994; and Heuberger, F., and Nash, L. (eds.). *A Fatal Embrace? Assessing Holistic Trends in Human Resources Programs*. New Brunswick: Transaction Publications, 1994.

2. This selection resembles most closely the classic description of the realm of the manager that was first identified by Chester I. Barnard in *The Functions of the Executive* (Cambridge: Harvard University Press, 1938). It divided organizations by cooperative situations and described four in relation to the corporation: (1) those that relate to aspects of the physical environment, (2) those that relate to aspects of the social environment, (3) those that relate to individuals, and (4) other variables. The details of the business realm given here combine these principles with typical functional descriptions used in companies today.

3. Management expert Herbert Simon made this point in his landmark *Administrative Behavior: A Study of Decision-Making Processes in Administrative Organization*. (3rd ed.) New York: Free Press, 1976. Simon noted (p. 38) that most descriptions of administration confined themselves too closely to mechanisms of authority, thereby creating a superficial, oversimplified, and unrealistic picture of why people behave the way they do.

4. Sethi, S. P., and Williams, O. *Economic Imperatives and Ethical Values in Global Business: The South African Experience and International*

Codes Today. Boston and Dordrecht: Kluwer Academic, 2000. For a good selection of denominational position papers on economics, see Stackhouse, M. L, Dennis, D. P., McCann, P., and Roels, S. J. (eds.), with Williams, P. *On Moral Business: Classical and Contemporary Resources for Ethics in Economic Life.* Grand Rapids, Mich.: Eerdmans, 1995.

5. As noted earlier, African American churches did not fit the patterns described here. Regardless of racial and ethnic differences, largely blue-collar congregations displayed extensive church activity in nuts-and-bolts economic counseling (use of credit cards, how to balance a checkbook, or ways to develop new job skills). Since this study is concentrating primarily on middle-class and top executives who have these skills, our discussion does not take up activities of this type.

Chapter Five

1. This quote and the event are taken from Bombardieri, M. "Bankers Come Up with Y2K Sermon." *Boston Globe,* Oct. 17, 1999, p. B4.

2. See especially Robert Wuthnow's extensive work on attitudes toward money in *God and Mammon in America.* New York: Free Press, 1994; *Poor Richard's Principle.* Princeton, N.J.: Princeton University Press, 1996; *The Crisis in the Churches: Spiritual Malaise, Fiscal Woe.* New York: Oxford University Press, 1997; and *Learning to Care: Elementary Kindness in an Age of Indifference.* New York: Oxford University Press, 1995. Our research confirmed many of his findings on the type of topic and reason for a sense of disconnect. Rather than repeat all aspects here, we try to enlarge his already in-depth analysis with discussion of how these attitudes were a key factor in the dynamics that caused businesspeople to feel unsupported by their churches in their attempt to integrate faith and their professional roles.

3. Were we to superimpose this conception of business on our integration framework, the shaded circle would be reduced to a dollar sign. In practice, this is how church depictions of business are often framed. Mark Ellingsen's study of public statements on social issues

by church groups from the 1960s to the 1990s revealed that in more than thirty years of activity on economic issues, only three statements frame the corporation as a potentially positive contributor to human well-being; the overwhelming majority voiced doubt as to any possibility of spiritual or moral contribution from business. See Ellingsen, M. *The Cutting Edge: How Churches Speak on Social Issues*. Geneva: Institute for Ecumenical Research, WCC Publications, and Grand Rapids, Mich.: Eerdmans, 1993.

4. Stackhouse, M. "Theology and the Economic Life of Society in a Global Era: On Mars, Eros, the Muses, Mammon, and Christ." *Public Policy Review and Civil Reform* (forthcoming).

5. For an extremely thorough and thoughtful explication of biblical views on wealth, passed through the "tainted" filter, see Wheeler, S. E. *Wealth as Peril and Obligation: The New Testament on Possessions*. Grand Rapids, Mich.: Eerdmans, 1995.

6. Although there seem to be Marxist echoes in the concern that capitalism has coopted the values of the establishment, no clergy and only a handful of seminarians directly referred to Marx in our interviews. Wuthnow reports that in his surveys of economic attitudes among religious professionals, the word that comes up most often when pastors talk about economic issues is *selfishness* (Wuthnow, 1997, p. 77).

7. According to the UN Development Program, the three richest people in the world (Bill Gates was number one, Warren Buffett was number three) have personal assets that together exceed the combined gross domestic product of the forty-eight least-developed nations in the world. See Knickerbocker, B. "Billionaires Giving to Get the Numbers Down." *Christian Science Monitor*, Sept. 30, 1999, p. 17. According to this same study, the world's 358 billionaires exceed the combined income of the countries that contain 45 percent of the world's population. Such numbers suggest a degree of injustice regarding the systemic mechanisms for balancing reward and effort that goes beyond any quibbles over differences in cost of living and the like.

8. Green, R. N. *Religion and Moral Reason: A New Method for Comparative Study*. New York: Oxford University Press, 1988, p. xv.

9. Pollard, W. C. "Bridging the Gulf." Speech delivered at Yale Berkeley Seminar, May 8, 1998, privately distributed, pp. 18, 19.

10. Stackhouse, M., with P. Paris (eds.) *God and Globalization*. Vol. 1. Harrisburg, PA: Trinity Press International, 2000, p. 19.

11. Tawney, R. H. *Religion and the Rise of Capitalism*. (A. B. Seligman, ed.) New Brunswick, N.J.: Transaction, 1998, p. 128.

12. Wilson, W. J. *When Work Disappears: The World of the New Urban Poor*. New York: Knopf, 1996.

13. Wuthnow (1997), pp. 93–98.

14. So, too, Wuthnow (1997), p. 77: "The word that comes up most often when pastors talk about economic issues is selfishness." Obviously, prosperity gospels were the exception to this view. They were not prevalent in our interviews.

15. Hough, J. C., Jr. "Theologian at Work." In C. S. Duley (ed.), *Building Effective Ministries*. New York: HarperCollins, 1983, p. 112. We are grateful to the Rev. Charles Bennison for calling our attention to this paper.

Chapter Six

1. This passage is quoted in Weber, M. *The Protestant Ethic and the Spirit of Capitalism*. (T. Parsons, trans.) New York: Scribner, 1958, p. 175.

2. Weiss, R. *The American Myth of Success*. Urbana, Ill.: University of Chicago Press, 1988, pp. 19ff.

3. See Mather, C. *Bonifacius: An Essay upon the Good*. (Edited, with an introduction by David Levin.) Cambridge, Mass.: Belknap Press of Harvard University Press, 1966.

4. As Daniel Bell so admirably demonstrated in *The Cultural Contradictions of Capitalism* (New York: Basic Books, 1976).

5. Baltzell, E. D. *The Protestant Establishment*. New Haven: Yale University Press, 1964, pp. 159ff.

6. Of the seventeen types of self-framed responses to the question "If you could, how would you like to minister to the businesspeople in your religious community?" almost 30 percent of students saw no

reason to believe that businesspeople needed any special ministering (twenty-one student responses; nine more answered either "don't know," "prefer to minister to the poor," or "not relevant to me"). The second most frequent responses were "seminars, sermons, and teaching" (fourteen) and "invite support, encourage, take an interest" (fourteen). The third most frequent answers were "creating opportunities for faith" (eleven students) and "help integrate faith and daily life" (eleven). The top two answers among faculty were "help integrate faith" and "encourage, take an interest." Cf. Wuthnow, R. *The Crisis in the Churches: Spiritual Malaise, Fiscal Woe.* New York: Oxford University Press, 1997, p. 72: "The clergy with whom we spoke uniformly regarded the economic realm as an important area of ministry." Alongside this interest, however, he reported that "most clergy consider [the economic world] troublesome. Many of them see it as an expansive, imperialistic world that seduces people, drawing them into it, tempting them to want more, work more and spend more" (pp. 76, 260, n. 4). In our survey, faculty and student answers to "How important do you feel it is for your curriculum to include ministry issues regarding businesses and businesspeople?" showed an interesting two-to-one split between "very important" and "not at all." Answers for "very important" correlated with those who saw business as bad or evil but might see themselves as needing to "encourage and support" businesspeople.

7. Summary of affirmative answers to the question "Have you been given (or assigned) any scripture passages to study with the explicit purpose of understanding God's message with respect to business or the responsibility of businesspeople?" The passages cited from the Old Testament, roughly paraphrased: (1) Gen. 22:17–18, "by your offspring shall all of the nations receive blessing"; (2) Lev. 25, regarding sabbatical year of rest; (3) Deut. 15:7–8, regarding sabbatical year; (4) Prov. 22:1, choose a good name rather than riches; (5) Prov. 22:26–69, do not be one of those who gives pledges; (6) Prov. 28.8, one who augments wealth by exorbitant interest and increase gathers it for him who is kind to the poor; (7) Ec. 4:9–10, two is better than one for they will look after one another; and (8) Ezek. 22–23–30, the people have practiced extortion and committed rob-

bery; they have oppressed the poor and needy. New Testament passages cited, roughly paraphrased: (1) Mt. 4:1–4, one does not live on
bread alone; (2) Mt. 5, Sermon on the Mount (cited as evidence of
preferential option for the poor); (3) Mt. 6:24, no one can serve two
masters; (4) Mt. 18:23–24, king settling account with his slaves; forgiveness; (5) Mt. 19:23, difficulty for a rich man to enter the kingdom of heaven; (6) Mt. 20:1–16, payment to the laborers in the
vineyard; (7) Mt. 21:12, Jesus drives the moneychangers out of the
temple; (8) Mt. 21:33–43, parable of the wicked tenants; (9) Mk.
10:41–45, whoever would be great among you must be your servant;
(10) Lk. 6:34–35, even sinners lend to sinners to receive much; but
love your enemies, and do good, and lend expecting nothing in
return; (11) Lk. 12:13–21, warning against covetousness; the man
who lays up treasure for himself and is not rich toward God; (12)
Lk. 19:11–17, parable of the ten pounds (mina); (13) Lk. 21:1–9,
the poor widow's contribution versus the gifts of the rich; (14) John
13:34, the new commandment, love one another; (15) Rev.
18:3–23, the fall of Babylon; (16) 1 Cor. 6:1–8, laying lawsuits
before those least esteemed by the church; finding fault with the
idea of needing to sue each other within the church; (17) 1 Cor.
11:17, factions inside the local church; selfishness of members concerning food and drink; (18) Eph. 6:5–9, slaves be obedient to your
earthly masters; masters forbear threatening; (19) Col 3:22–25,
slaves, obey your earthly masters; work heartily as if serving the
Lord, knowing you will receive inheritance from the Lord; and (20)
1 Tim. 6:17, charge the rich not to be haughty, but to set their
hopes on God; they should do good and be generous. A number of
general references also appeared: most frequently to the Sermon on
the Mount, the "option for the poor," and the rich man not serving
two masters. Acts was cited as a generally relevant biblical model.

8. Some of the congregants we interviewed who had participated on
church committees interviewing new pastors suggested that today's
clergy are generally biased against concrete, practical religion. Commented one: "They have these pat abstractions, like 'community,'
with a pat conceptual framework. They trot it out, but you get no
sense that they really have any interest in knowing what your

specific religious community is about. And they seem to be unaware that there's a difference."

9. Greenhouse, S. "Labor and Clergy are Reuniting to Help the Underdogs of Society." *New York Times*, Aug. 18, 1996, p. 1.

10. This pattern surfaced clearly in the initial support for Cesar Chavez's United Farm Workers movement within business and the media, and the subsequent withdrawal of support. As they backed away from endorsing the union claims, while some churches were still actively boycotting grapes and lettuce, businesspeople characterized the churches as "not understanding" the full issues. *Time* went so far as to say it was a fight between unions in which the church should not be involved.

11. See, for example, John A. Ryan, "The Church and the Working-man." *The Catholic World*. September 1909, pp. 776-782.

12. Vaill, P. B. "The Learning Challenges of Leadership." *Kellogg Leadership Studies Project*, July 1997, p. 74.

13. Ammerman, N. T., with Farnsley, A. E., II, and Adams, T. *Congregation and Community*. New Brunswick, N.J.: Rutgers University Press, 1997.

14. These attitudes are well attested in Roof, W. C., with Greer, B. *A Generation of Seekers: The Spiritual Journeys of the Baby Boom Generation*. San Francisco: HarperSanFrancisco, 1993.

15. Wyszynski, S. C. *All You Who Labor: Work and the Sanctification of Daily Life*. Sophia Institute Press, 1995.

Chapter Seven

1. Gomes, P. J. *The Good Book: Reading the Bible with Mind and Heart*. New York: Morrow, 1998.

2. See Seglin, J. L. *The Good, The Bad, and Your Business: Choosing Right When Ethical Dilemmas Pull You Apart*. New York: Wiley, 2000.

3. Greenleaf, R. *Servant Leadership: A Journey into the Nature of Legitimate Power and Greatness*. New York: Paulist Press, 1983, 45.

4. See especially Kaufman, G. *Critical Terms for Religious Studies*. (M. Taylor, ed.) Chicago: University of Chicago Press, 1998; and Beckley, H. R., and Swezey, C. M. (eds.). *James M. Gustafson's Theocentric Ethics: Interpretations and Assessments*. Macon, Ga.: Mercer University Press, 1988. The separate problem Kaufman raises—whether the doctrinal terms and concepts of Christianity are still justifiable in the modern world—is beyond the scope of this discussion.

5. Novak, M. *The Catholic Ethic and the Spirit of Capitalism*. New York: Free Press, 1993, p. 23.

6. Korten, D. C. *When Corporations Rule the World*. San Francisco: Berrett-Koehler, 1995, pp. 70, 271.

7. Larsen, D. V. "Confessions of a Christian Professional." *Vocatio* 1.1. Vancouver: Gent College Foundation, Feb. 1998, p. 8.

8. The directional biases quoted here should not be seen as absolute. The doctor quoted also moved to additive tasks, describing how he subsequently accepted a position to establish health care in KwaZulu-Natal. So too, appeals to give away money are followed by additive recommendations about where to give it. The business executive's emphasis on enabling "tasks"—love the Lord, honor my wife, encourage my kids, use my talents—was tempered in his actual life by extremely active financial and personal governance contributions to a national faith-based social service organization. This commitment "took away" financial assets and time from his family. For selection of concretized language of religion and work among the new lay-initiated efforts, see, for example, Brink, B., and Specht, D. (eds.). *The Bridge: Field Notes for Seeing Things Whole*. Shelburne Falls, Mass., a project affiliated with the Robert K. Greenleaf Center for Servant Leadership.

9. Ulcer, S. "Guilty of a Lesser Love. Missionaries for Christ or Prosperity?" *Regeneration Quarterly*, Winter 1996, p. 24. See also Brueggemann, W., Parks, S., and Groome, T. H. *To Act Justly, Love Tenderly, Walk Humbly: An Agenda for Ministers*. New York: Paulist Press, 1986.

10. In *Good Intentions Aside: A Manager's Guide to Resolving Ethical Problems* (Cambridge: Harvard Business School Press, 1993), Laura Nash noted that successful businesspeople with inherently strong convictions seemed to focus on enabling relationships as their key problem-solving paradigm. Essentially, this concept reflects the additive approach discussed here and underscores a focus on interests that go beyond the material to psychology and community.

11. Tillich, P. *Dynamics of Faith*. New York: HarperCollins, 1965, p. 49.

12. See Olson, D. "Fellowship Ties and the Transmission of Religious Identity." In J. Carroll and W. C. Roof (eds.), *Beyond Establishment: Protestant Identity in a Post-Protestant Age*. Westminster: John Knox Press, 1993. Olson was also kind enough to share his conclusions on pluralism from a study that was about to be published. For a more positive view of pluralism's effect on religion, see Stark, R., and Finke, R. *Acts of Faith: Explaining the Human Side of Religion*. Berkeley: University of California Press, 2000.

13. Hunter, J. D. *Evangelicalism: The Coming Generation*. Chicago: University of Chicago Press, 1987.

14. Warren Buffett's remarks, quoted in *HARBUS*. Boston: Harvard Business School, Sept. 19, 1999, p. 1.

15. Jones, L. B. "He was a Turnaround Specialist." Chapter in *Jesus CEO* (1995).

16. Chaves, M., and Miller, S. L. (eds.). *Financing American Religion*. Walnut Creek, Calif.: Alta Mira Press, 1999.

17. Smith, J. A., III. "Polemical and Dialogical Approaches to Issues." Private paper, May 1999.

18. Smith, J. A., III. "Religious Activism and Economic Power: Assessing 25 Years of the Interfaith Center on Corporate Responsibility." Private paper, Jan. 7, 1998.

19. ibid.

20. Childs, J. M., Jr. *Ethics in Business*. Faith at Work. Minneapolis: Fortress Press 1999, p. 51.

Chapter Eight

1. Merriam, D. *Trinity: A Church, a Parish, a People*. New York: Cross River Press, 1996, pp. 9, 11.

2. Letter from Beth Robinson (consultant to the Trinity Church Wall Street Dialogues), July 13, 1999.

3. Burnham, F. B. "Dialogue Lives: A Wall Street Story." *Trinity News*, 1998, 45(1), pp. 10–11.

4. See especially Mitroff and Denton (2000). For further examples, see Seglin (2000).

5. The paradoxical demands of free religious expression in a diverse society have been widely discussed. See especially Marty (1997); Rouner, L. S., and Langford, J. (eds.). *Philosophy, Religion, and Contemporary Life: Essays on Perennial Problems*. Notre Dame, Ind.: University of Notre Dame Press, 1996; Thiemann, R. F. *Constructing a Public Theology: The Church in a Pluralistic Culture*. Louisville, Ky.: Westminster/John Knox Press, 1991; Wolfe, A. *One Nation After All: What Middle-Class Americans Really Think About God, Country, Family, Racism, Welfare, Immigration, Homosexuality, Work, the Right, the Left, and Each Other*. New York: Viking, 1998.

6. McCoy, B. "The Parable of the Sadhu." *Harvard Business Review*, Sept.-Oct. 1983.

7. Gallup and Jones (2000), pp. 184–185.

8. Templeton, J. M. *Discovering the Laws of Life*. New York: Continuum, 1994.

9. For discussion of this power as a positive aspect of pluralism, see Berger, P. L. *A Far Glory: The Quest for Faith in an Age of Credulity*. New York: Free Press, 1992.

10. For a discussion of the differences between industrial forms of expertise and the "intellective" skills needed in today's business environment, see Zubof, S. *In the Age of the Smart Machine: The Future of Work and Power*. New York: Basic Books, 1988.

11. See Chappell, T. *The Soul of a Business: Managing for Profit and the Common Good*. New York: Bantam Books, 1993.

Chapter Nine

1. Wuthnow (1997).

2. For similar evidence and conclusions, see Wuthnow (1997), pp. 96–97.

3. Gustafson, J. M., and Johnson, E. W. "The Corporate Leader and the Ethical Resources of Religion: A Dialogue." In O. Williams and J. Houck (eds.), *The Judeo–Christian Vision and the Modern Corporation*. Notre Dame, Ind.: University of Notre Dame Press, 1982.

Suggested Reading

General Books on Spirituality and Effectiveness (Secular and Christian)

Buchanan, C. *Choosing to Lead: Women and the Crisis of American Values.* Boston: Beacon, 1996.

Canfield, J., and others. *Chicken Soup for the Soul at Work.* Deerfield Beach, Fla.: Health Communications, 1996.

Carlson, R. *Don't Sweat the Small Stuff . . . and It's All Small Stuff.* New York: Hyperion, 1997.

Chopra, D. *The Seven Spiritual Laws of Success: A Practical Guide to the Fulfillment of Your Dreams.* San Rafael, Calif.: Amber-Allen, 1994.

Chopra, D. *How to Know God: The Soul's Journey into the Mystery of Mysteries.* New York: Crown, 2000.

Covey, S. R. *The Seven Habits of Highly Effective People.* New York: Simon & Schuster, 1989.

Covey, S. R. *Principle-Centered Leadership.* New York: Fireside, 1992.

Covey, S. R., with Merrill, A. R., and Merrill, R. R. *First Things First.* New York: Simon & Schuster, 1994.

Das, Lama Surya. *Awakening the Buddha Within*. New York: Broadway, 1997.

Edelman, J., and Crain, M. B. *The Tao of Negotiation*. New York: HarperCollins, 1993.

Garfield, C. *Peak Performers: The New Heroes of American Business*. New York: Avon, 1986.

Handy, C. *The Hungry Spirit*. New York: Broadway, 1998.

Harner, M. *The Way of the Shaman*. (3rd ed.) San Francisco: HarperSanFrancisco, 1990.

Hendricks, G., and Ludeman, K. *The Corporate Mystic: A Guidebook for Visionaries with Their Feet on the Ground*. New York: Bantam, 1996.

Hillman, J. *The Soul's Code: In Search of Character and Calling*. New York: Warner, 1996.

Kaminer, W. *Sleeping with Extra-Terrestrials: The Rise of Irrationalism and Perils of Piety*. New York: Pantheon Books, 1999.

Redfield, J., and Adrienne, C. *The Celestine Prophecy: An Experiential Guide*. New York: Warner, 1995.

Whyte, D. *The Heart Aroused: Poetry and the Preservation of the Soul*. New York: Currency/Doubleday, 1994.

Wilber, K. *Spirituality: A Brief History of Everything*. Boston: Shambala, 1996.

New Science and Religion and/or Business

Jaworski, J. *Synchronicity: The Inner Path of Leadership*. San Francisco: Berrett-Koehler, 1996.

Kauffman, S. *At Home in the Universe*. New York: Oxford University Press, 1995.

Noble, D. F. *The Religion of Technology: The Divinity of Man and the Spirit of Invention*. New York: Knopf, 1998.

Wheatley, M. J. *Leadership and the New Science: Learning About Organization from an Orderly Universe*. San Francisco: Berrett-Koehler, 1992.

Wilber, K. *The Marriage of Sense and Soul: Integrating Science and Religion*. New York: Random House, 1998.

Business Leadership and Religion

Autry, J. *Confessions of an Accidental Businessman*. San Francisco: Berrett-Koehler, 1996.

Beckett, J. D. *Loving Monday*. Downers Grove, Ill.: Inter-Varsity, 1998.

Blanchard, K., Hybels, B., and Hodges, P. *Leadership by the Book: Tools to Transform Your Workplace*. New York: Morrow, 1999.

Blanchard, K., and Peale, N. V. *The Power of Ethical Management*. New York: Morrow, 1988.

Block, P. *Stewardship: Choosing Service over Self-Interest*. San Francisco: Berrett-Koehler, 1993.

Buford, B. *Half Time*. Grand Rapids, Mich.: Zondervan, 1994.

Buford, B. *Game Plan*. Grand Rapids, Mich.: Zondervan, 1997.

Chappell, T. *The Soul of a Business: Managing for Profit and the Common Good*. New York: Bantam, 1993.

Childs, J. M., Jr. *Ethics in Business: Faith at Work*. Minneapolis: Fortress, 1995.

De Pree, M. *Leadership Is an Art*. New York: Doubleday, 1989.

Greenleaf, R. *Servant Leadership: A Journey into the Nature of Legitimate Power and Greatness*. New York: Paulist Press, 1983.

Griffiths, B. *The Creation of Wealth: A Christian's Case for Capitalism*. Downers Grove, Ill.: Inter-Varsity, 1984.

Guinness, O. *The Call: Finding and Fulfilling the Central Purpose of Your Life*. Nashville, Tenn.: Word, 1998.

Jones, L. B. *Jesus CEO: Using Ancient Wisdom for Visionary Leadership*. New York: Hyperion, 1995.

Komisar, R., with Lineback, K. *The Monk and the Riddle*. Boston: Harvard Business School Press, 2000.

Mitroff, I. I., and Denton, E. A. *A Spiritual Audit of Corporate America: A Hard Look at Spirituality, Religion, and Values in the Workplace*. San Francisco: Jossey-Bass, 2000.

Novak, M. *Business as a Calling*. New York: Free Press, 1996.

Pollard, C. W. *The Soul of the Firm*. New York: HarperBusiness/ Zondervan, 1996.

Stackhouse, M. L., and others (eds.). *On Moral Business*. Grand Rapids, Mich.: Eerdmans, 1995.

Social Analysis of U.S. Religious Trends, Especially Relating to Business

Baltzell, E. D. *The Protestant Establishment*. New Haven: Yale University Press, 1964.

Bellah, R. N., and others. *Habits of the Heart: Individualism and Commitment in American Life*. Berkeley: University of California Press, 1996.

Berger, P. L. *The Sacred Canopy*. Garden City, N.Y.: Doubleday, 1967.

Campbell, C. *The Romantic Ethic and the Spirit of Modern Consumerism*. New York: Blackwell, 1987.

Cimino, R. P., and Lattin, D. *Shopping for Faith: American Religion in the New Millennium*. San Francisco: Jossey-Bass, 1998.

Colson, C., with Vaughn, E. S. *Against the Night*. Ann Arbor, Mich.: Vine Books, 1989.

Cox, H. *Fire from Heaven: The Rise of Pentecostal Spirituality and the Reshaping of Religion in the Twenty-First Century*. Reading, Mass.: Addison-Wesley, 1995.

Ellingsen, M. *The Cutting Edge: How Churches Speak on Social Issues*. Geneva: Institute for Ecumenical Research, WCC Publications, and Grand Rapids: Eerdmans, 1993.

Fogel, R. *The Fourth Great Awakening and the Future of Egalitarianism*. Chicago: University of Chicago Press, 2000.

Gallup, G., Jr., and Castelli, J. *The People's Religion: American Faith in the '90s*. New York: Macmillan, 1989.

Hunter, J. D. *The American Culture Wars*. (J. L. Nolan, Jr., ed.) Charlottesville: University Press of Virginia, 1996.

James, W. *The Varieties of Religious Experience*. New York: Collier, 1961. (Originally published 1902)

Jones, T., and Gallup, G., Jr. *The Next American Spirituality: Finding God in the Twenty-First Century*. Colorado Springs, Colo.: Cook Communications, 2000.

Roof, W. C. *Spiritual Marketplace: Baby Boomers and the Remaking of American Religion*. Princeton: Princeton University Press, 1999.

Rouner, L. (ed.). *Civility*. Notre Dame, Ind.: University of Notre Dame Press, 2000.

Stackhouse, M. L. *Christian Social Ethics in a Global Era*. Nashville, Tenn.: Abingdon Press, 1995.

Tawney, R. H. *Religion and the Rise of Capitalism*. (A. B. Seligman, ed.) New Brunswick, N.J.: Transaction, 1998.

Weber, M. *The Protestant Ethic and the Spirit of Capitalism*. (2nd ed., T. Parsons, ed.) London: Allen & Unwin, 1976.

Wolfe, A. *One Nation After All: What Middle-Class Americans Really Think About God, Country, Family, Racism, Welfare, Immigration, Homosexuality, Work, the Right, the Left, and Each Other*. New York: Viking, 1998.

Wuthnow, R. *The Crisis in the Churches*. New York: Oxford University Press, 1997.

The Authors

Laura Nash is senior research fellow at the Harvard Business School and has been a consultant on corporate values to a number of leading businesses for twenty years.

Prior to joining the HBS faculty in 2000, she was program director on business and religion at Harvard Divinity School's Center for the Study of Values in Public Life. For ten years, she was on the faculty at Boston University's Institute for the Study of Economic Culture and taught in BU's School of Management and School of Theology. She was president of the Society for Business Ethics in 1996-97.

Nash has published numerous books and articles on corporate ethics, personal values, and religion. Among her books are *Good Intentions Aside: A Manager's Guide to Resolving Ethical Dilemmas* and *Believers in Business: Resolving the Tensions Between Christian Faith, Business Ethics, Competition, and our Definitions of Success.*

She has a Ph.D. in classical philology from Harvard University and lives in Cambridge with her husband and two children.

Scotty McLennan is the dean for religious life at Stanford University. From 1984 to 2000 he was the university chaplain at Tufts University, and from 1988 to 2000 on a part-time basis he was a senior lecturer in the area of business leadership, ethics, and religion at the Harvard Business School. He is the author of *Finding Your Religion: When the Faith You Grew Up with Has Lost Its Meaning.*

He graduated from Yale University (B.A.) in 1970, the Harvard Divinity School (M.Div.) in 1975, and the Harvard Law School (J.D.) also in 1975. He was ordained to the Unitarian Universalist (UU) ministry in 1975 and also admitted to the Massachusetts bar that year. He remains a UU minister and a Massachusetts lawyer in good standing. For nine years before going to Tufts, he practiced law under church sponsorship in a low-income area of Boston.

Index

A

Activism, church-based, 67, 106, 112–114, 138, 240, 242; economic, 75–77, 111–115, 167–168

African American congregation, 278–279

American Bankers Association (ABA), 127

Ammerman, N., 174

Asceticism, wealth accumulation and, 158, 159

Atomists, business-religion integration and, 53–55, 61–62

Austin, R., 218–219, 220

B

Baby boomers, values and spirituality of, 11

Banks, R., 217–218, 219, 220

Beliefnet.com, 26, 38

Believers in Business (Nash), 41, 276

Bellah, R., 82

Berger, P., 45, 55

Blanchard, K., 221, 236

Block, P., 17

Buddhist practice, 44, 250

Buffett, W., 204

Business, community in, 28–29, 99

Business congregant: clergy/church interactions with, 9–10, 77–78, 164–165, 174–175; and church's bias toward business, 159–163, 167; coping strategies of, 42–60; relational realms of, 96–99, *104*; religious language use of, 186–187, 195–196; and spiritual calling, 248

Business culture: Calvinist values in, 138–139; of efficiency and pragmatism, 139–140; optimistic and self-reliant bias in, 143, 147–149

Business gurus, 13–14, 236

Business prayer groups, 110

Business role models, biblical, 145, 166–167

Business-church relationship: authority and power structures in, 171–173; and businesspeople's coping strategies, 42–60; businesspeople's criticisms in, 164–165, 175–176; capitalist critique in, 156–157, 158–161, 164; church's bias and criticisms in, 159–163, 167; church's financial accountability and, 177–182; and church's standard modes of guidance, 74–81; and clergy's coping strategies, 60–65; clergy's corruption and wrongdoing in, 175–177; cultural conflicts in, 126–143; and cultural pluralism, 200–202; economic

Church on Sunday, Work on Monday

The Challenge of Fusing Christian Values with Business Life:
A GUIDE TO REFLECTION

Laura Nash and Scotty McLennan

$4.95 Paperback
ISBN: 0787960721

Businesspeople and professionals have a strong and growing interest in the relationship between work and spirit, and many actively seek ways to improve the integration between their deepest beliefs and their daily work. But surprisingly few find the church to be of resource in their explorations. Why is this? And how can the church respond more effectively to businesspeople's needs?

In *Church on Sunday, Work on Monday*, Harvard-based experts Laura Nash and Scotty McLennan assess the distance between pew and pulpit; articulate how it is that the church is 'turning off' business leaders and professional people; and make concrete recommendations about how church leaders and lay businesspeople can work together to bridge the gap.

This practical guide helps businesspeople revitalize their spirits at work by discussing the four central spiritual needs: to create constant awareness of the sacred self, to achieve harmony and balance, to connect with community, and to practice faith-based business ethics. Each chapter offers questions for reflection and discussion and suggests actions you might take as a group as well as individually, providing a sturdy framework that readers can use as a jumping-off point while they find their own way to connect the worlds of business and faith.

LAURA NASH is Senior Research Fellow on the faculty at Harvard Business School. Prior to joining HBS in the Fall of 2000, she was Visiting Lecturer and Program Director on Business and Religion at the Center for the Study of Values in Public Life at Harvard Divinity School.

SCOTTY MCLENNAN is the Dean for Religious Life at Stanford. From 1984–2000, he was the University Chaplain at Tufts University and from 1988–2000, he was a senior lecturer in the area of business leadership, ethics and religion at Harvard Business School.